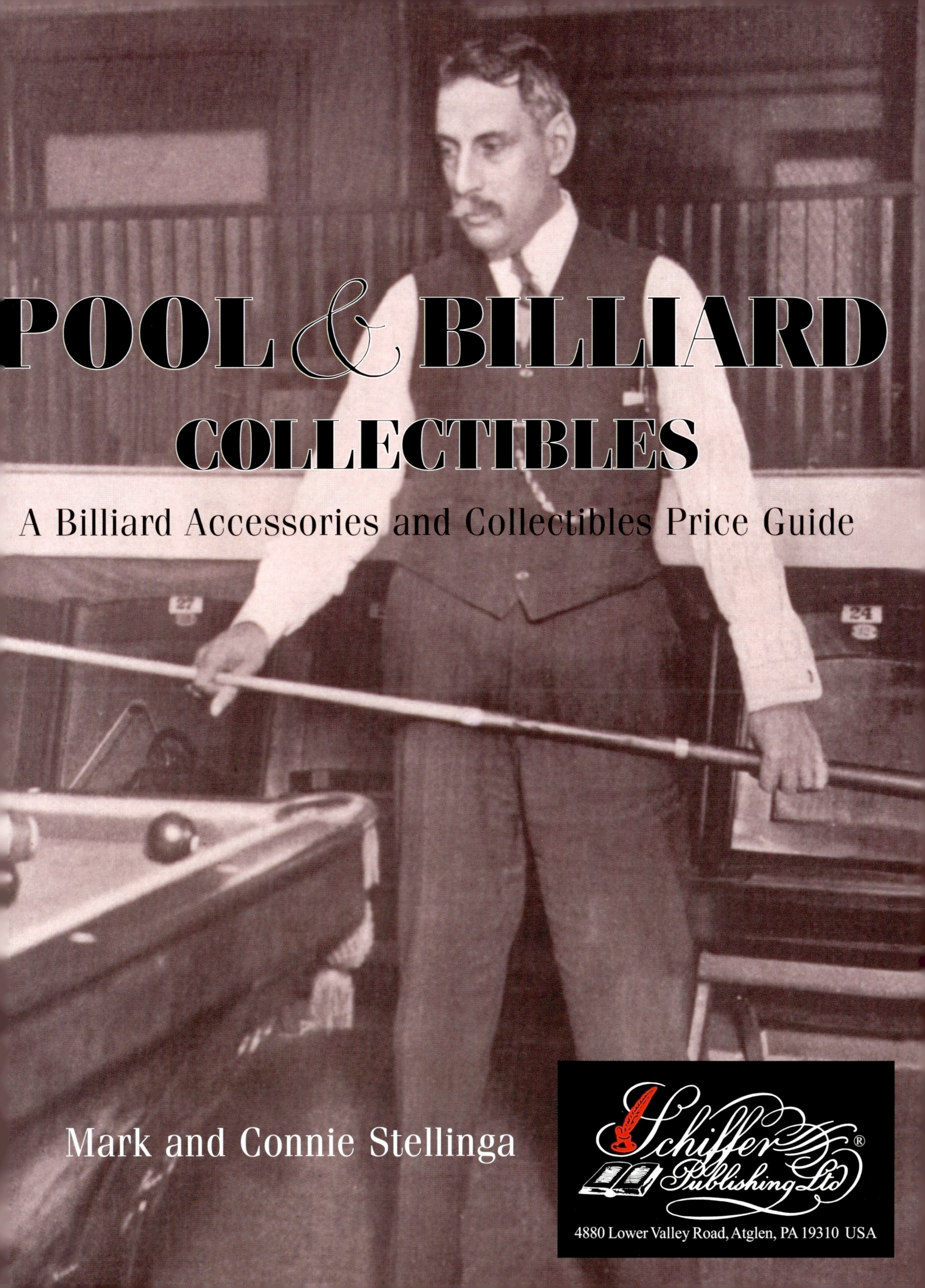

POOL & BILLIARD COLLECTIBLES

A Billiard Accessories and Collectibles Price Guide

Mark and Connie Stellinga

Schiffer Publishing Ltd®
4880 Lower Valley Road, Atglen, PA 19310 USA

Dedication

We dedicate this book to our mothers and fathers, from whom we each acquired both the pit-bull tenacity for serious acquisitioning, and a seemingly unquenchable thirst for learning.

These characteristics have proven to be two of the most important prerequisites to locating, purchasing, and restoring fine antiques.

Library of Congress Cataloging-in-Publication Data

Stellinga, Mark.
Pool & billiard collectibles: a billiard accessories and collectibles price guide/by Mark and Connie Stellinga.
p. cm.
ISBN 0-7643-1700-8 (Hardcover)
1. Billiards—Collectibles. 2. Pool (Game)—Collectibles. I. Title: Pool and billiard collectibles. II. Stellinga, Connie. III. Title.
NK3654.7.S74 2003
794.7'3'028—2003
2002012026

Designed by John P. Cheek
Cover design by Bruce M. Waters
Type set in Zapf Chancery Bd BT/Goudy OISt BT

ISBN: 0-7643-1700-8
Printed in China
1 2 3 4

Published by Schiffer Publishing Ltd.
4880 Lower Valley Road
Atglen, PA 19310
Phone: (610) 593-1777; Fax: (610) 593-2002
E-mail: Schifferbk@aol.com
Please visit our web site catalog at **www.schifferbooks.com**
We are always looking for people to write books on new and related subjects. If you have an idea for a book please contact us at the above address.

This book may be purchased from the publisher.
Include $3.95 for shipping.
Please try your bookstore first.
You may write for a free catalog.

In Europe, Schiffer books are distributed by
Bushwood Books
6 Marksbury Ave.
Kew Gardens
Surrey TW9 4JF England
Phone: 44 (0)20-8392-8585
Fax: 44 (0)20-8392-9876
E-mail: Bushwd@aol.com
Free postage in the UK. Europe: air mail at cost

Contents

Acknowledgments

I wish to thank my wonderful wife, Connie, for her thirty years of support and relentless encouragement. As our collecting endeavors invariably involved hour upon hour and day upon day of logistical coordination, Connie quietly oversaw it all. Without her continual hands on involvement, not the least of which entailed her finely tuned navigational skills, we could, without a doubt, never have acquired and ultimately restored the hundreds of antiques that we have. Not with just cookies, but with "homemade" cookies, I was endlessly plied as she, ever so diplomatically would remind me, "You've got work to do, fella!" Also, we wish to give special thanks to our good friend, Charlie Miller, for his many years of top quality, meticulous furniture repair, and expert advice, with whom we so often teamed to carefully revive our sometimes rather intimidating projects.

Preface

What's It Worth?

Over twenty-six years of experience wheeling and dealing in antique collectibles has helped us to understand one sure thing about what a given item is worth. To a great extent, an item's value is, though often confusingly so, relative to but three basic factors. These are, in the order of importance I feel they best present themselves, desirability, scarcity, and condition.

Scarcity and condition are irrelevant if desirability is not there. Desirability can be somewhat diminished if an item is relatively common, but it is still the most important factor in determining a collectible's monetary value.

Once an item falls into the category of desirable, the next most important factor becomes its scarcity. Virtually ANY collectible item will obviously increase in worth relative to the degree of difficulty in procuring one. And finally, once it is decided that you simply aren't going to be able to live if you don't find one, and, you have indeed subsequently found one, you are, quite understandably, going to kill for the opportunity to acquire the most perfect example known to exist. Condition serves only to increase the item's value as it improves.

For the most part, these three factors will dictate what an antique item will sell for. However, pricing an item as close to what the basic antique collector perceives as "reasonable" for that particular piece is what typically consummates a sale. This is where price guides come into the picture.

We purchased nearly every item we collected in the past quarter of a century, even those we bought to resell, without the support of a price guide. All price guides, including this one, are just that, ONLY GUIDES. By far, most dealers and collectors alike firmly believe that value is a totally personal concept. In an era when Picasso paintings and particular homerun baseballs fetch in the millions of dollars, and lovingly restored, spectacular Victorian homes bring only hundreds of thousands, I'm still putting my money on the homes. My advice is to stick with your instincts and buy what you like. And PAY what you like.

You've all heard these two sayings: "Nothing is worth one penny more than what someone is willing to give you for it!" and "Everything's for sale for a price!" The first is generally true. The second is NOT! Ever tried to buy a family heirloom from an inheritor who needs the blessing of the entire remaining family to say, "Sure, why not," to the sale of grandma's or grandpa's last bequeathed whatever? Don't hold your breath. And that's a good thing, as far as we're concerned.

But the daunting task of assigning a value to each of the many, early billiard collectibles you'll find in this book is based completely on only OUR personal experiences in buying and selling them over the past many years. We've tried to bear in mind the three factors mentioned earlier, but any given price may be the subject of some dispute. As prospective collectors, we wanted to lean toward slightly conservative figures. As daily sellers of this type of merchandise, exaggerated numbers were tempting. We tried to compromise for the good of all concerned. If a price seems high to you, be sure you are taking into consideration its desirability. What you may not perceive to be an important item may be something we are called about with surprising frequency. You also may not be aware of the difficulty involved in procuring some of these items. Rare is also a relative consideration. You may have seen MANY more of a given item than we have, therefore our values could differ considerably. And, as far as condition goes, as far as we're concerned, most people should save the term "MINT" for one of their favorite flavors of ice cream. The words "ANTIQUE" and "MINT" are undoubtedly two of the most abused words in every language around the world.

Now let's talk about one other sometimes abused term: RESTORED! Contrary to what most of us have heard, or seen on TV, in many instances, properly cleaned and/or professionally restored pieces sell much more quickly and, very often, for somewhat higher prices than their typical "original condition" counterparts. We're asked all the time, "Doesn't restoring a piece reduce its value?" What we've found consistently for twenty-six years running, in every part of the country, is that most collectors and dealers alike extensively clean or, unless in literally outstanding condition, totally restore ALL of their finest pieces. That is *every*where, *every*body, and *every* piece good enough to warrant the work and expense of the restoration.

Those who leave top quality antiques to wither and die are normally either too lazy or too cheap to do the required work, in our opinion, or just too foolish to realize the betrayal this represents to the craftsmen who created them for future generations to enjoy. It does cut into the profit margin, but that has never stopped US. Antique homes, fine antique automobiles, and even the greatest paintings by the masters are restored without hesitation when deemed economically feasible. Don't ever be afraid to purchase an antique that has been professionally restored; but let me emphasize professionally, you don't want to settle for what the handy man THINKS constitutes genuine restoration. There is a market for practically anything, in ANY condition. You can't go wrong if you simply use common sense. It does, however, always make us a little sad to hear someone say. "I'll bet that was a really beautiful piece way back when!" NOTE: Generally speaking, the dates we assign to these collectibles somewhat closely reflect the period in which each item first became available as we show it. The poem that follows was derived from an actual experience we overheard at an antique show!

On Original Condition

"What is the price on your big antique clock?"
I asked of the dealer, who said to my shock,
"There isn't a thing on that clock I would touch.
If you leave it alone, I will tell how much."
"It COULD use a cleaning," I said in surprise.
I felt the disgust from the glare in his eyes.
"If you don't like the way that it looks, take a hike!"
he quipped, as he quickly got harder to like.
"I only was thinking of wiping it down."
"It's fine like it is," he snapped with a frown.
"Most of this dirt," he went on to explain,
has been there for years, you must be insane!"
"You'd lose the *patina*, and making it WORK
would ruin its value, man, what a jerk."
"So now you are saying, its value is *hurt*
if I get it to run, and I take off the dirt?"
"That's right," he proclaimed! I was stunned, couldn't speak!
Distraught by his theory about his "antique,"
I wanted to kill him, but thought I'd be nice,
and just told him, "Thanks," for his expert advice.
Then added, "I'll bet it would even sell higher
if you busted the glass and then set it on fire!"

Introduction

Until recently, many antique enthusiasts were relatively unaware of the surprisingly prolific and diverse selection of truly exciting collectibles that once graciously adorned the early and highly revered world of the billiard connoisseur. Many an eighteenth and nineteenth century Victorian ballroom shared its beautiful parquet floor with one of these stunning, highly carved and/or inlaid, exotic masterpieces. Fabulous estates of the upper class factions, in an otherwise relatively puritanical inner society, proudly displayed their ostentatious billiard tables, along with many equally impressive accoutrements of the game.

As with many of the once, for the average wage earner, unaffordable "toys" of the incredible renaissance era, some of these fabulous billiard and pocket billiard tables have fallen into the hands of lucky heirs and descendants and, sometimes, those of astute antique furniture lovers.

Because the industrialization of America saw several relatively to extremely successful billiard table manufacturers establish their factories and countless distribution outlets throughout the United States, these marvelous, utilitarian antiques can be found virtually anywhere. For more than one hundred years, only outnumbered perhaps by barber shops and taverns—which were more often than not actually located in the same buildings as the billiard parlors and pool halls (and there was a difference), the game of pool could be found in even the most diminutive of communities.

From the Newport mansions to the fabulous homes of California's "gold coast," and from the Carnegies to the Vanderbilt's, billiard rooms were, for a few hundred years, among the most lavishly furnished and well-used rooms in their castles.

Both beautiful *and* practical, still today there are undoubtedly a few extraordinary examples silently languishing in the dark, dusty attics and ballrooms of some of our country's much too often neglected Victorian estates. Finding them and putting them back into an attractive and useable condition is our intent. WHY we do that quickly becomes apparent as the reader reviews the images in this book.

The billiard collectibles field is both interesting and diverse, and, as you will see, encompasses a surprisingly wide range of categories. Despite the fact that clay, composition, and even ivory carom and numbered balls were available for nearly 200 years, and the basic appearance of some of the billiard cues you'll see in this book stood unchanged for even longer than that, do not hold your breath waiting to find similar examples. Twenty-six years of relentless, nationwide purchasing of pre-1910 billiard tables and their accompanying accessories, combined with regular appearances at countless higher quality antique auctions and shows, is the only way we were able to build a collection as comprehensive as we have. Both antique dealers and fellow billiard collectors alike will readily testify to the claim that acquiring the finer, and often elusive, antique billiard items shown in this book will demand these three things of the devoted curator: persistence, great patience, and, sometimes, a pretty big hit on the piggy bank. Only a fraction of what is out there is found between these covers, and the values assigned are no more than our personal opinions; but, nevertheless, we feel you'll agree, as a collectible, billiards is hard to beat. Enjoy!

Chapter I
Ephemera (Paper Collectibles)

A truly diverse, yet nevertheless *scant* category, it's out there, as they say, but amazingly elusive. Any longtime advertising dealer will tell you he, "just can't find good, early billiard paper items!" Very seldom, but sometimes, a small amount of better quality, early billiard merchandise surfaces. When it does, if you truly want some, get your paddle up.

Great postcard image of upscale billiard parlor, c. 1880s room, $65.

Postcard with image of none other than Mark Twain, an avid billiards enthusiast. The price assumes the postcard is in good condition (as will ALL the prices for the following pieces of ephemera), $35.

Image depicting players playing the game of "pin pool." That makes it RARE, $85.

Image shows a Narragansett table, a pin pool scoreboard, and several Collender style billiard chairs, $85.

Image of the rare "Northern" model pool tables, great racks and chairs too, $125.

Image shows a large advertisement for a local pool tournament, along with great and rarely seen shot of a "Billiard Experts" poster, $50.

A special very early scene showing some great racks and the front end of a Monarch pool table, $65.

Image of all St. Bernard Mission model pool tables and several mission style billiard lights, $55.

Magnificent table, cue rack, and chandelier testifying to the amazing opulence found in the private billiard rooms of the affluent members of the aristocracy, $55.

Another great table and chandelier image, $45.

Great table and chandelier: this early table is equipped with rare "mechanical" drop pockets made of brass that tip down to return the ball to the shooter. $55.

Gorgeous, early hotel billiard parlor depicted, $65.

A room full of Rochester model tables with great brass lights, $60.

Twenty-seven Madison style tables with brass lights, a great image on this postcard, $55.

Nice room with Saratoga tables and elongated metal lights, lots of goodies, $50.

Rare interior shot of the famous "Bott Bros." pool room in Columbus, Ohio, c. 1900s. There were forty tables on the second floor, $50.

Exterior view of the extravagantly decorated Bott Bros. Billiard Parlor, rare postcard, $45.

Huge room boasting SIXTY tables, ALL are the rare Arcade model. Super image, $55.

Image of some Madison model tables and cue racks, and a rare shot of a billiard cue cupboard (holds 120 cues in drawers), $50.

A group of Rochester models, again with two cue/coat closets and some wonderful mission style lights, $45.

A manufacturer's advertising postcard, super image, common card, $18.

A rare two-piece card celebrating the 1909 Alaska-Yukon Exposition in Seattle, unused example, issued by Brunswick-Balke-Collender, good condition, $175.

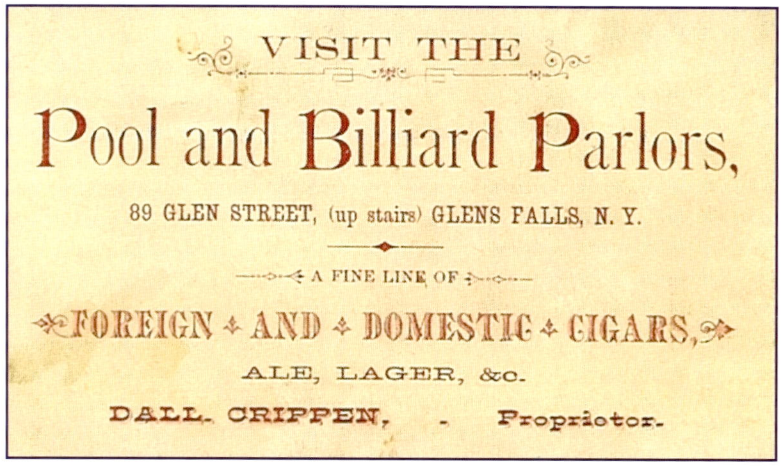

Nice Victorian tradecard, fair condition, $85.

Early tradecard for Los Angeles pool hall — note the 2 1/2¢ per cue charge. Nice pool table image in color, $135.

Limited edition fairly contemporary postcard with a fabulous image of a 1700s 6' x 12' snooker table, $20.

Tradecard, rooms for $1.25 to $2.00!!! Napa City, California, $90.

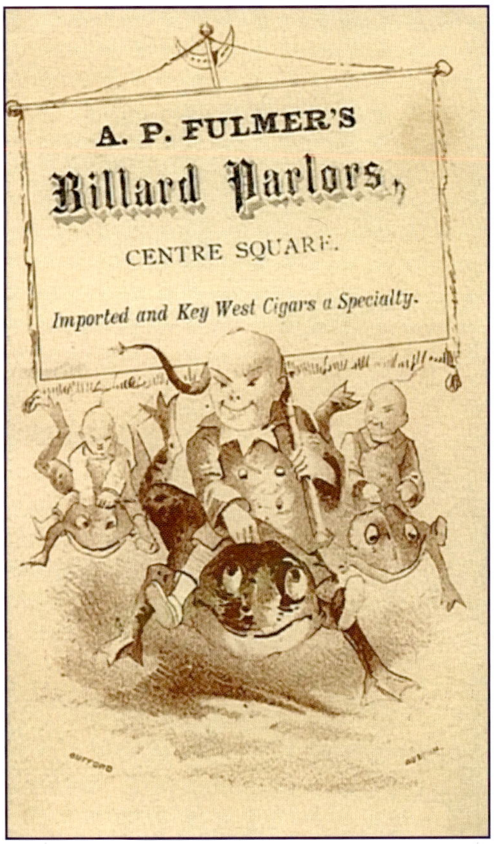

Tradecard with frogs, $125.

Middle 1800s tradecard, rare, fair condition, $165.

Rare excellent condition 1860s tradecard boasting six Julius Balke pool tables! $350.

Great monkey image on a 1911 tradecard advertising a local fair, $45.

Two category card (postcard and tradecard), great color graphics, some very interesting reference material, $65.

Tradecard from the "M. Bast & Bros." pool room, Canton, Ohio, $45.

A set of FOUR beautifully colored and graphically amusing tradecards for Wm. J. Mendence Billiards and Pool, excellent condition, c. 1881, $400 for the set.

Matched set of two tradecards, Chas. H. Cone Billiard Hall, showing their age, $90 for the pair.

Rare Iowa City, Iowa, tradecard, F. J. Epeneter Billiard Parlor, $80.

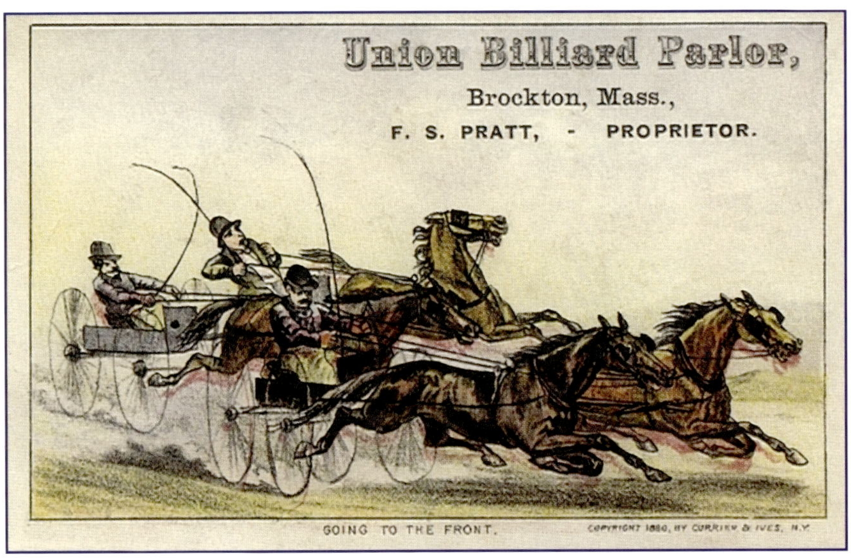

One example from a large series of Currier & Ives imaged tradecards from the Union Billiard Parlor, Brockton, Mass., c. 1880s, excellent condition, $150.

Very early tradecard from New Hampshire!!! Approximately 1860s, rare, $195.

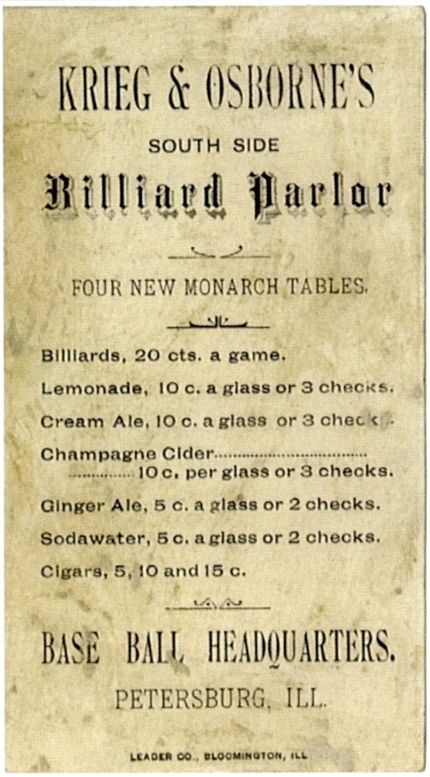

Great color image and very interesting text on the obverse of this early tradecard, $125.

Nice Victorian image on this 1882 tradecard, fair condition, $65.

Flier designed to ridicule the playing of billiards, with a cute poem, unusual piece, $55.

A billiard themed image from a set of twenty-five authorized issues from "Puck" to the W. Duke Sons & Co. for their smoking and chewing tobacco, some wear, $80.

Tradecard for the Mayer Shoe Co., good condition, nice color image, $55.

Arbuckle Bros. Coffee tradecard, copyrighted 1893, from a series of fifty different images, this is #6, $45.

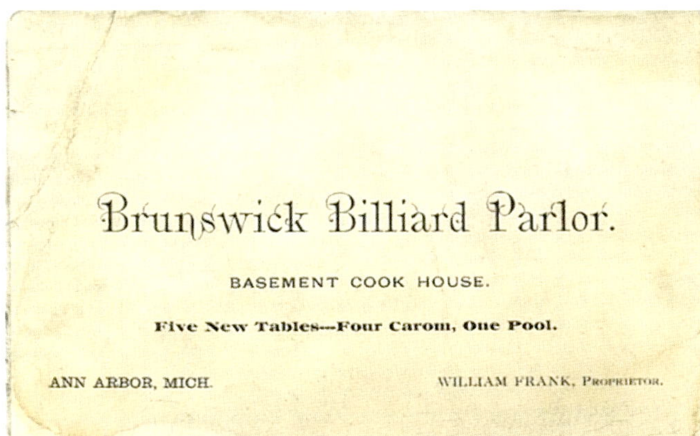

Ultra rare J. M. Brunswick & Balke Co. tradecard, advertising a Brunswick Billiard Parlor, c. 1870s, fair condition, $500+.

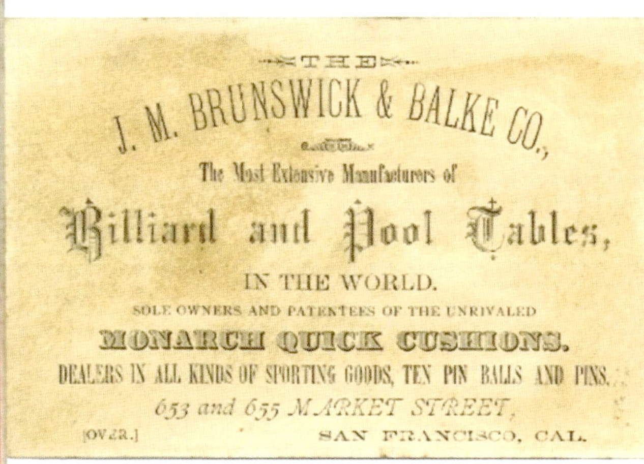

Great, and rare, 1881 J. M. Brunswick & Balke Co. tradecard, $375+.

Another very rare 1881 J. M. Brunswick & Balke Co. tradecard, $375+.

RARE example of a Portland, Oregon, "Brunswick Balke Collender Co." factory advertisement tradecard showing their Brilliant Novelty model pool table. Super image, rare location, fair condition, $295+.

A rare "A. Hand" Billiard Table Co. tradecard, great table image, $195.

Spectacular "National Billiard Mfg. Co." tradecard, oversized at 3.5" x 5.5". Excellent condition, outstanding graphics. Note the name of "A. Gunklach & Co.," a related firm based in California in the late 1800s. Super card, $400+.

"Chas, Passow & Sons" factory tradecard, fabulous graphics, very good condition, very hard card to find, $450.

Rare, complete, four piece set of 1881 "Benedict Billiard Table Co." tradecards, good condition, $600 for the set.

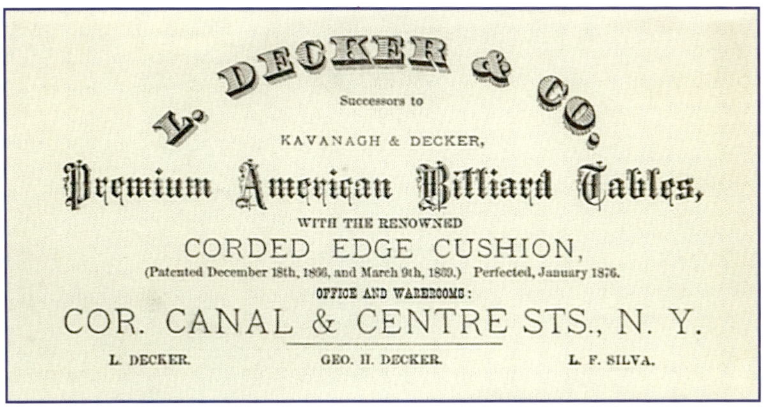

Extremely rare 1870s "L. Decker & Co." tradecard, excellent condition, $350.

Following are ten different examples of "stereocards" or "stereoviews." This type of card with a billiard image on it is ultra rare. This group of ten was collected over a twenty-six year period with the tenth being found only a few months prior to this writing. This first one shows a great early table with mechanical tip-down brass pockets, c. 1840s. The card is in good condition, $300.

This card, though it does NOT show in this photo, is in full color and is truly stunning to view. The stereoviewers give these cards the amazing sensation of a three dimensional image. You actually feel as though you are standing in the room with the billiard table(s). Very good condition, $300.

An early, ornate pool table is centered on this card. Rather worn condition, $200.

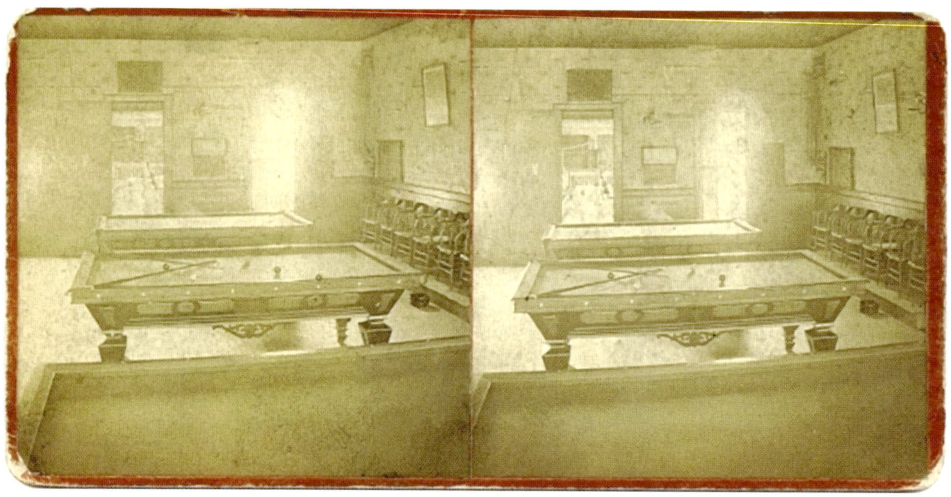

Great table, wonderful pool cue rack, and outstanding light. Very good condition, $300.

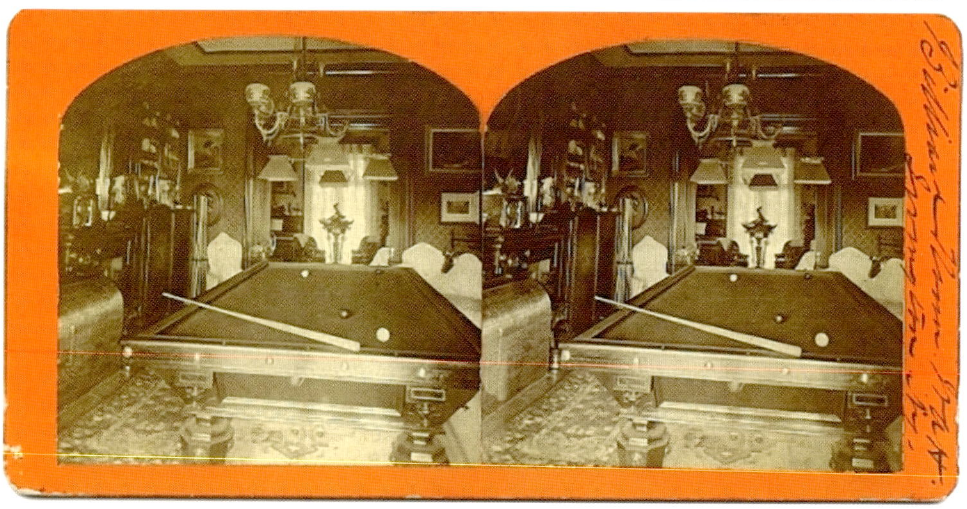

Nice table and light, several spectator chairs, and ceiling bead scorekeeper, $325.

Baldwin's Hotel, San Francisco, interior shot of a fabulous billiard parlor. One of two different examples, $350.

Different view of the Baldwin's Hotel billiard parlor, from the late 1800s, in San Francisco, $350.

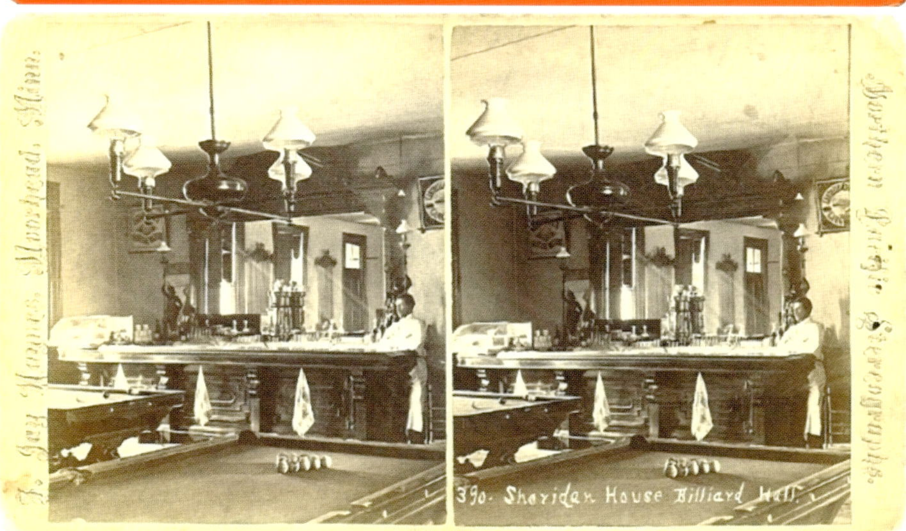

"Sheridan House Billiard Hall," awesome pool image, great bar with a pair of spectacular large figural kerosene lamps, Monarch pool tables, fabulous billiard light, $350.

Image shows several antique tables, four antique cue racks, and a lot of enthusiastic players posing for this 1870s stereocard, $350.

A palatial French chateau billiard room of unbelievable opulence. This card is one of the thin tissue types that are in glorious full color. This example can be found with the massive chandelier either covered for the winter season, or uncovered when the matriarch is "in house"! One of the finest billiard rooms to ever exist. Super stereocard, great conditon, $400.

These comprise a full set of the fifteen Mecca Tobacco Company's cards from the early 1900s that depict the important pool and billiard players of that era. Individually averaging around $40 to $50 EACH for a good specimen, a superior example can fetch somewhat more. Some cards are more difficult to locate and that, too, will drive the value up a bit.

This is a full set of the nine late-1800s issue of billiard themed tobacco cards from the Allen & Ginter Tobacco Co. In very good condition, and based on scarcity to a degree, these average around $95 to $150 each.

This is the full set of six billiard themed "Old Judge & Gypsy Queen" tobacco cards. In very good condition, these have been averaging around $150 to $175 per card. Full sets in mint condition can bring as much as $1,200+.

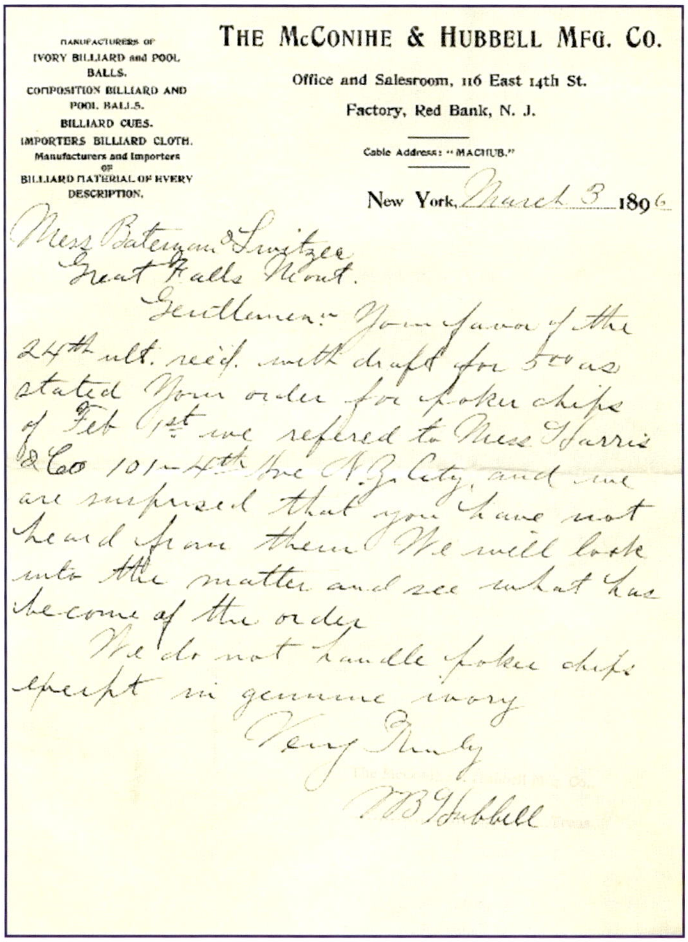

MANUFACTURERS OF
IVORY BILLIARD and POOL BALLS.
COMPOSITION BILLIARD AND POOL BALLS.
BILLIARD CUES.
IMPORTERS BILLIARD CLOTH.
Manufacturers and Importers OF BILLIARD MATERIAL OF EVERY DESCRIPTION.

THE McCONIHE & HUBBELL MFG. CO.

Office and Salesroom, 116 East 14th St.
Factory, Red Bank, N. J.

Cable Address: "MACHUB."

New York, March 3 1896

Mess Bateman & Switzer
Great Falls Mont.

Gentlemen:- Your favor of the 24th ult. rec'd. with draft for 5.00 as stated. Your order for poker chips of Feb 1st we refered to Mess Harris & Co 101-4th Ave N.Y. City, and we are surprised that you have not heard from them. We will look into the matter and see what has become of the order.

We do not handle poker chips except in genuine ivory.

Very Truly
W B Hubbell

Letterhead values typically correlate to a combination of their age, condition, and—most significantly—the company represented, along with WHO'S signature is at the end of the correspondence. The following values are based on the assumption that the piece is in very good to excellent condition. This McConihe & Hubble Mfg. Co. document happens to have been signed by Mr. Hubble. Dated 1896, very good condition, $50.

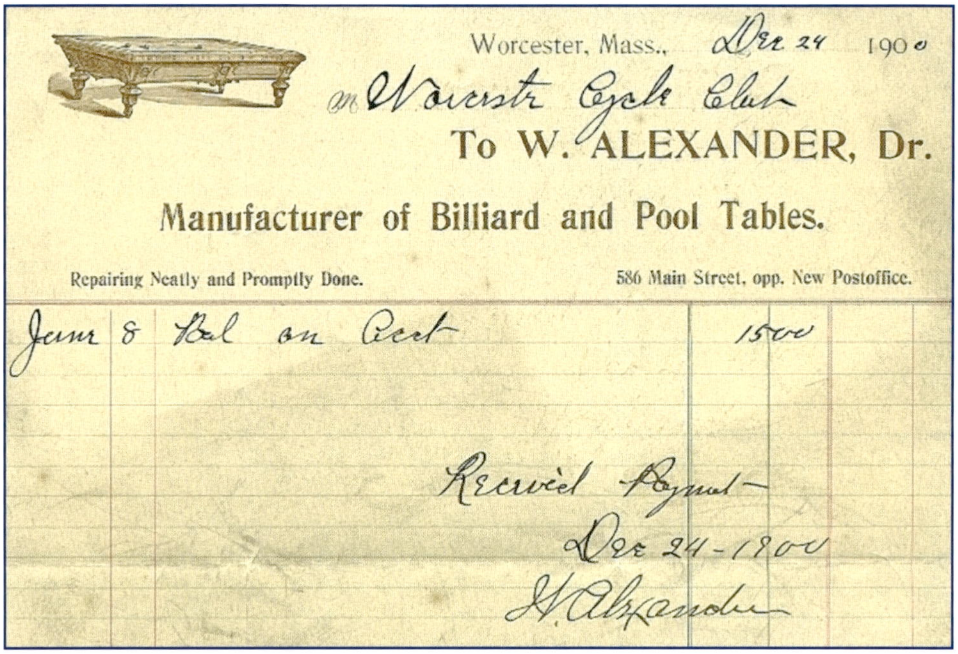
Worcester, Mass., Dec 24 1900

M Worcester Cycle Club

To W. ALEXANDER, Dr.

Manufacturer of Billiard and Pool Tables.

Repairing Neatly and Promptly Done. 586 Main Street, opp. New Postoffice.

June 8 Bal on Acct 15.00

Received Payment
Dec 24-1900
W. Alexander

Nice pool table graphic on this Christmas Eve, 1900s letterhead receipt, signed by Mr. Alexander himself. Tacky and soiled, $90.

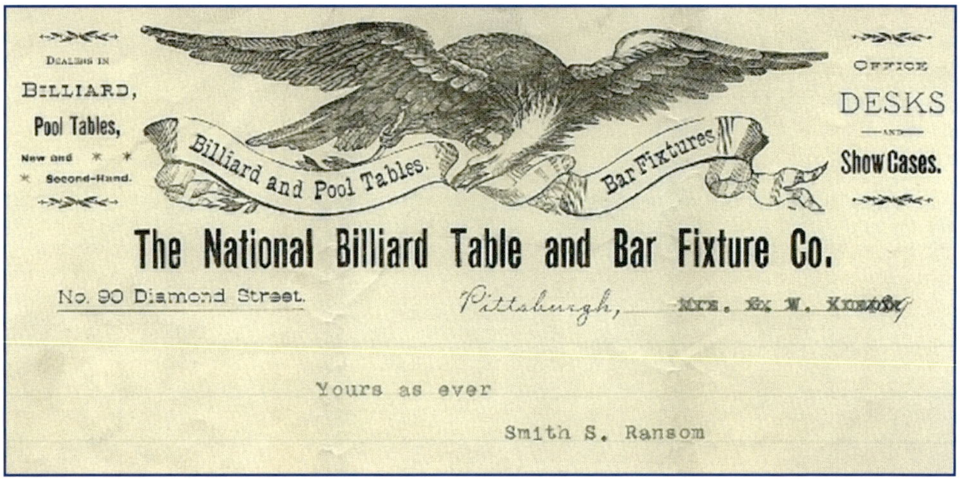
Dealers in BILLIARD, Pool Tables, New and Second-Hand.

Billiard and Pool Tables. Bar Fixtures

Office DESKS and Show Cases.

The National Billiard Table and Bar Fixture Co.

No. 90 Diamond Street. Pittsburgh,

Yours as ever

Smith S. Ransom

Nice "National Billiard Table & Bar Fixture Co.," c. 1890s, $95.

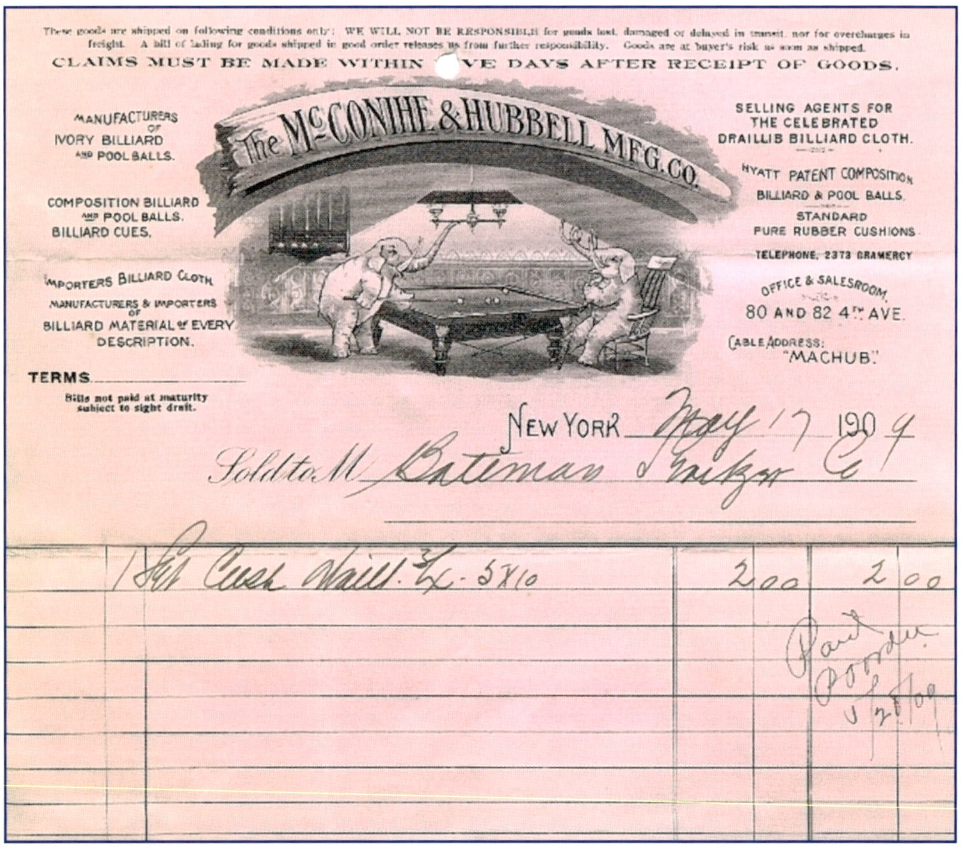
These goods are shipped on following conditions only: WE WILL NOT BE RESPONSIBLE for goods lost, damaged or delayed in transit, nor for overcharges in freight. A bill of lading for goods shipped in good order releases us from further responsibility. Goods are at buyer's risk as soon as shipped.

CLAIMS MUST BE MADE WITHIN FIVE DAYS AFTER RECEIPT OF GOODS.

The McCONIHE & HUBBELL MFG. CO.

MANUFACTURERS OF IVORY BILLIARD AND POOL BALLS.

COMPOSITION BILLIARD AND POOL BALLS. BILLIARD CUES.

IMPORTERS BILLIARD CLOTH. MANUFACTURERS & IMPORTERS OF BILLIARD MATERIAL OF EVERY DESCRIPTION.

SELLING AGENTS FOR THE CELEBRATED DRAILLIB BILLIARD CLOTH.

HYATT PATENT COMPOSITION BILLIARD & POOL BALLS. STANDARD PURE RUBBER CUSHIONS.

TELEPHONE, 2373 GRAMERCY

OFFICE & SALESROOM, 80 AND 82 4TH AVE.

CABLE ADDRESS: "MACHUB."

TERMS

Bills not paid at maturity subject to sight draft.

NEW YORK May 17 1909

Sold to M Bateman

1 Set Cush Nails 5X10 2.00 2.00

Light pink colored, 1900s example, with outstanding graphics, $75.

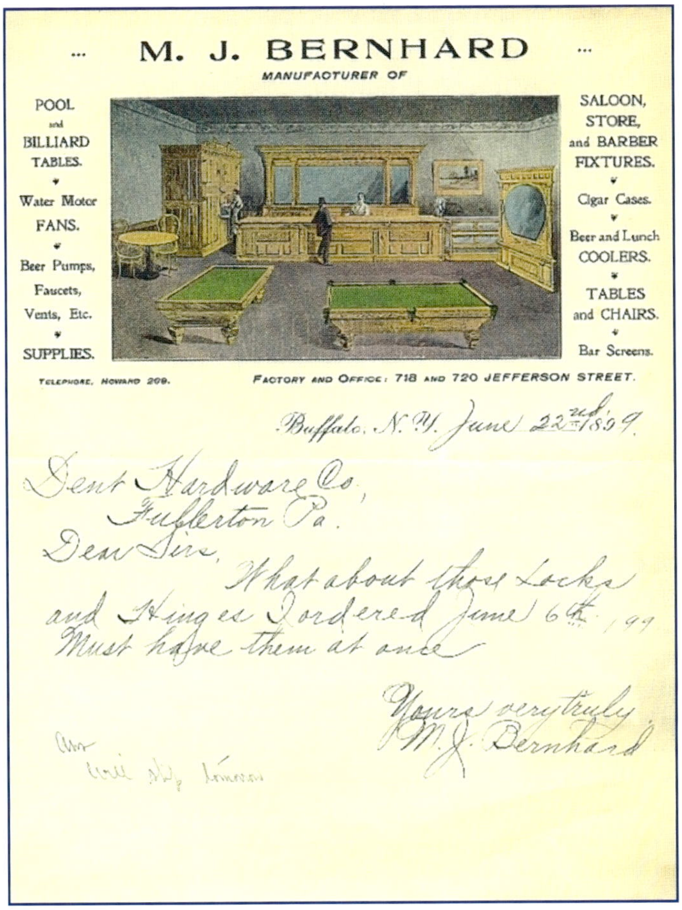

M. J. BERNHARD

MANUFACTURER OF

POOL and BILLIARD TABLES.
Water Motor FANS.
Beer Pumps, Faucets, Vents, Etc.
SUPPLIES.

SALOON, STORE, and BARBER FIXTURES.
Cigar Cases.
Beer and Lunch COOLERS.
TABLES and CHAIRS.
Bar Screens.

TELEPHONE, HOWARD 209. FACTORY AND OFFICE: 718 AND 720 JEFFERSON STREET.

Buffalo, N.Y. June 22nd 1899.

Dent Hardware Co,
Fullerton Pa.

Dear Sirs,

What about those Locks and Hinges I ordered June 6th '99. Must have them at once

Yours very truly
M. J. Bernhard

Signed by the "boss," M. J. Bernhard, 1899 date, fabulous colored billiard and barroom graphics, $130.

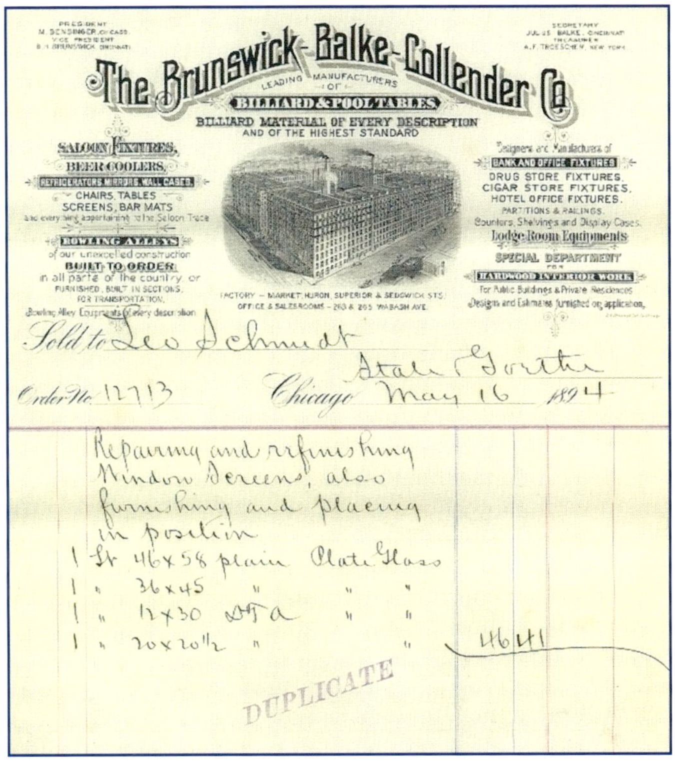

PRESIDENT M. BENSINGER, CHICAGO. VICE PRESIDENT B. H. BRUNSWICK, CINCINNATI

SECRETARY JULIUS BALKE, CINCINNATI. TREASURER A. F. TROESCHER, NEW YORK.

The Brunswick-Balke-Collender Co

LEADING MANUFACTURERS OF BILLIARD & POOL TABLES

BILLIARD MATERIAL OF EVERY DESCRIPTION AND OF THE HIGHEST STANDARD

SALOON FIXTURES, BEER COOLERS, REFRIGERATORS, MIRRORS, WALL CASES. CHAIRS, TABLES SCREENS, BAR MATS and everything appertaining to the Saloon Trade

BOWLING ALLEYS of our unexcelled construction BUILT TO ORDER in all parts of the country or FURNISHED, BUILT IN SECTIONS, FOR TRANSPORTATION. Bowling Alley Equipments of every description

Designers and Manufacturers of BANK AND OFFICE FIXTURES DRUG STORE FIXTURES, CIGAR STORE FIXTURES, HOTEL OFFICE FIXTURES. PARTITIONS & RAILINGS. Counters, Shelvings and Display Cases. Lodge Room Equipments

SPECIAL DEPARTMENT FOR HARDWOOD INTERIOR WORK For Public Buildings & Private Residences Designs and Estimates furnished on application.

FACTORY — MARKET, HURON, SUPERIOR & SEDGWICK STS. OFFICE & SALESROOMS — 263 & 265 WABASH AVE.

Sold to Leo Schmidt
State & Forthe

Order No. 12713 Chicago May 16 1894

Repairing and refinishing Window Screens, also furnishing and placing in position

1 St 46x58 plain Plate Glass
1 " 36x45 " " "
1 " 12x30 DSA " "
1 " 20x20½ " " 46.41

DUPLICATE

An 1890s version of a Brunswick-Balke-Collender Co.'s letterhead, very good condition, $45.

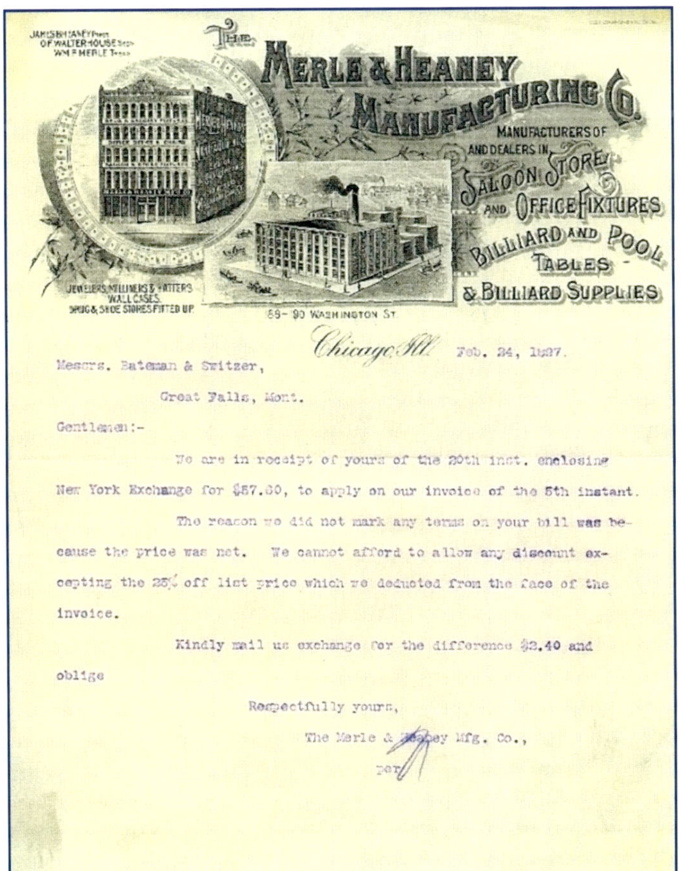

JAMES HEANEY Pres.
OF WALTER HOUSE Secy.
WM. F. MERLE Treas.

THE MERLE & HEANEY MANUFACTURING CO.

MANUFACTURERS OF AND DEALERS IN SALOON, STORE AND OFFICE FIXTURES BILLIARD AND POOL TABLES & BILLIARD SUPPLIES

JEWELERS, MILLINERS & HATTERS WALL CASES. DRUG & SHOE STORES FITTED UP

88–90 WASHINGTON ST

Chicago Ill. Feb. 24, 1897.

Messrs. Bateman & Switzer,

Great Falls, Mont.

Gentlemen:-

We are in receipt of yours of the 20th inst. enclosing New York Exchange for $57.60, to apply on our invoice of the 5th instant.

The reason we did not mark any terms on your bill was because the price was net. We cannot afford to allow any discount excepting the 25% off list price which we deducted from the face of the invoice.

Kindly mail us exchange for the difference $2.40 and oblige

Respectfully yours,

The Merle & Heaney Mfg. Co.,

per

An 1897 Merle & Heaney Manufacturing Co. super letterhead, very rare maker, $125.

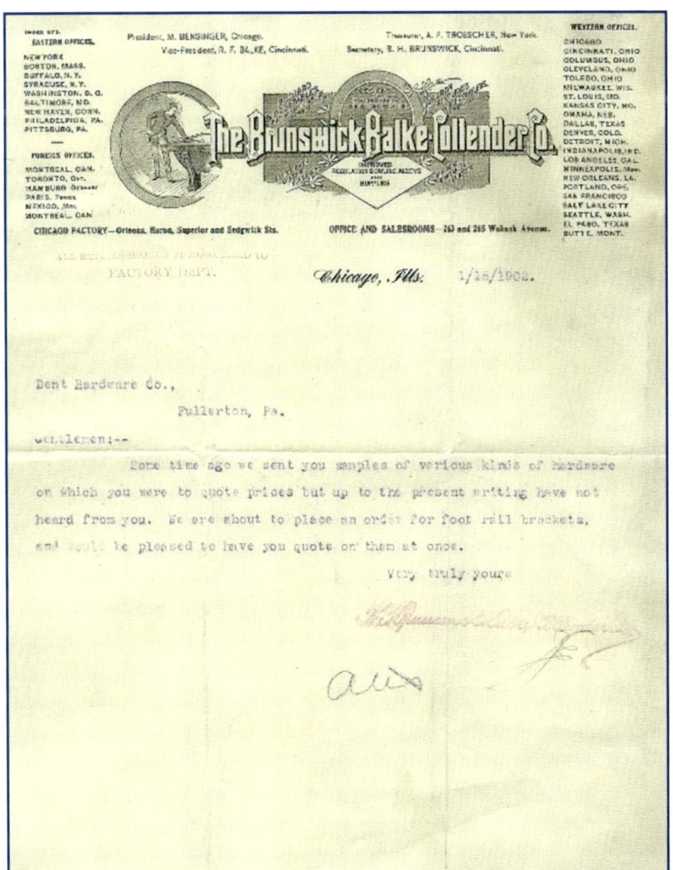

EASTERN OFFICES. NEW YORK, BOSTON, MASS., BUFFALO, N.Y., SYRACUSE, N.Y., WASHINGTON, D.C., BALTIMORE, MD., NEW HAVEN, CONN., PHILADELPHIA, PA., PITTSBURG, PA.

FOREIGN OFFICES. MONTREAL, CAN., TORONTO, ONT., HAMBURG, PARIS, MEXICO, MONTREAL, CAN.

President, M. BENSINGER, Chicago. Vice-President, R. F. BALKE, Cincinnati. Treasurer, A. F. TROESCHER, New York. Secretary, B. H. BRUNSWICK, Cincinnati.

WESTERN OFFICES. CHICAGO, CINCINNATI, OHIO, COLUMBUS, OHIO, CLEVELAND, OHIO, TOLEDO, OHIO, MILWAUKEE, WIS., ST. LOUIS, MO., KANSAS CITY, MO., OMAHA, NEB., DALLAS, TEXAS, DENVER, COLO., DETROIT, MICH., INDIANAPOLIS, IND., LOS ANGELES, CAL., MINNEAPOLIS, MINN., NEW ORLEANS, LA., PORTLAND, ORE., SAN FRANCISCO, SALT LAKE CITY, SEATTLE, WASH., EL PASO, TEXAS, BUTTE, MONT.

The Brunswick-Balke-Collender Co.

CHICAGO FACTORY—Orleans, Huron, Superior and Sedgwick Sts. OFFICE AND SALESROOMS—263 and 265 Wabash Avenue.

FACTORY DEPT.

Chicago, Ills. 1/16/1902.

Dent Hardware Co.,

Fullerton, Pa.

Gentlemen:--

Some time ago we sent you samples of various kinds of hardware on which you were to quote prices but up to the present writing have not heard from you. We are about to place an order for foot rail brackets, and would be pleased to have you quote on them at once.

Very truly yours

Early 1900s sampling of a Brunswick-Balke-Collender letterhead, $35.

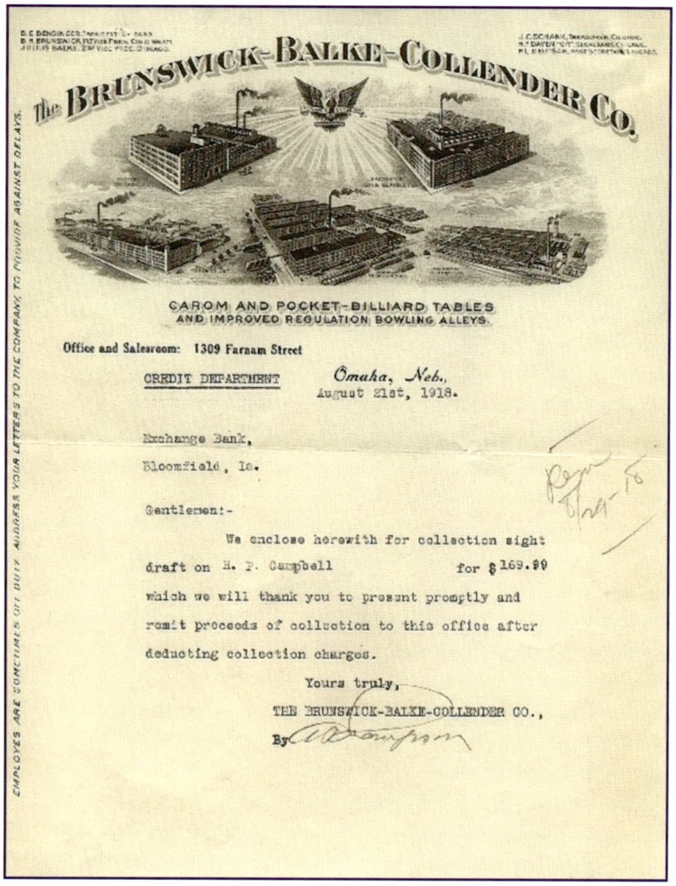
THE BRUNSWICK-BALKE-COLLENDER CO.

CAROM AND POCKET-BILLIARD TABLES
AND IMPROVED REGULATION BOWLING ALLEYS.

Office and Salesroom: 1309 Farnam Street

CREDIT DEPARTMENT

Omaha, Neb.,
August 21st, 1918.

Exchange Bank,

Bloomfield, Ia.

Gentlemen:-

We enclose herewith for collection sight draft on H. P. Campbell for $169.99 which we will thank you to present promptly and remit proceeds of collection to this office after deducting collection charges.

Yours truly,

THE BRUNSWICK-BALKE-COLLENDER CO.,

By

EMPLOYES ARE SOMETIMES OUT OF DUTY. ADDRESS YOUR LETTERS TO THE COMPANY, TO PROVIDE AGAINST DELAYS.

Later version Brunswick piece, dated 1918, $25.

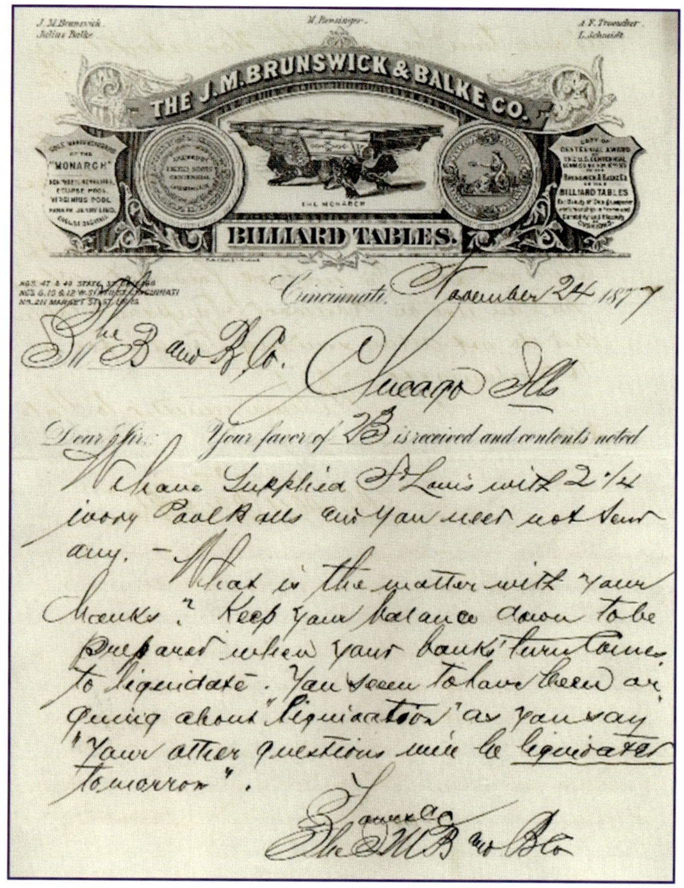
THE J. M. BRUNSWICK & BALKE CO.

BILLIARD TABLES.

Cincinnati, November 24 1877

Dear Sir: Your favor of 23 is received and contents noted

Graphically great 1877 letterhead showing Brunswick's "Monarch" pool table, very good condition, from one Brunswick employee to another!! $225.

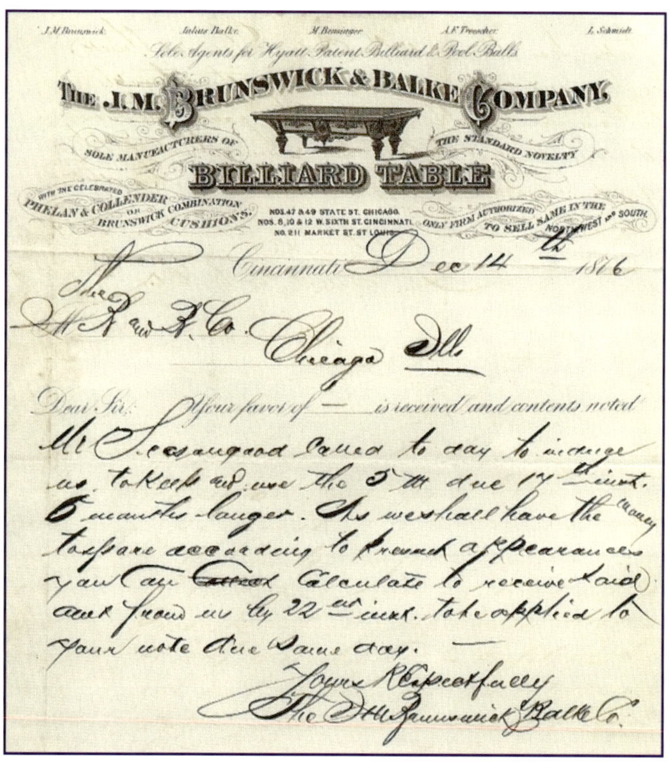
THE J. M. BRUNSWICK & BALKE COMPANY.

Sole Agents for Hyatt Patent Billiard & Pool Balls

SOLE MANUFACTURERS OF THE STANDARD NOVELTY BILLIARD TABLE

Cincinnati, Dec 14th 1876

Chicago Ill.

Dear Sir: Your favor of — is received and contents noted

Yours Respectfully

The J. M. Brunswick & Balke Co.

Super 1876 "J. M. Brunswick & Balke Company" letterhead, rare and in good condition, shows a Non-Pariel pool table, $175.

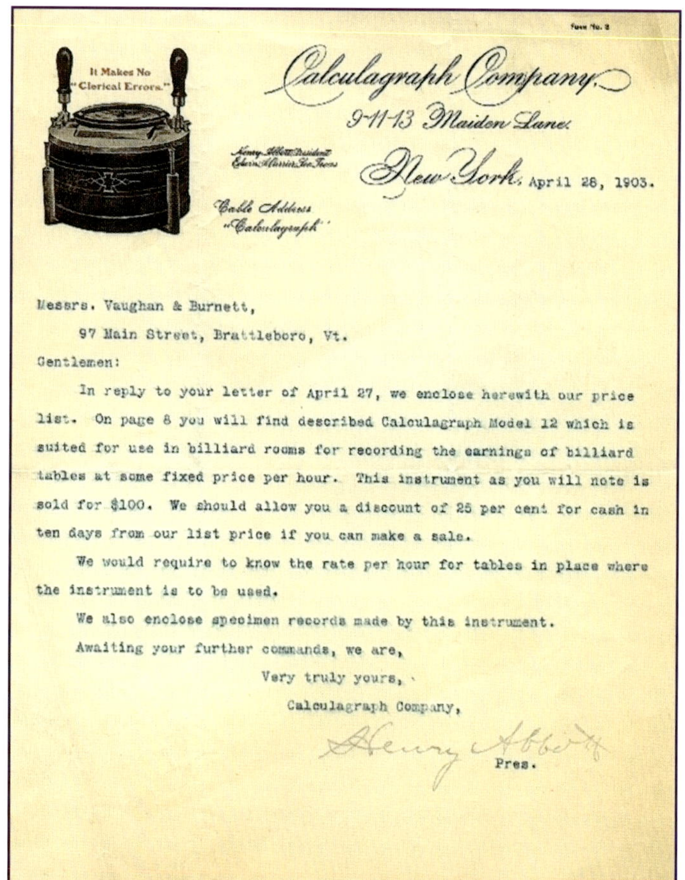

Calculagraph Company.

9-11-13 Maiden Lane.

Cable Address "Calculagraph"

New York, April 28, 1903.

Messrs. Vaughan & Burnett,

97 Main Street, Brattleboro, Vt.

Gentlemen:

In reply to your letter of April 27, we enclose herewith our price list. On page 8 you will find described Calculagraph Model 12 which is suited for use in billiard rooms for recording the earnings of billiard tables at some fixed price per hour. This instrument as you will note is sold for $100. We should allow you a discount of 25 per cent for cash in ten days from our list price if you can make a sale.

We would require to know the rate per hour for tables in place where the instrument is to be used.

We also enclose specimen records made by this instrument.

Awaiting your further commands, we are,

Very truly yours,

Calculagraph Company,

Henry Abbott
Pres.

Dated 1903, this Calculagraph Co. letterhead is a tricky one to find, $40.

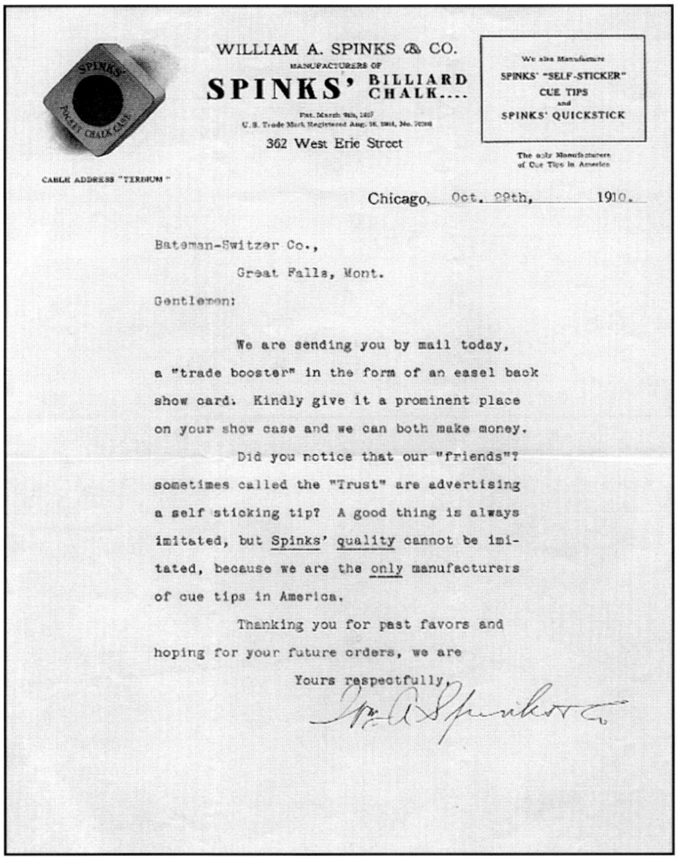

WILLIAM A. SPINKS & CO.
MANUFACTURERS OF
SPINKS' BILLIARD CHALK....
362 West Erie Street

We also Manufacture
SPINKS' "SELF-STICKER" CUE TIPS
and
SPINKS' QUICKSTICK

The only Manufacturers of Cue Tips in America

CABLE ADDRESS "TERBIUM"

Chicago, Oct. 29th, 1910.

Bateman-Switzer Co.,
Great Falls, Mont.

Gentlemen:

We are sending you by mail today, a "trade booster" in the form of an easel back show card. Kindly give it a prominent place on your show case and we can both make money.

Did you notice that our "friends"? sometimes called the "Trust" are advertising a self sticking tip? A good thing is always imitated, but Spinks' quality cannot be imitated, because we are the only manufacturers of cue tips in America.

Thanking you for past favors and hoping for your future orders, we are

Yours respectfully,
Wm. A. Spinks & Co.

Rare W. A. Spinks & Co. letterhead, neat graphic, $50.

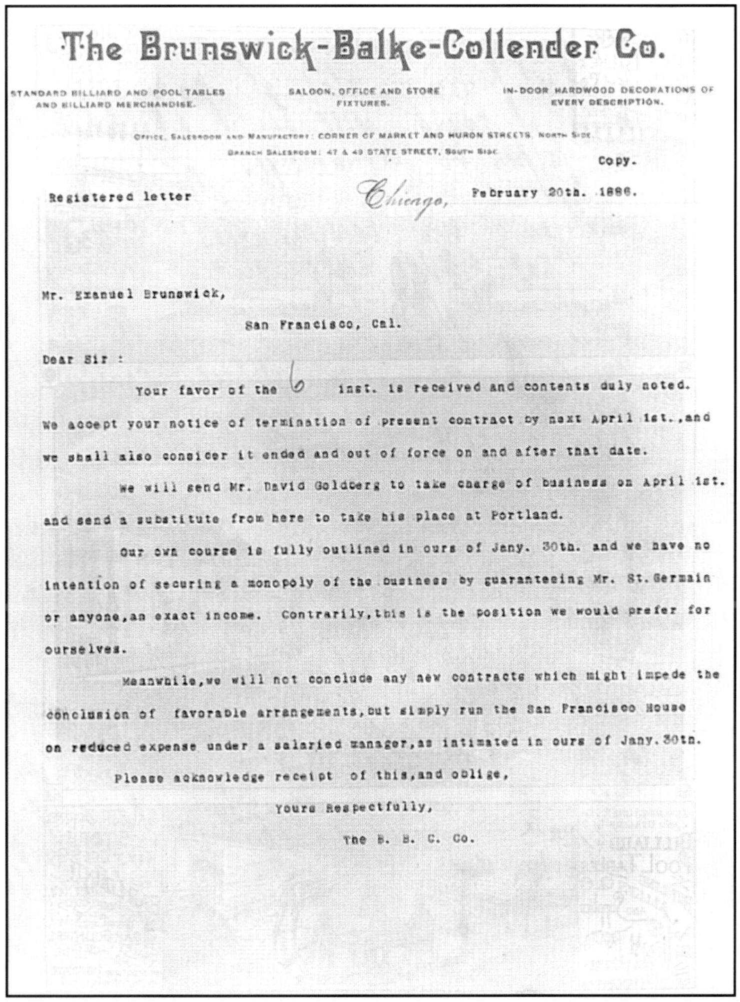

The Brunswick-Balke-Collender Co.

STANDARD BILLIARD AND POOL TABLES AND BILLIARD MERCHANDISE. SALOON, OFFICE AND STORE FIXTURES. IN-DOOR HARDWOOD DECORATIONS OF EVERY DESCRIPTION.

OFFICE, SALESROOM AND MANUFACTORY: CORNER OF MARKET AND HURON STREETS, NORTH SIDE.
BRANCH SALESROOM: 47 & 49 STATE STREET, SOUTH SIDE.

Copy.

Registered letter Chicago, February 20th. 1886.

Mr. Emanuel Brunswick,
San Francisco, Cal.

Dear Sir :

Your favor of the 6 inst. is received and contents duly noted. We accept your notice of termination of present contract by next April 1st.,and we shall also consider it ended and out of force on and after that date.

We will send Mr. David Goldberg to take charge of business on April 1st. and send a substitute from here to take his place at Portland.

Our own course is fully outlined in ours of Jany. 30th. and we have no intention of securing a monopoly of the business by guaranteeing Mr. St. Germain or anyone,an exact income. Contrarily,this is the position we would prefer for ourselves.

Meanwhile,we will not conclude any new contracts which might impede the conclusion of favorable arrangements,but simply run the San Francisco House on reduced expense under a salaried manager,as intimated in ours of Jany. 30th.

Please acknowledge receipt of this,and oblige,

Yours Respectfully,
The B. B. C. Co.

An 1886 dated letter from the Brunswick-Balke-Collender Co. in Chicago to Mr. Emanuel Brunswick in California, a brother to Mr. John Moses Brunswick himself. Very rare, $350.

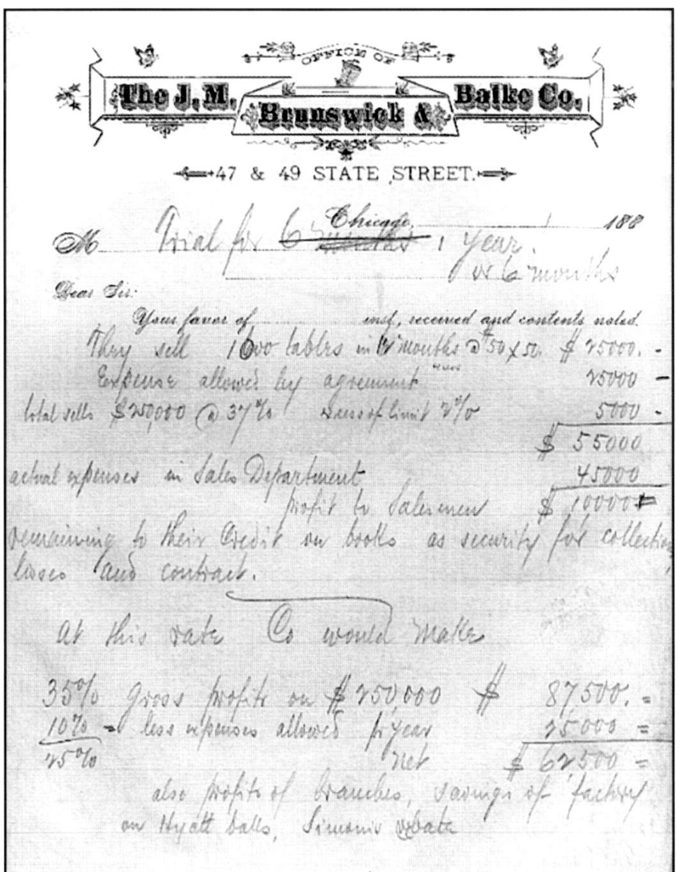

OFFICE OF
The J. M. Brunswick & Balke Co.
47 & 49 STATE STREET.

Chicago, 188

M Trial for 6 ~~months~~ 1 year or 6 months

Dear Sir:

Your favor of inst, received and contents noted.

They sell 1000 tables in 6 months @ 50 x 50 $ 25000.
Expense allowed by agreement 25000
total sells $250,000 @ 3% Sum of limit 2% 5000
$ 55000
actual expenses in Sales Department 45000
profit to Salesmen $ 10000
remaining to their Credit on books as security for collections losses and contract.

At this rate Co would make

35% gross profit on $ 250000 $ 87500.
10% less expenses allowed p/year 25000
25% net $ 62500
also profits of branches, savings of factory on Hyatt balls, Simonis & Data

An 1880s example of a letterhead the Brunswick & Balke Co. was using at that time, decent condition, from their earliest address in Chicago! $150.

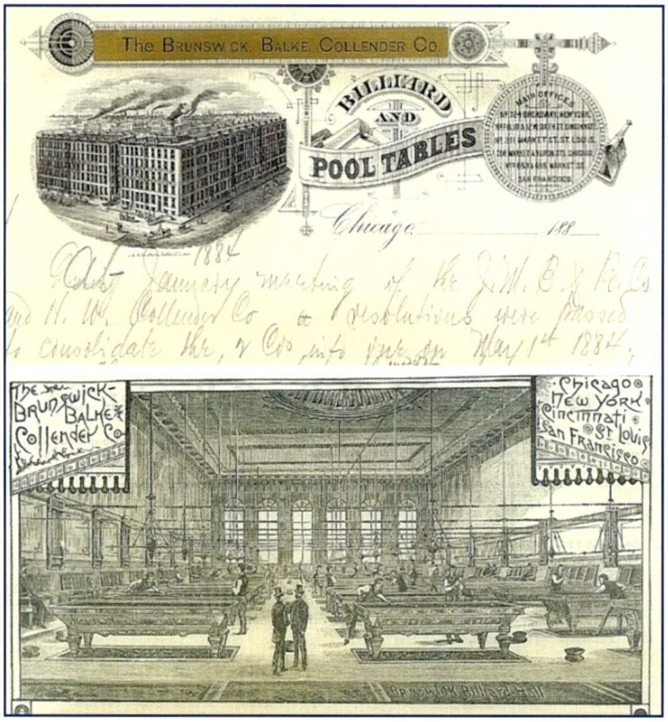

Outstanding letterhead (the top shot is on the front of the letter, and the bottom shot is just the top of the back part of the letter), superb piece of ephemera, extremely rare, $300+.

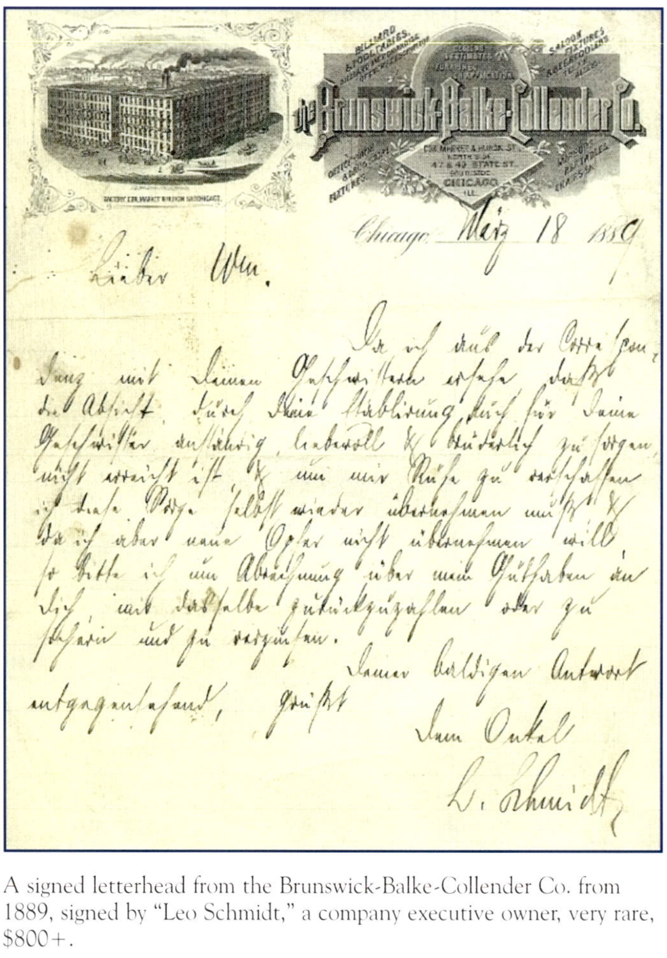

A signed letterhead from the Brunswick-Balke-Collender Co. from 1889, signed by "Leo Schmidt," a company executive owner, very rare, $800+.

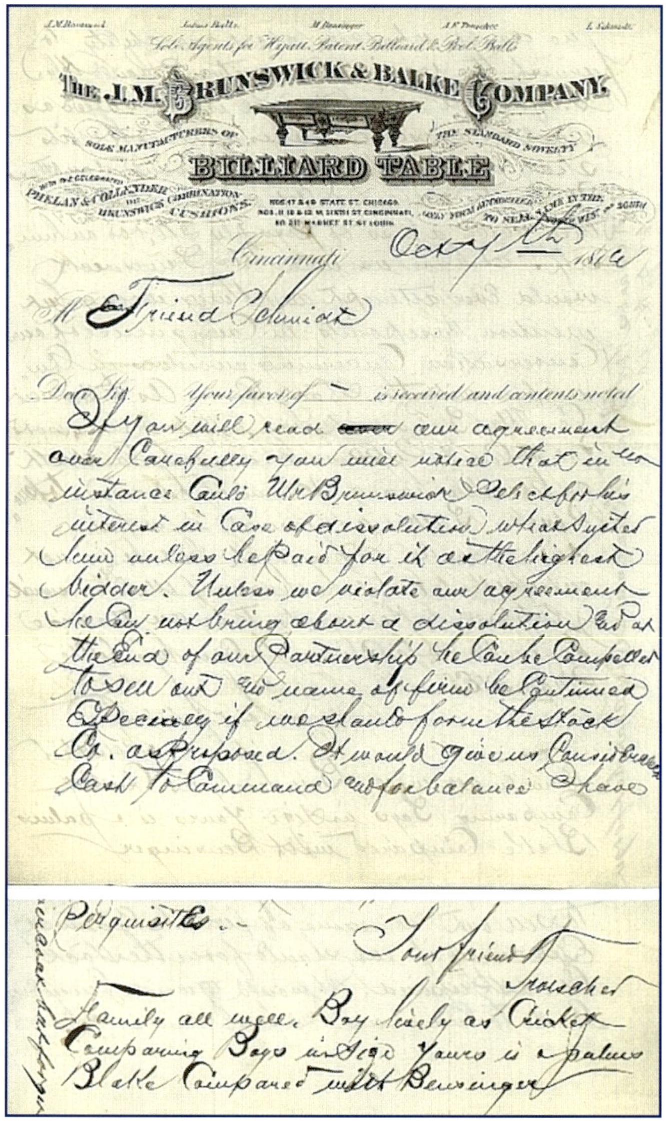

Another signed letterhead, this one by (A. F.) Troescher, 1876, very rare, $875+.

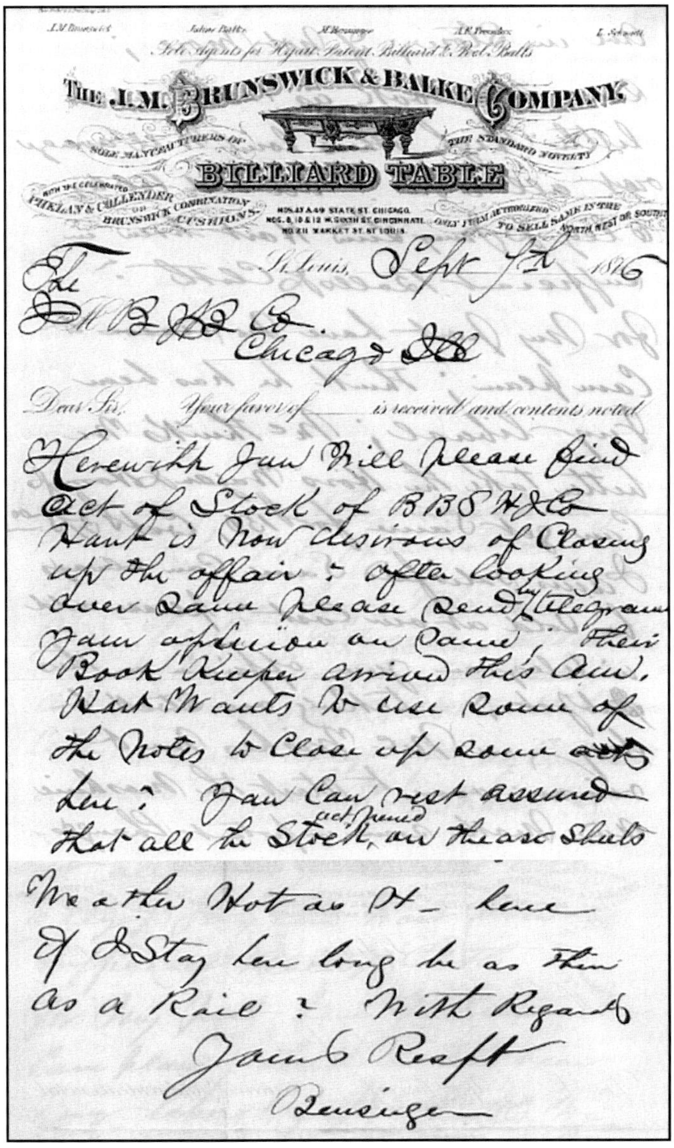

The J. M. Brunswick & Balke Company.

Billiard Table

St. Louis, Sept 7th 1876

The J M B & B Co
Chicago Ill

Dear Sir, Your favor of ______ is received and contents noted.

Herewith You Will please find act of Stock of B B & H & Co Hant is now desirous of Closing up the affair: after looking over Same please Send telegram your opinion on Same. Their Book Keeper arrived this am. Hart Wants to use Some of the Notes to Close up Some [illegible] here: You Can rest assured that all the Stock, on these Sheets Weather Hot as H— here If I Stay here long be as thin as a Rail: With Regards

Jacob Resft

Bensinger

Another signed letterhead from B. & B. Co., 1876, (M.) Bensinger, very rare, $875+.

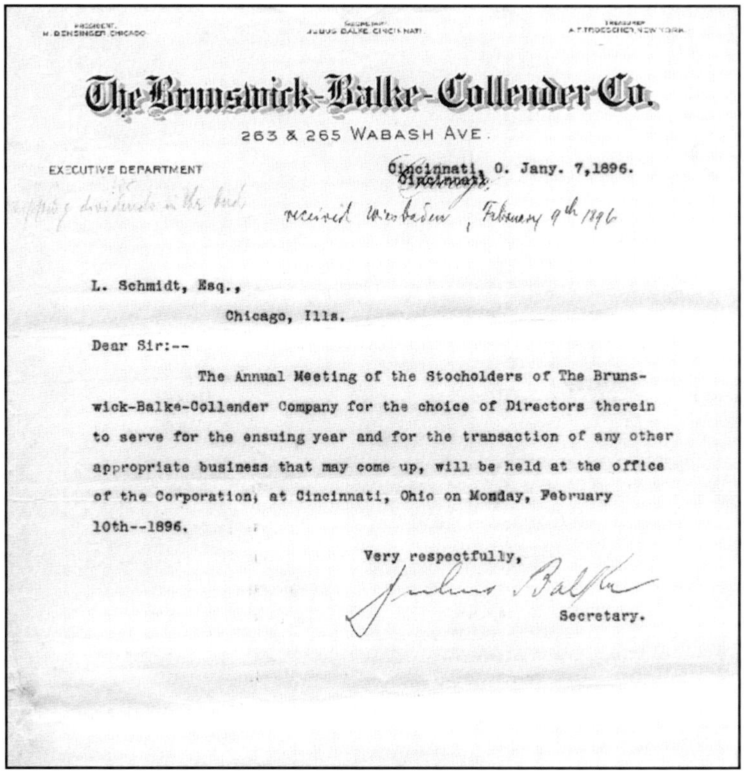

The Brunswick-Balke-Collender Co.

263 & 265 WABASH AVE.

EXECUTIVE DEPARTMENT

Cincinnati, O. Jany. 7,1896.

received Wiesbaden, February 9th 1896

L. Schmidt, Esq.,

Chicago, Ills.

Dear Sir:--

The Annual Meeting of the Stocholders of The Brunswick-Balke-Collender Company for the choice of Directors therein to serve for the ensuing year and for the transaction of any other appropriate business that may come up, will be held at the office of the Corporation, at Cincinnati, Ohio on Monday, February 10th--1896.

Very respectfully,

Julius Balke

Secretary.

One of the three best signatures available, very rare, of course. This letterhead is signed by Julius Balke, dated 1896, $1,500+.

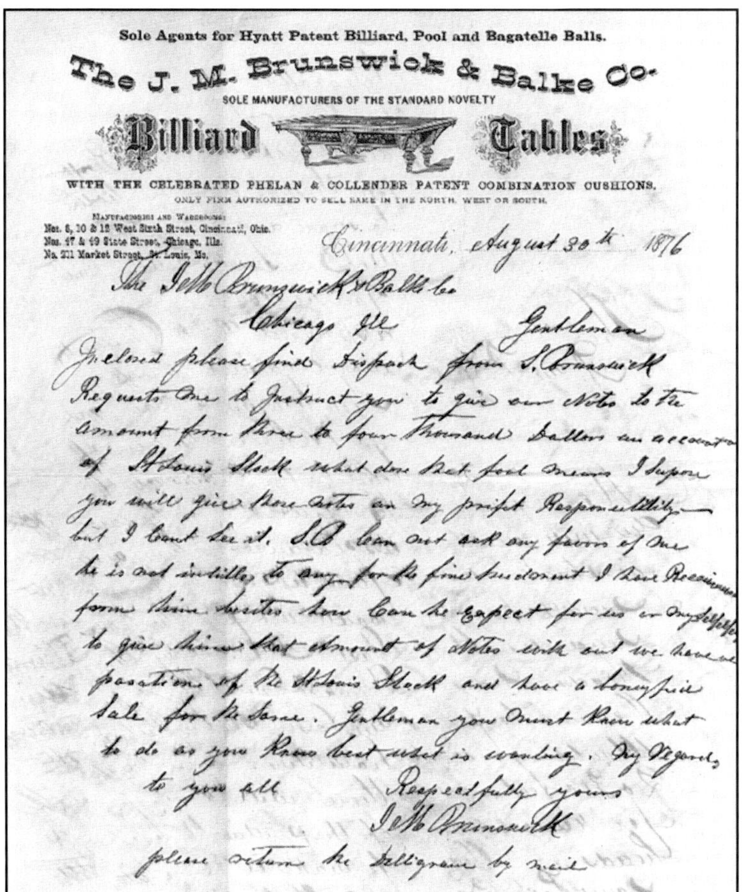

Sole Agents for Hyatt Patent Billiard, Pool and Bagatelle Balls.

The J. M. Brunswick & Balke Co.

SOLE MANUFACTURERS OF THE STANDARD NOVELTY

Billiard Tables

WITH THE CELEBRATED PHELAN & COLLENDER PATENT COMBINATION CUSHIONS.

ONLY FIRM AUTHORIZED TO SELL SAME IN THE NORTH, WEST OR SOUTH.

Manufactories and Warerooms:
Nos. 8, 10 & 12 West Sixth Street, Cincinnati, Ohio.
Nos. 47 & 49 State Street, Chicago, Ills.
No. 211 Market Street, St. Louis, Mo.

Cincinnati, August 30th 1876

The J M Brunswick & Balke Co
Chicago Ill Gentleman

Inclosed please find Dispatch from S. Brunswick Requests me to instruct you to give our Notes to the amount from three to four Thousand Dollars on account of St Louis Stock what does that fool means I suppose you will give those Notes on my private Responsibility but I dont see it. S.B. can not ask any favors of me he is not entitled to any for the fine treatment I have Received from their hands how can he expect for us or myself to give them that amount of Notes with out we have possession of the St Louis Stock and have a bonafide Sale for the Same. Gentleman you must know what to do as you know best what is wanting. My Regards to you all Respectfully yours

J M Brunswick

please return the telligram by mail

The most desirable signature to be found, John Moses Brunswick himself, on a very early letterhead, 1876, featuring a beautiful Non-Pariel billiard table, good condition, $2,000+.

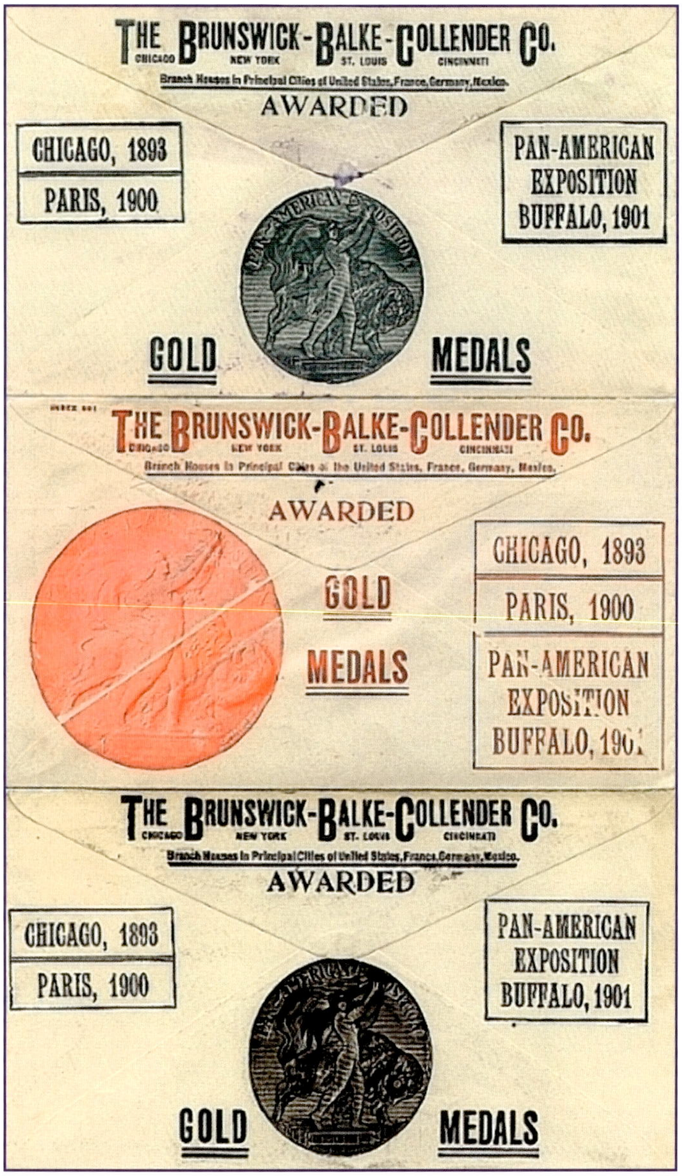

Three early 1900s Brunswick Co. envelopes, great graphics for an envelope, $65+ each.

T: An 1894 Brunswick-Balke-Collender Co. envelope with a Brilliant Novelty displayed, rare, $145. B: An 1895 B. B. C. envelope, $85+.

T: Ultra rare O. D. Benjamin envelope with a very unusual miniature business directory on the other side, good condition. Because of special text feature, $250+. B: 1899 Chas. Passow & Sons envelope, super graphics, $150.

1893 and 1895 dates on these two awesome B. A. Stevens envelopes, $155+ each.

T: 1870s J. M. Brunswick & Balke Co. envelope, the pool table is the "Monarch," very rare, $175. B: An unusual envelope with *embossed lettering* by B. B. C. from what appears to be 1888(?), good condition, $130.

A group of early hotel "blotters," c. 1860s to 1890s, for blotting messy ink signatures when signing in at a hotel. These always had several advertisements for the more prominent local businesses. The left edge of the left three, and the center section of the front blotter, show ads for billiard establishments near, or in, the hotel. All are in nice condition, $55 each.

A blotter provided by the Chas. Passow & Sons Billiard & Pool Table Co. for use in any business office of the day, c. 1890s. Nice condition, quite rare as a blotter, $375+.

Beautifully colored blotter, complete with a 1918 calendar, rare, and super condition, $135+.

Chapter II
Magazine Ads, Catalogs, and Books

This chapter covers three specific categories. Shown first, some partial to full page advertisements from the early to late 1800s, followed by some "interior" shots from a few hard to find examples of early billiard catalogs and supply price guides (prices are for good complete catalogs), and finally a small group of early books about the game.

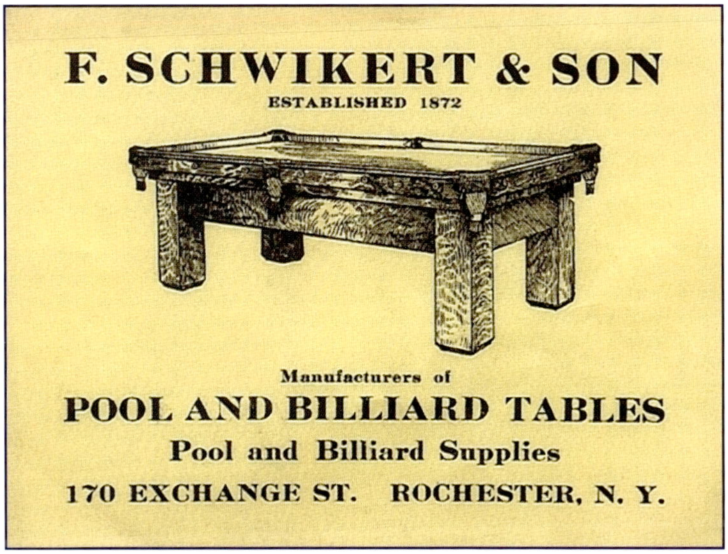

3.5" x 4.75" flier ad, fair condition, $15.

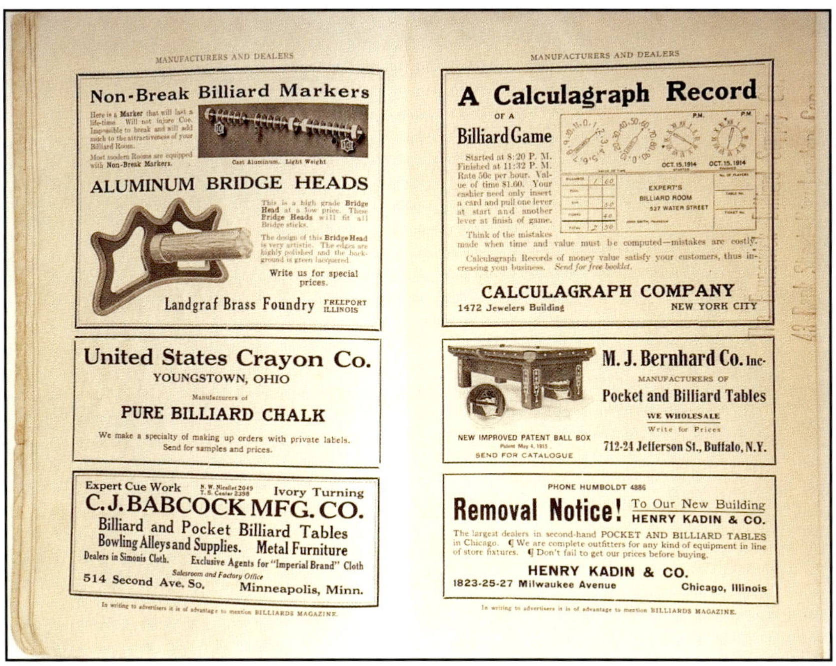

Typical ad from an issue of *Billiard's Magazine*, 1915. These magazines are literally seething with great billiard images, stories, and tournament results, unparalleled for reference material, $250 / issue.

Article from an 1863 issue of *Frank Leslie's Illustrated Newspaper*, great image, $30.

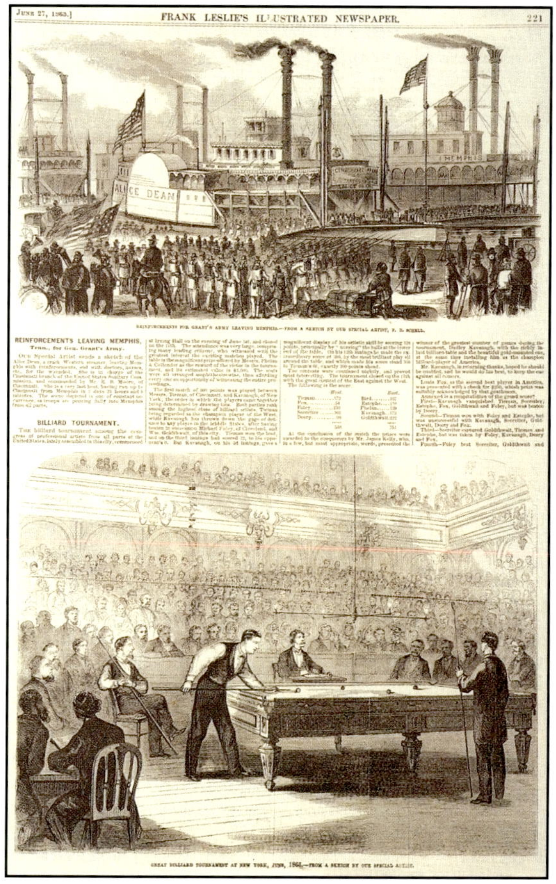

June 27, 1863.] FRANK LESLIE'S ILLUSTRATED NEWSPAPER. 221

REINFORCEMENTS LEAVING MEMPHIS, TENN., FOR GEN. GRANT'S ARMY.

BILLIARD TOURNAMENT.

HARPER'S WEEKLY. VOLUME XXVI, NO. 1312.

SLOSSON AND VIGNAUX.

THE BILLIARD MATCH BETWEEN SLOSSON AND VIGNAUX—CHEERING THE VICTOR.

Article about, and showing a bird's-eye view of, a February 1882 billiard tournament, from an issue of *Harper's Weekly*, $35.

HARPER'S WEEKLY.

THE BLACKVILLE BILLIARD CLUB—A MENACE TO VIGNAUX.

"If Mr. Johnsing make dat shot, we'll bick him agin de hull Chicago Turnupment."

Drawn by Sol. Eytinge, Jun.

Another *Harper's Weekly* article that makes reference to an impending 1883 world billiard tournament to be held in Chicago. The "fellas" in the image are hoping their hero, who is attempting a shot, will get a chance to compete. Charming period theme, suitable to frame as a print, $65.

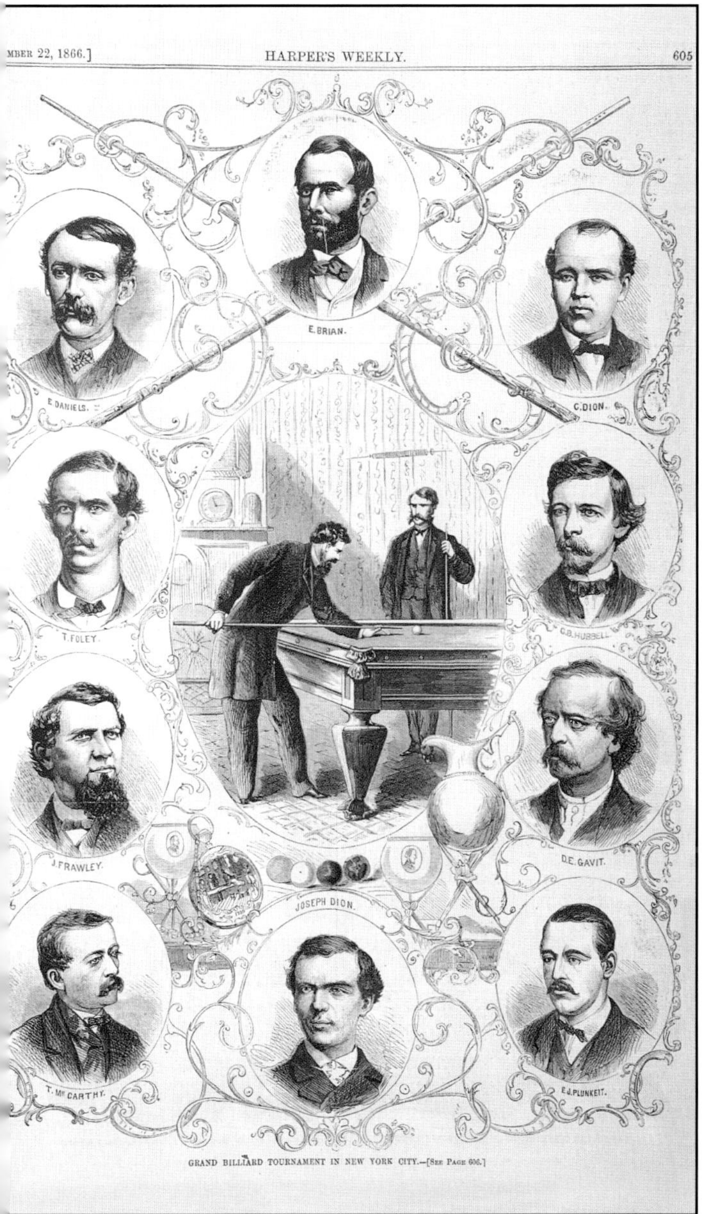

A *Harper's Weekly* full page print commemorating the "Grand Billiard Tournament In New York City," showing all the contenders and the champion. Fabulous and coveted image, dated September 22, 1866, $110.

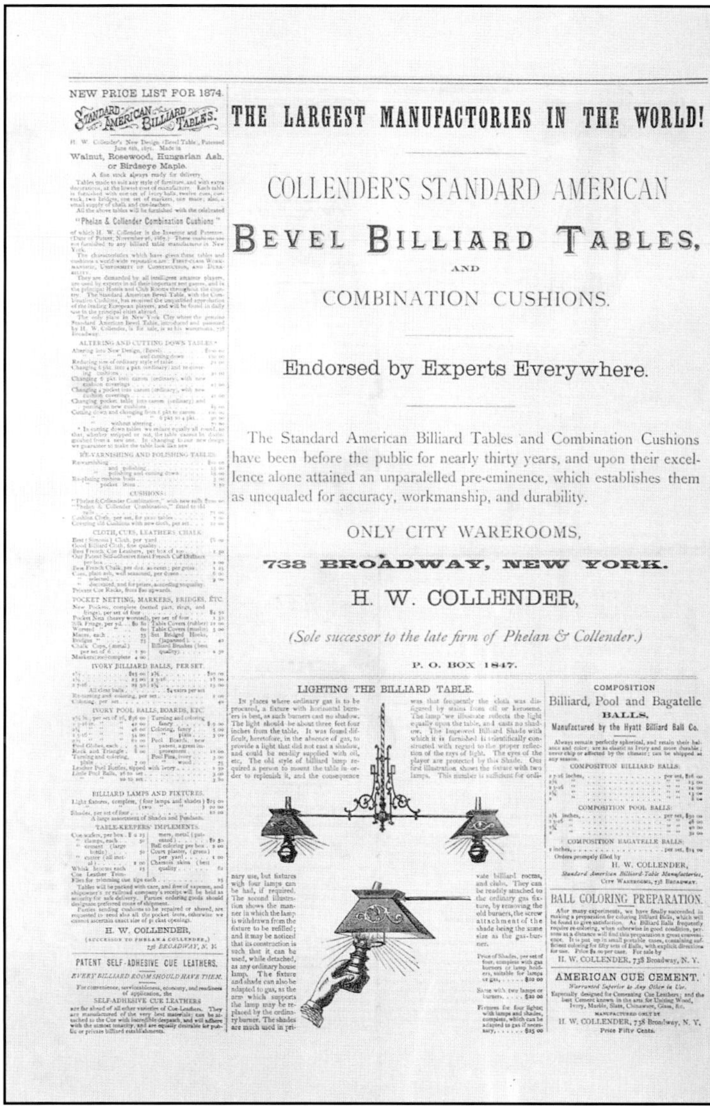

Definitely the most coveted billiard periodical there ever was, *The Billiard Cue* was devoted entirely to the royal sport of billiards. This is full page ad (from an 1874 issue) from the H. W. Collender Co., long before he merged with the J. M. Brunswick Co. in 1883. Very rare, $900+ for the entire paper.

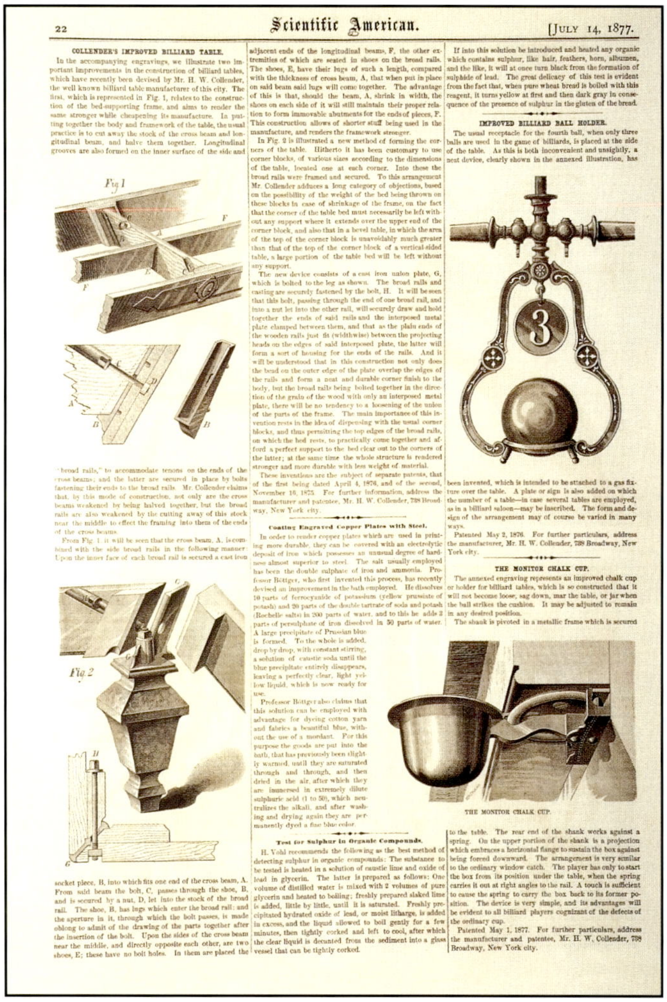

22 Scientific American. [July 14, 1877.

COLLENDER'S IMPROVED BILLIARD TABLE.

IMPROVED BILLIARD BALL HOLDER.

Coating Engraved Copper Plates with Steel.

THE MONITOR CHALK CUP.

Test for Sulphur in Organic Compounds.

Article from an 1877 issue of *Scientific American* magazine showing "improvements and patents" from H. W. Collender. Excellent condition, $45.

586 The Spirit of the Times, Dec. 24,

DECKER'S BILLIARD AND POOL TABLES with the New Corded Edge Cushion. The best now made! Warerooms, 726 Broadway, N.Y.

The J. M. Brunswick & Balke Co

PARKER'S GINGER TONIC

PARKER'S HAIR BALSAM.

Veuve Clicquot Ponsardin. Yellow Label Dry. White Label Rich. Champagne.

Grand Vintage 1878.

COLLENDER BILLIARD TABLES

THE H. W. COLLENDER COMPANY,

30 DAYS TRIAL ALLOWED.

I. H. SMITH'S SONS

HOPE FOR THE DEAF

ASTHMA Quickly and Permanently CURED

WM. H. GRIFFITH & CO.

F. GROTE & CO

TURNERS AND DEALERS IN IVORY.

BILLIARD BALLS, CLOTH, CUES,

WAREROOMS, 900 BROADWAY, NEW YORK.

MATHEY CAYLUS CAPSULES

L.S.L.

LOUISIANA STATE LOTTERY CO.

The J. M. Brunswick & Balke Co

724 BROADWAY, NEW YORK.

BILLIARD & POOL TABLES.

MAKE HENS LAY.

A POSITIVE CURE

M. Crichton & Co., DISTILLERS, Baltimore.

REPRESENTED BY J. D. W. SHERMAN, 62 Water Street, New York.

A full page ad from *The Spirit of the Times / A Gentleman's Magazine*, replete with advertisements from some of the leading billiard table manufacturers of the period, dated 1881, $95.

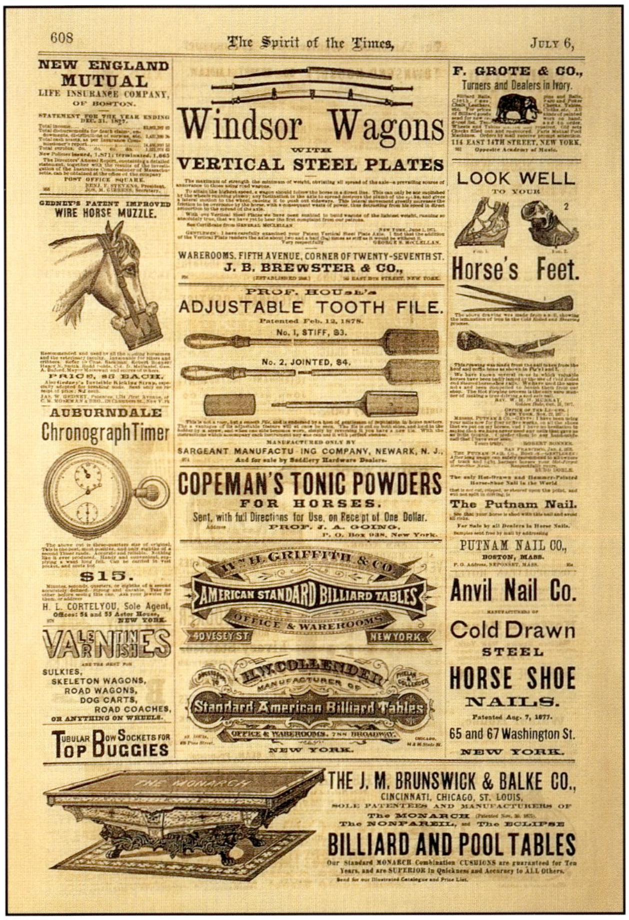

Very early example of *The Spirit of the Times*, dated 1878, showing one of the oldest versions of the famous "Monarch" model billiard table, showing that they were still the Brunswick & Balke Co. at this time. Large ad, good condition, very rare image, $125.

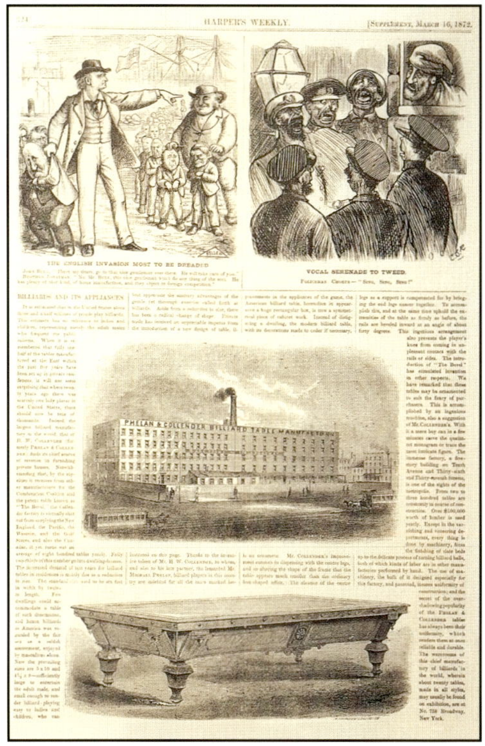

Harper's Weekly, dated 1872, showing the "Phelan & Collender Table Manufactory." Great example of one of their finer table models. Excellent condition, $80.

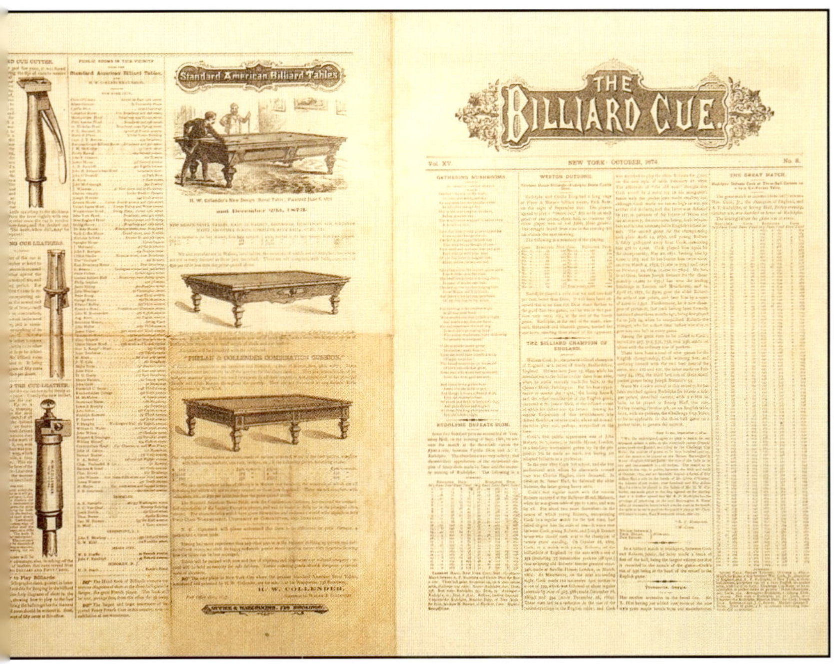

Opened to reveal both the front and back pages, this is another example of *The Billiard Cue* periodical. Dated 1874, $900+ for the entire paper.

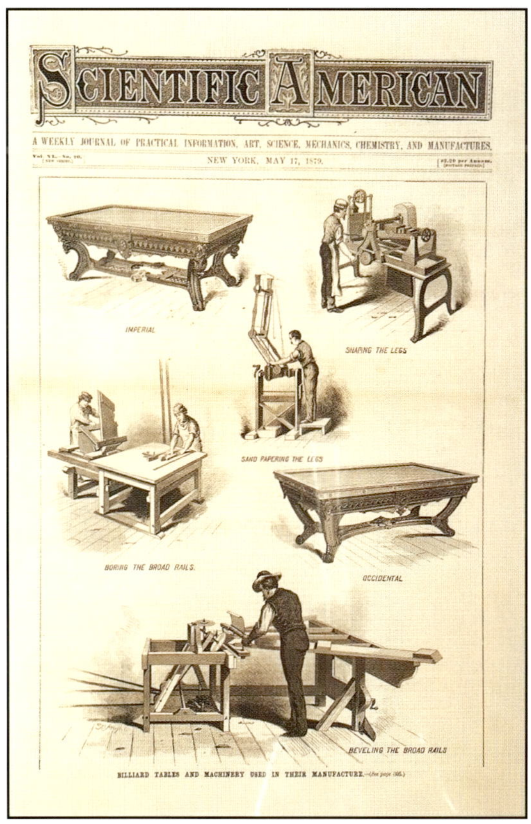

COVER page from an 1879 issue of the *Scientific American* journal. This is an article depicting a few different steps in the H. W. Collender's methods of manufacturing, and two super images of the most spectacular tables they ever produced. Rare and coveted, $110.

An ad from 1876 for "J. Schaffer & Bro. Billiard Table Co.," good condition, $20.

An 1871 ad from a book of prose and poetry, interesting early image, $25.

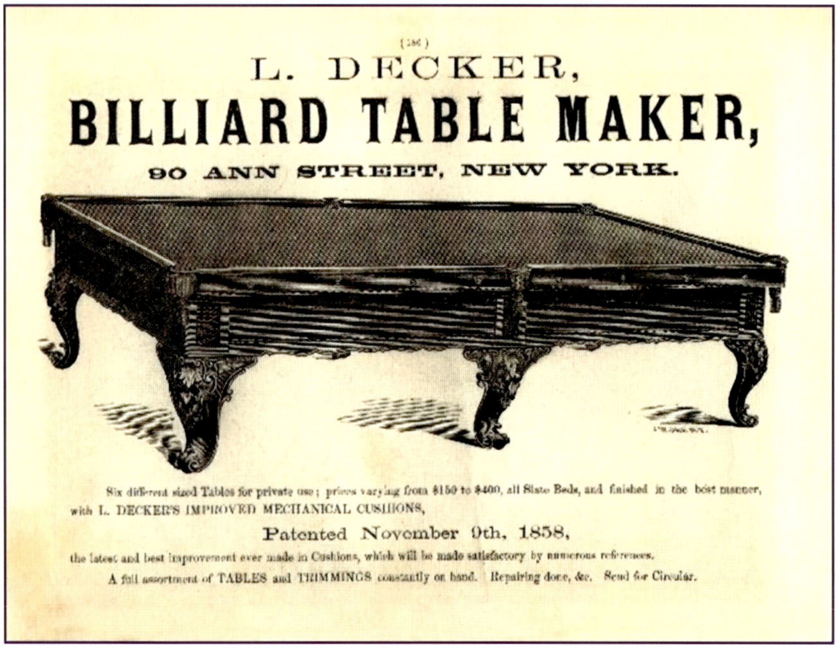

A 6.5" x 9" full page ad from an 1860s vintage periodical (pat. 1858 on table), very good condition, $80.

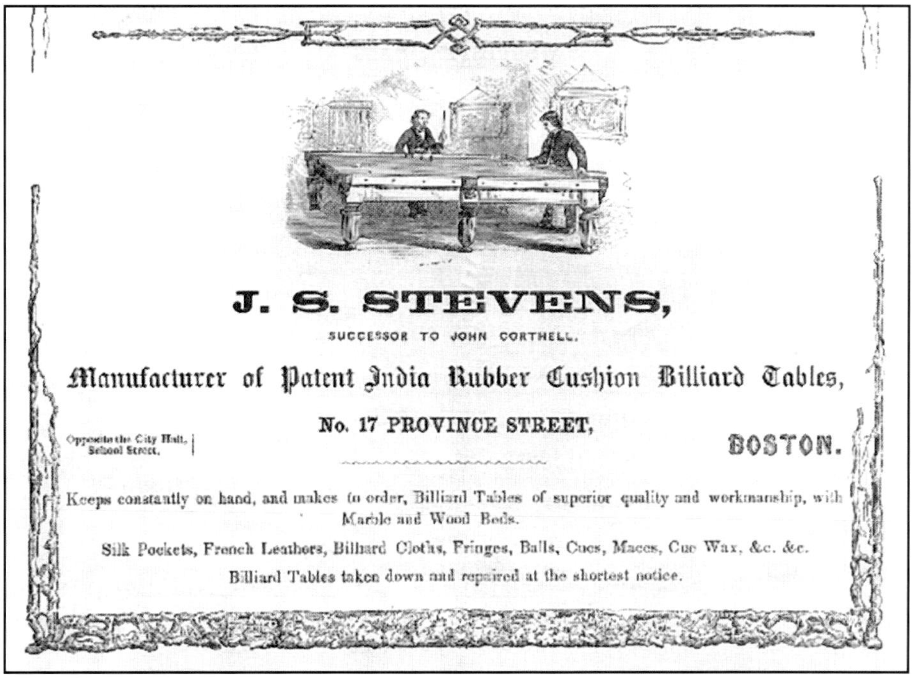

An ad for an 1850s to1860s period manufacturer. It is hard to find pieces this early, $65.

Another 1850s and 1860s period manufacturer's advertisement, nice condition, $55.

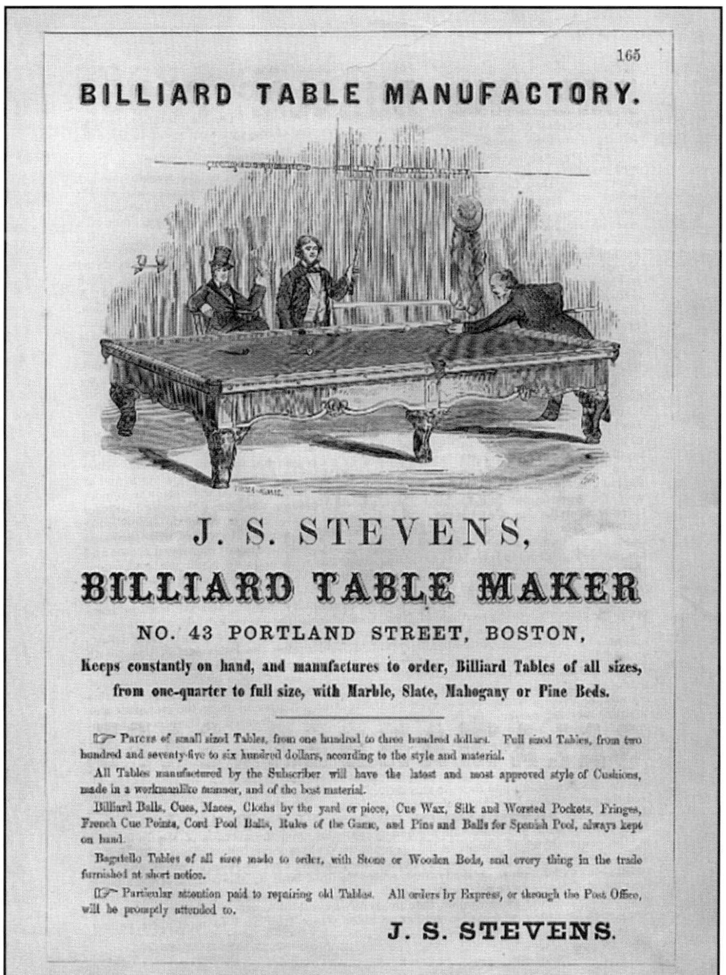

An 1860s period ad, full page piece, offering beds made from marble, slate, mahogany, or pine!! Interesting fact indeed. Rare ad, $155.

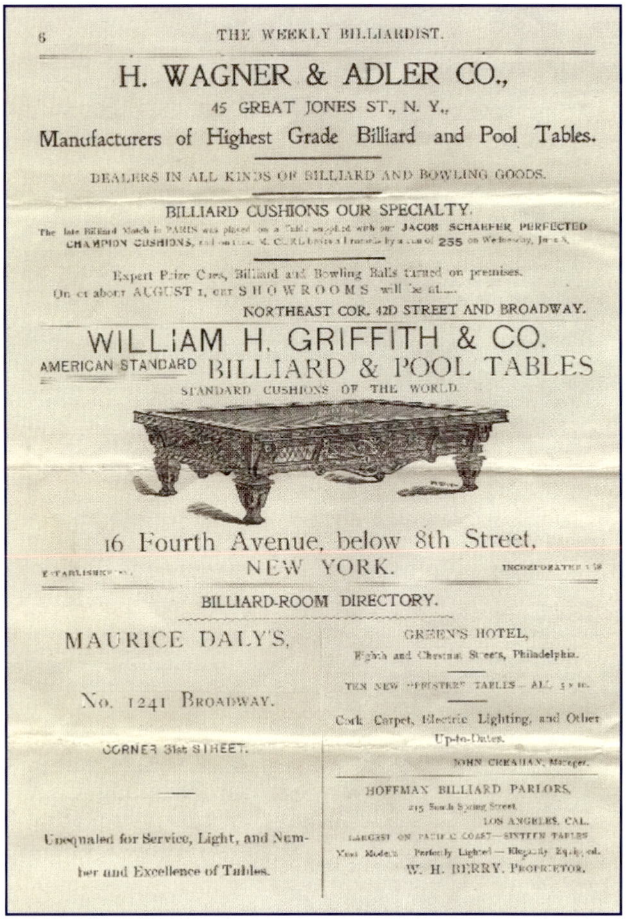
6 THE WEEKLY BILLIARDIST.

H. WAGNER & ADLER CO.,

45 GREAT JONES ST., N. Y.,

Manufacturers of Highest Grade Billiard and Pool Tables.

DEALERS IN ALL KINDS OF BILLIARD AND BOWLING GOODS.

BILLIARD CUSHIONS OUR SPECIALTY.

Expert Prize Cues, Billiard and Bowling Balls turned on premises.

On or about AUGUST 1, our SHOWROOMS will be at....

NORTHEAST COR. 42D STREET AND BROADWAY.

WILLIAM H. GRIFFITH & CO.

AMERICAN STANDARD BILLIARD & POOL TABLES

STANDARD CUSHIONS OF THE WORLD.

16 Fourth Avenue, below 8th Street,

NEW YORK.

BILLIARD-ROOM DIRECTORY.

MAURICE DALY'S,

No. 1241 BROADWAY.

CORNER 31st STREET.

Unequaled for Service, Light, and Number and Excellence of Tables.

GREEN'S HOTEL,

Eighth and Chestnut Streets, Philadelphia.

Cork Carpet, Electric Lighting, and Other Up-to-Dates.

JOHN CREAHAN, Manager.

HOFFMAN BILLIARD PARLORS,

LOS ANGELES, CAL.

W. H. BERRY, PROPRIETOR.

Three pages from *The Weekly Billiardist* magazine from the early 1900s. This magazine is elusive and coveted for its wealth of interesting reference material. A good condition issue will bring $175+.

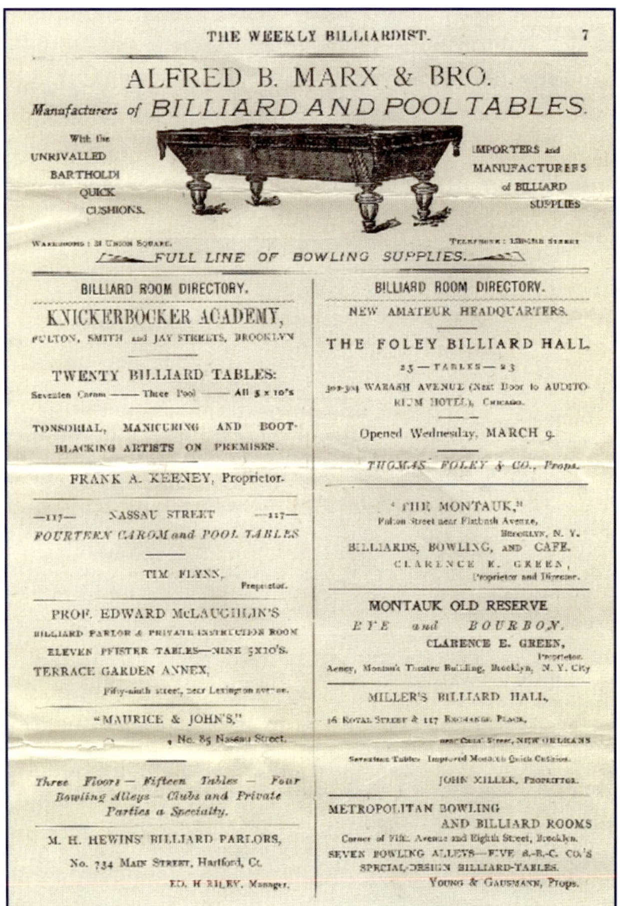
THE WEEKLY BILLIARDIST. 7

ALFRED B. MARX & BRO.

Manufacturers of *BILLIARD AND POOL TABLES.*

With the UNRIVALLED BARTHOLDI QUICK CUSHIONS.

IMPORTERS and MANUFACTURERS of BILLIARD SUPPLIES

WAREROOMS: 31 UNION SQUARE.

FULL LINE OF BOWLING SUPPLIES.

BILLIARD ROOM DIRECTORY.

KNICKERBOCKER ACADEMY,

FULTON, SMITH and JAY STREETS, BROOKLYN

TWENTY BILLIARD TABLES:

Seventeen Carom —— Three Pool —— All 5 x 10's

TONSORIAL, MANICURING AND BOOT-BLACKING ARTISTS ON PREMISES.

FRANK A. KEENEY, Proprietor.

—117— NASSAU STREET —117—

FOURTEEN CAROM and POOL TABLES

TIM FLYNN, Proprietor.

PROF. EDWARD McLAUGHLIN'S

BILLIARD PARLOR & PRIVATE INSTRUCTION ROOM

ELEVEN PFISTER TABLES—NINE 5X10'S.

TERRACE GARDEN ANNEX,

Fifty-ninth street, near Lexington avenue.

"MAURICE & JOHN'S,"

No. 85 Nassau Street.

Three Floors — Fifteen Tables — Four Bowling Alleys — Clubs and Private Parties a Specialty.

M. H. HEWINS' BILLIARD PARLORS,

No. 734 MAIN STREET, Hartford, Ct.

ED. H RILEY, Manager.

BILLIARD ROOM DIRECTORY.

NEW AMATEUR HEADQUARTERS.

THE FOLEY BILLIARD HALL.

23 — TABLES — 23

WABASH AVENUE (Next Door to AUDITORIUM HOTEL), CHICAGO.

Opened Wednesday, MARCH 9.

THOMAS FOLEY & CO., Props.

"THE MONTAUK,"

Fulton Street near Flatbush Avenue, BROOKLYN, N. Y.

BILLIARDS, BOWLING, AND CAFE.

CLARENCE E. GREEN, Proprietor and Director.

MONTAUK OLD RESERVE

RYE and BOURBON.

CLARENCE E. GREEN, Proprietor.

Montauk Theatre Building, Brooklyn, N. Y. City

MILLER'S BILLIARD HALL,

16 ROYAL STREET & 117 EXCHANGE PLACE,

near Canal Street, NEW ORLEANS

JOHN MILLER, PROPRIETOR.

METROPOLITAN BOWLING AND BILLIARD ROOMS

Corner of Fifth Avenue and Eighth Street, Brooklyn.

SEVEN BOWLING ALLEYS—FIVE B.-B.-C. CO.'S SPECIAL-DESIGN BILLIARD-TABLES.

YOUNG & GAUSMANN, Props.

THE WEEKLY BILLIARDIST.

The Brunswick-Balke-Collender Co.,

LEADING MANUFACTURERS OF

STANDARD BILLIARD AND POOL TABLES

Fitted with their CELEBRATED and always RELIABLE

MONARCH CUSHIONS. (PATENTED.)

Always on Hand a Large Assortment of New and Second Hand Billiard and Pool Tables At Prices and Terms to Suit Purchasers.

BILLIARD MATERIAL OF EVERY DESCRIPTION

OF OUR OWN MANUFACTURE AND IMPORTATION.

PRINCIPAL OFFICES AND WAREROOMS:

NEW YORK,	CHICAGO,	CINCINNATI,	ST. LOUIS,	SAN FRANCISCO
FOURTH AVENUE, cor. 13TH ST.	263 & 265 WABASH AVE.	130 & 132 EA. SIXTH STR.	106 SO. FOURTH STR.	653 & 655 MARKET STR.

Branch Offices and Warerooms in all Leading Cities of the United States.

TELEPHONE 568 18TH ST

F. GROTE & CO.,

ESTABLISHED IN 1847

TURNERS AND DEALERS IN

IVORY

Manufacturers and Importers of BILLIARD MATERIAL.

Builders of the "GROTE STANDARD" BOWLING ALLEYS

114 EAST FOURTEENTH ST., OPPOSITE ACADEMY OF MUSIC NEW YORK

FOR PARLOR USE.

PRICES.

Young America Table, for Children,	$1.50	No. 2 Table, size 2x4, Extra,	$10.00
No. 1 Table, size 2x4,	5.00	No. 2 Table, size 2x4, Extra, with Stand,	12.00
No. 1 Table, size 2x4, with Stand,	7.00	No. 3 Table, size 2½x5, Extra,	14.00

No. 3 Table, size 2½x5, Extra, with Stand, $16.00. Large size Ivory Balls, $3.00 per set.

☞ Furnish with all the above Tables, 4 Balls, 2 Cues, Spirit Level, Pool Outfit, and Counters. Delivered to any part of the city.

A Billiard Table suitable for the parlor, whereby the popular game of Billiards can be enjoyed within the family circle is a want that has long been felt, and we have endeavored to supply that want.

The game of Billiards has become a national game throughout the civilized globe, and the objections heretofore urged that its fascination and interest keep young men out frequently until a late hour in the evening, is entirely overcome by our Parlor Tables. Every house, no matter of what order, the Hotel, Boarding House, Private dwelling, should all possess them for the comfort, health, amusement and diversion of the game to all, no matter how delicate. The call upon every father and mother in the land is, make home, the sacred family circle, the most joyous place on earth. The Billiard Table does much to accomplish this result. It adds new joy to the home, binds the family circle, makes the morning and evening of every household rejoice. The temptation offered at Billiard halls to dissipation and the ruin of the brother and the son are largely overcome by having in the family one of our Billiard Tables. The desire to spend the evening away from home is taken away. The boys and girls both unite in saying, no place like home, sweet home.

Our Billiard Tables are made after the most approved of the larger and more costly ones, and we sell them at so small prices, that they are within the reach of every family.

Frames are of black walnut, the cushions are rubber, perfect in every respect, and the whole outfit complete. They can be laid upon the centre table in the parlor, or breakfast table in the dining room, as shown in the above cut, and are ample in size to enable two persons, or even four, to play the game as satisfactorily in every respect as they could upon the larger Tables now in use throughout the country.

The **Akam Billiard Table** has been endorsed by the most noted Billiard Table Manufacturers in the country, who say it is the most perfect and the best Table for the purpose for which it is designed ever introduced in the market. We make them perfect, we abhor a sham, and we never send a Table out unless we know it is right and will last for years.

C. G. AKAM, Inventor & Manufacturer,
22 East Adams Street, CHICAGO.

On Exhibition and Sale at ....

Cover page for a very rare, original 1870s "Akam Billiard Table Co." catalog, four pages, good condition, $550+.

30 Years Practical Experience.

THE

National Billiard Mfg. Co.

ESTABLISHED 1860.

A. GUNKLACH & CO.

96 WEST CANAL STREET. - - - CINCINNATI, O.

MANUFACTURERS OF

BILLIARD & POOL TABLES,

SUPPLIED WITH OUR

IMPROVED "FAMOUS" CUSHIONS.

NEVER EXCELLED.

NEVER EQUALLED.

Importers and Dealers in a full and complete line of Billiard Supplies.

MANUFACTURERS AND PATENTEES OF THE COMPOSITION

MONARCH POOL BALLS.

ILLUSTRATIONS OF BILLIARD AND POOL TABLES AND PRICES FURNISHED ON APPLICATION.

Rare, original "National Billiard Mfg. Co." 1880s catalog, very good condition, well known maker of very fine goods, $895+.

R. HERRMANN'S

NEW YORK PRICE LIST

OF

BILLIARD BALLS, BILLIARD MATERIAL, REPAIRS, ETC.

2¼ Inches Ivory Billiard Balls, per set,	$—— $24.50
2⅜ " " " " "	from $20 to 23.00
2 1 16 " " " " for Parlor tables,	8 to 12.00
2¼ " Ivory Pool Balls, per set of 15 balls, " "	50 to 55.00
2¼ " " " " " " (old Ivory) "	35 to 45 00
2⅜ " Compressed Ivory Billiard Balls, per set, "	9 00
Turning and Coloring 1 Set Billiard Balls (best workmanship guaranteed,)	1.50
Turning and coloring 15 Pool Balls, No. 1, per set,	10 00
Coloring 15 Pool Balls, No. 1,	6.00
Turning, coloring and numbering 15 old Billiard Balls,	15.00
2 Inches Ivory Bagatell Balls, 9 balls per set, from	$15 00 to 20.00
1⅞ " " " " " " "	13 00 to 18.00
6-8 " Numbered Pool Balls, Ivory, 20 per set,	4.00
6-8 " " " " " 16 "	3.00
6-8 " " " Comp. Ivory, 20 "	2.00
6 8 " " " Boxwood, 20 "	1.50
Pool Pins, Ivory, per set,	4 00
" Boxwood, per set,	75
Ivory *Checks*, per hundred.	22.00
Bone " white, "	3.00
Bone " col'd, "	4.00

BILLIARD GOODS.

Billiard Table Cloth, Simonis No. 1, (sold for cash only) per yard, - - - - - - - - - $8.00

Cues, fancy and inlaid,	from 3.00 to 10.00 each
Cues, fine ash wood, per dozen,	5.00
French self-adhesive Cue Leathers, per box,	only 1 75
French Cue Leather, No. 1, per box,	only 1.50
French Billiard Chalk, per gross,	only 1.25
Cue Cutters,	from 1.50 to 2.50 each
Billiard Brushes, No. 1,	2.50
Leather Pool Boxes, each,	1.25

Ten Pin Balls are always kept on hand and made to order.

Ten Pin Balls re-adjusted, - - - 50 to 75 cts. each

I keep constantly on hand a large assortment of fine walking canes. Malace Cane with Ivory and Walrus handles, Sword Canes, Ebony Canes, handles inlaid with Gold and Silver; Hickory Canes at different prices; Fancy walking Canes, of every description made to order and repaired on short notice.

Instructions for the use of self adhesive Cue Leather: Remove from the Cue the old glue, wet the glue on the new leather lightly and then press it on the Cue.

In ordering *Billiard Table Cloth*, please send the length and width of the bed of your table, and I shall send the exact quantity of Simonis Cloth, No 1, and of the same quality as the sample furnished you at the price of $8.00 per yard.

Having had an experience of sixteen years as practical workman in the largest Ivory and Billiard establishments in New York and other cities, those favoring me with their patronage may rest assured that all work entrusted to me, will be executed in the very best workmanship, and on short notice.

In coloring Ivory Balls, I take such material as will in no way affect the quality and durability of the Ivory.

Balls sent to me for turning and coloring, will in all cases be done immediately, and will be sent back within twenty-four hours after receiving them.

Please write your address very plain, to avoid delay.

☞ Compare this Price List with those of other establishments, and you will find it your advantage to give me a call before purchasing elsewhere.

I guarantee best workmanship in all cases.

R. HERRMANN,

MANUFACTURER OF AND DEALER IN

Ivory Balls, and all other Billiard Material, Walking Canes, Etc.

OFFICE--No. 162 SENECA ST., (Up Stairs.)

Scarce, early 1870s, four page catalog from the "R. Herrmann's Billiard Supply Co." Neat graphics, some soiling, $550.

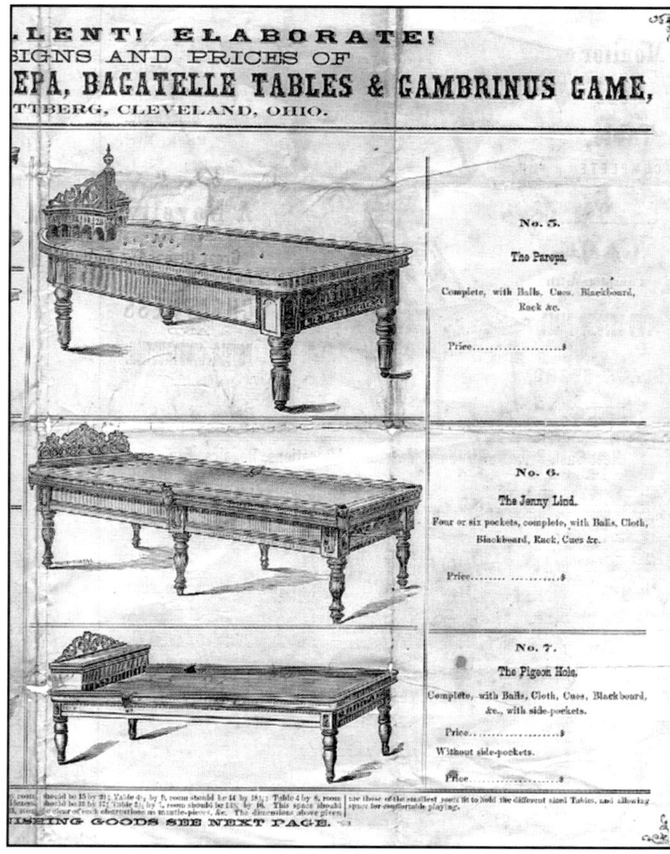

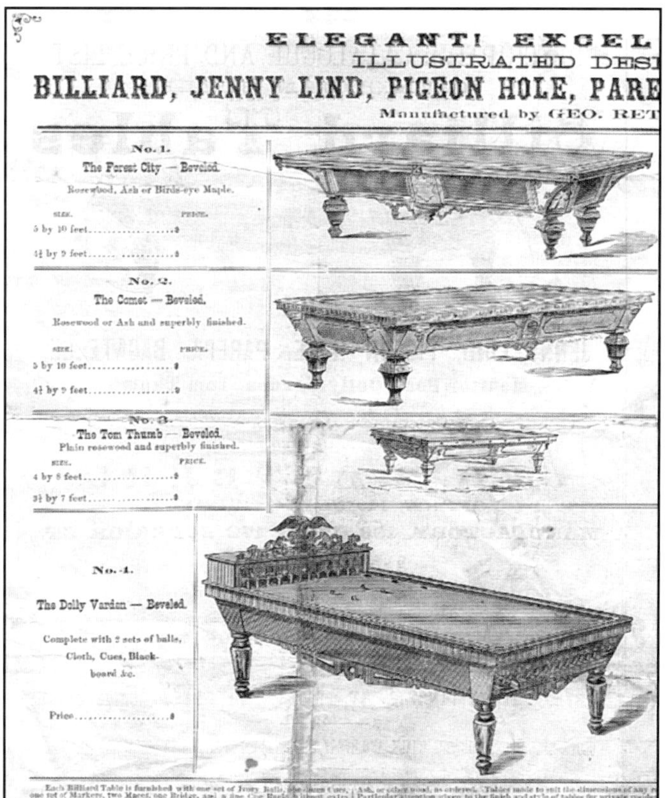

Ultra rare, 1870s, four page catalog from the "Geo. Rettberg" Billiard Table Co. Outstanding images of several of the truly unique tables that were available in the Victorian period. Poor condition, but a highly coveted piece of ephemera. As is, $350+. If found in excellent condition, $850+.

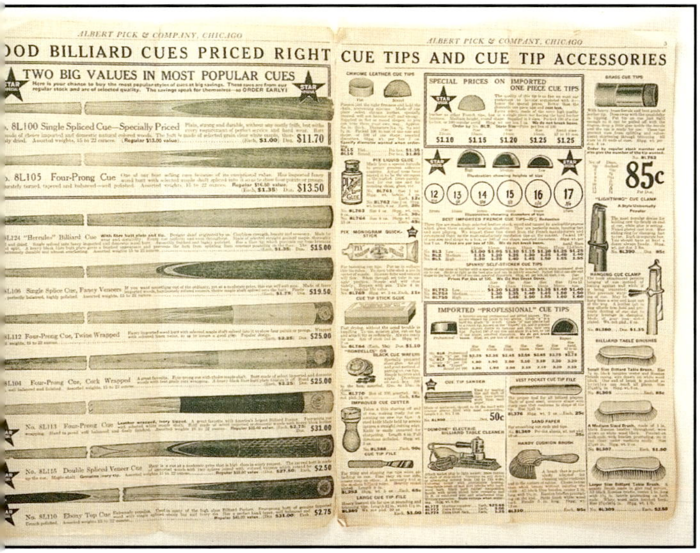

A 1923 supply catalog from the "The Albert Pick Co.," demonstrating their line of billiard supplies. Twelve pages, fair condition, $300.

A couple of pages from a sixty-three page billiard supply catalog from W. A. Spinks & Co. (WASCO), c. 1920s(?). Some color, one page is partially clipped, otherwise very good condition, $250.

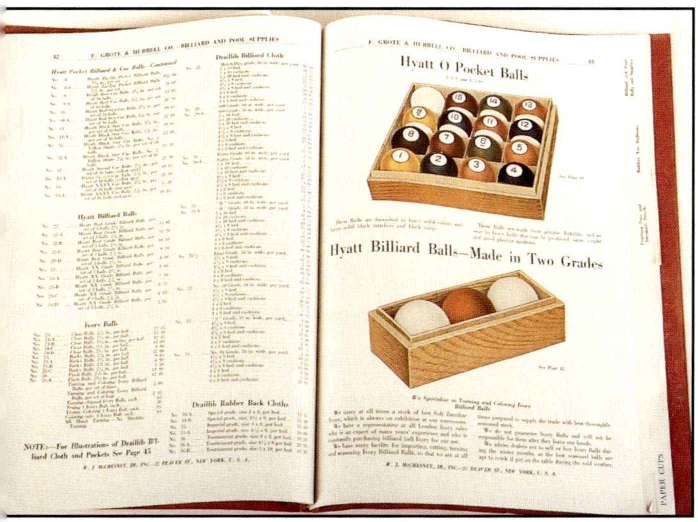

Single page from an F. Grote and Hubble sales brochure (from one chapter of goods in a merchants general catalog), with fifteen additional pages of their billiard items, some in color, with prices, complete sales book, very good condition, $75.

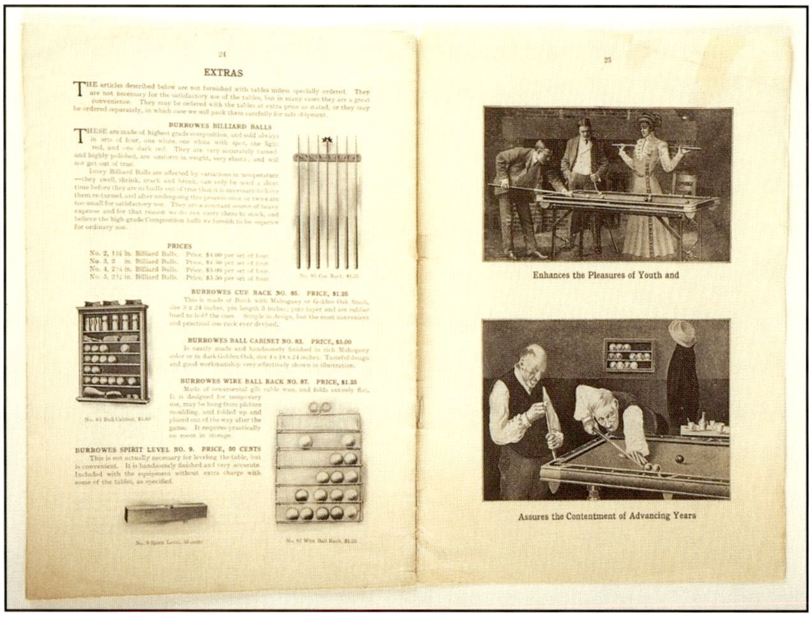

Two pages from a "Burrowes Billiard Table Co." supply catalog, featuring two of the wall décor prints they offered at the turn of the twentieth century. Shows tables and supplies as well. Catalog in good condition, $225.

Two pages from a twenty-two page, color, 1890s, "Merle & Heaney Mfg. Co." billiard and pool table catalog. Fair condition, $800+.

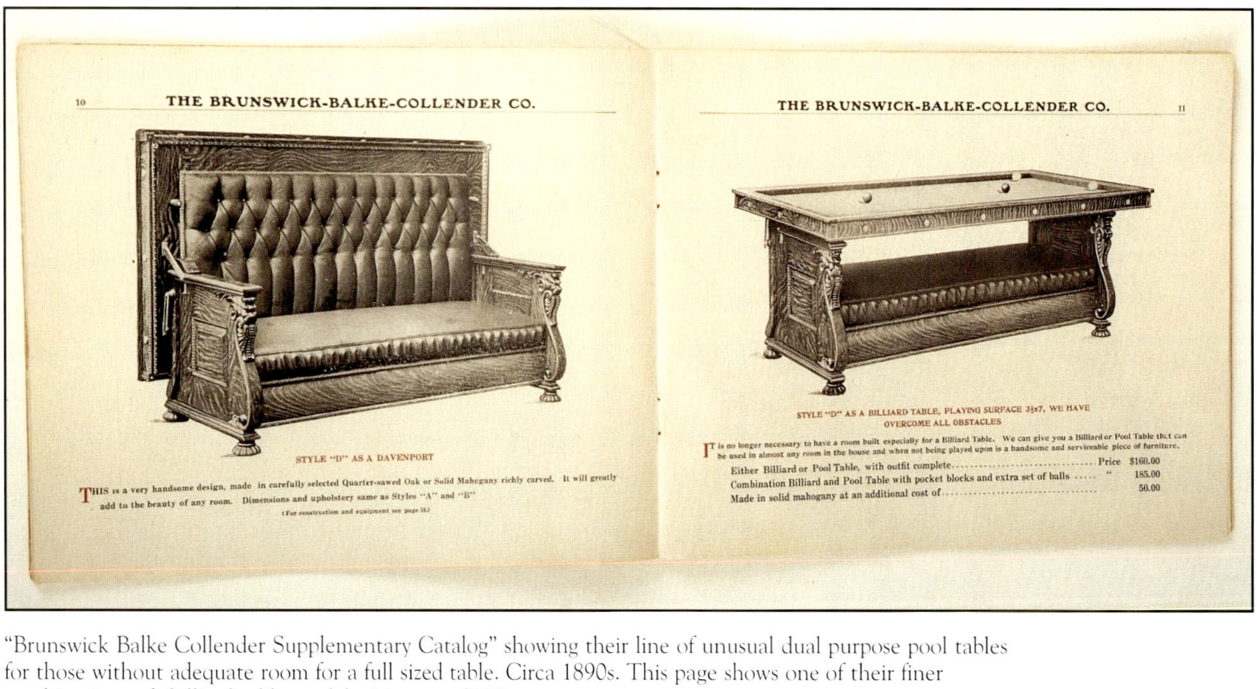

"Brunswick Balke Collender Supplementary Catalog" showing their line of unusual dual purpose pool tables for those without adequate room for a full sized table. Circa 1890s. This page shows one of their finer combination sofa/billiard table models. 24 pages, $500.

Turn of the century (1900) "Alfred B. Marx & Bro." Billiard and Pool Table Co. catalog. 24 pages, pretty good condition, $475+.

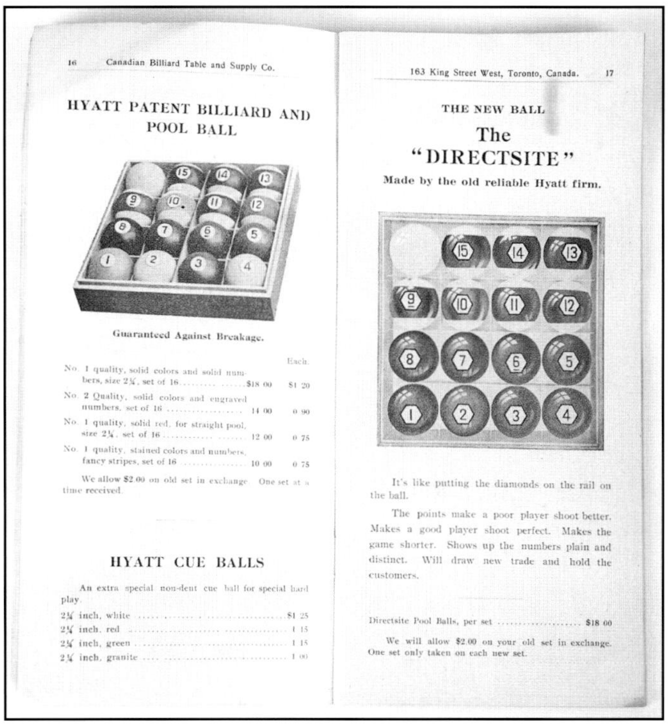

Four pages from a 1916 "Canadian Billiard Table and Supply Co." 70 pages, good condition, $150.

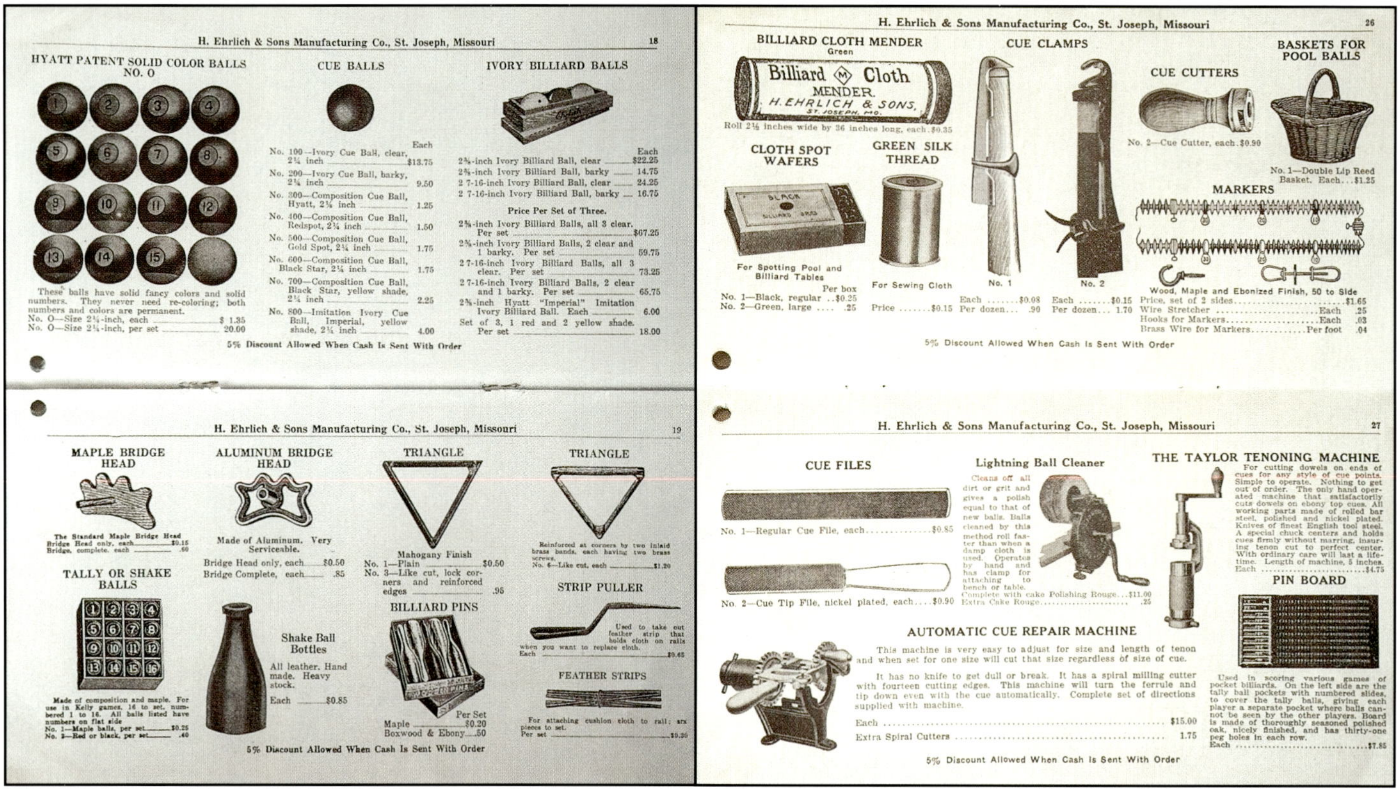

H. Ehrlich & Sons Manufacturing Co., St. Joseph, Missouri 18

HYATT PATENT SOLID COLOR BALLS NO. O

These balls have solid fancy colors and solid numbers. They never need re-coloring; both numbers and colors are permanent.
No. O—Size 2¼-inch, each .... $ 1.35
No. O—Size 2¼-inch, per set 20.00

CUE BALLS

	Each
No. 100—Ivory Cue Ball, clear, 2¼ inch	$13.75
No. 200—Ivory Cue Ball, barky, 2¼ inch	9.50
No. 300—Composition Cue Ball, Hyatt, 2¼ inch	1.25
No. 400—Composition Cue Ball, Redspot, 2¼ inch	1.50
No. 500—Composition Cue Ball, Gold Spot, 2¼ inch	1.75
No. 600—Composition Cue Ball, Black Star, 2¼ inch	1.75
No. 700—Composition Cue Ball, Black Star, yellow shade, 2¼ inch	2.25
No. 800—Imitation Ivory Cue Ball, Imperial, yellow shade, 2¼ inch	4.00

IVORY BILLIARD BALLS

	Each
2⅜-inch Ivory Billiard Ball, clear	$22.25
2⅜-inch Ivory Billiard Ball, barky	14.75
2 7-16-inch Ivory Billiard Ball, clear	24.25
2 7-16-inch Ivory Billiard Ball, barky	16.75

Price Per Set of Three.

2⅜-inch Ivory Billiard Balls, all 3 clear. Per set	$67.25
2⅜-inch Ivory Billiard Balls, 2 clear and 1 barky. Per set	59.75
2 7-16-inch Ivory Billiard Balls, all 3 clear. Per set	73.25
2 7-16-inch Ivory Billiard Balls, 2 clear and 1 barky. Per set	65.75
2⅜-inch Hyatt "Imperial" Imitation Ivory Billiard Ball. Each	6.00
Set of 3, 1 red and 2 yellow shade. Per set	18.00

5% Discount Allowed When Cash Is Sent With Order

H. Ehrlich & Sons Manufacturing Co., St. Joseph, Missouri 26

BILLIARD CLOTH MENDER
Green

Billiard Cloth MENDER. H. EHRLICH & SONS, ST. JOSEPH, MO.

Roll 2½ inches wide by 36 inches long, each $0.35

CLOTH SPOT WAFERS

For Spotting Pool and Billiard Tables

	Per box
No. 1—Black, regular	$0.25
No. 2—Green, large	.25

GREEN SILK THREAD

For Sewing Cloth

Price $0.15

CUE CLAMPS

No. 1		No. 2	
Each	$0.08	Each	$0.15
Per dozen	.90	Per dozen	1.70

CUE CUTTERS

No. 2—Cue Cutter, each $0.90

BASKETS FOR POOL BALLS

No. 1—Double Lip Reed Basket. Each ... $1.25

MARKERS

Wood, Maple and Ebonized Finish, 50 to Side

Price, set of 2 sides		$1.65
Wire Stretcher	Each	.25
Hooks for Markers	Each	.03
Brass Wire for Markers	Per foot	.04

5% Discount Allowed When Cash Is Sent With Order

H. Ehrlich & Sons Manufacturing Co., St. Joseph, Missouri 19

MAPLE BRIDGE HEAD

The Standard Maple Bridge Head
Bridge Head only, each $0.15
Bridge, complete, each .... .60

ALUMINUM BRIDGE HEAD

Made of Aluminum. Very Serviceable.
Bridge Head only, each $0.50
Bridge Complete, each .... .85

TRIANGLE

Mahogany Finish
No. 1—Plain $0.50
No. 3—Like cut, lock corners and reinforced edges .... .95

TRIANGLE

Reinforced at corners by two inlaid brass bands, each having two brass screws.
No. 6—Like cut, each $1.20

TALLY OR SHAKE BALLS

Made of composition and maple. For use in Kelly games, 16 to set, numbered 1 to 16. All balls listed have numbers on flat side
No. 1—Maple balls, per set $0.25
No. 3—Red or black, per set .... .40

Shake Ball Bottles

All leather. Hand made. Heavy stock.
Each $0.85

BILLIARD PINS

	Per Set
Maple	$0.20
Boxwood & Ebony	.50

STRIP PULLER

Used to take out feather strip that holds cloth on rails when you want to replace cloth.
Each $0.65

FEATHER STRIPS

For attaching cushion cloth to rail; six pieces to set.
Per set $0.30

5% Discount Allowed When Cash Is Sent With Order

H. Ehrlich & Sons Manufacturing Co., St. Joseph, Missouri 27

CUE FILES

No. 1—Regular Cue File, each $0.85
No. 2—Cue Tip File, nickel plated, each $0.90

Lightning Ball Cleaner

Cleans off all dirt or grit and gives a polish equal to that of new balls. Balls cleaned by this method roll faster than when a damp cloth is used. Operates by hand and has clamp for attaching to bench or table.
Complete with cake Polishing Rouge ... $11.00
Extra Cake Rouge .... .25

THE TAYLOR TENONING MACHINE

For cutting dowels on ends of cues for any style of cue points. Simple to operate. Nothing to get out of order. The only hand operated machine that satisfactorily cuts dowels on ebony top cues. All working parts made of rolled bar steel, polished and nickel plated. Knives of finest English tool steel. A special chuck centers and holds cues firmly without marring, insuring tenon cut to perfect center. With ordinary care will last a lifetime. Length of machine, 5 inches.
Each $4.75

AUTOMATIC CUE REPAIR MACHINE

This machine is very easy to adjust for size and length of tenon and when set for one size will cut that size regardless of size of cue.

It has no knife to get dull or break. It has a spiral milling cutter with fourteen cutting edges. This machine will turn the ferrule and tip down even with the cue automatically. Complete set of directions supplied with machine.

Each $15.00
Extra Spiral Cutters 1.75

PIN BOARD

Used in scoring various games of pocket billiards. On the left side are the tally ball pockets with numbered slides, to cover the tally balls, giving each player a separate pocket where balls cannot be seen by the other players. Board is made of thoroughly seasoned polished oak, nicely finished, and has thirty-one peg holes in each row.
Each $7.85

5% Discount Allowed When Cash Is Sent With Order

Four pages from an "H. Ehrlich & Sons Manufacturing Co." supply catalog from 1922. 40 pages, good condition though loose at binding, $185.

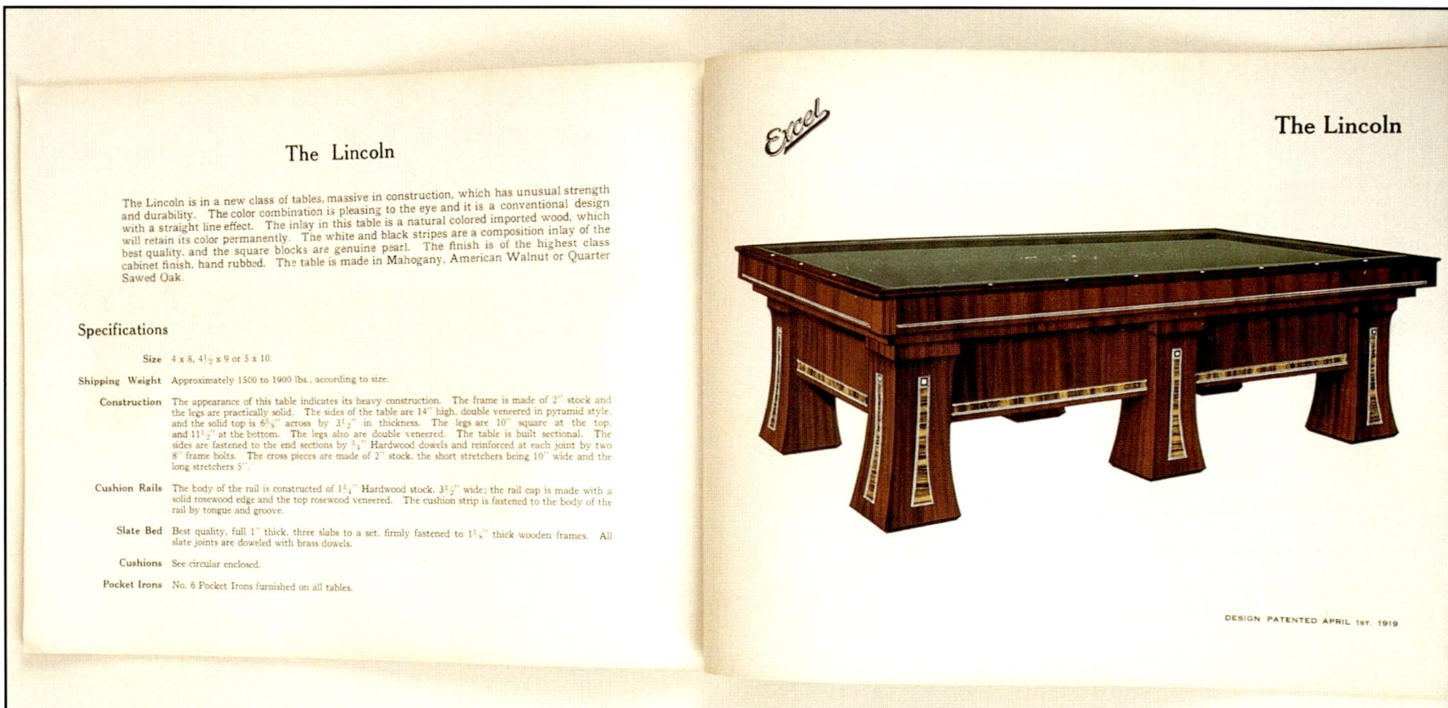

The Lincoln

The Lincoln is in a new class of tables, massive in construction, which has unusual strength and durability. The color combination is pleasing to the eye and it is a conventional design with a straight line effect. The inlay in this table is a natural colored imported wood, which will retain its color permanently. The white and black stripes are a composition inlay of the best quality, and the square blocks are genuine pearl. The finish is of the highest class cabinet finish, hand rubbed. The table is made in Mahogany, American Walnut or Quarter Sawed Oak.

Specifications

Size	4 x 8, 4½ x 9 or 5 x 10.
Shipping Weight	Approximately 1500 to 1900 lbs., according to size.
Construction	The appearance of this table indicates its heavy construction. The frame is made of 2" stock and the legs are practically solid. The sides of the table are 14" high, double veneered in pyramid style, and the solid top is 6⅝" across by 3½" in thickness. The legs are 10" square at the top, and 11½" at the bottom. The legs also are double veneered. The table is built sectional. The sides are fastened to the end sections by ¾" Hardwood dowels and reinforced at each joint by two 8" frame bolts. The cross pieces are made of 2" stock, the short stretchers being 10" wide and the long stretchers 5".
Cushion Rails	The body of the rail is constructed of 1¾" Hardwood stock, 3½" wide; the rail cap is made with a solid rosewood edge and the top rosewood veneered. The cushion strip is fastened to the body of the rail by tongue and groove.
Slate Bed	Best quality, full 1" thick, three slabs to a set, firmly fastened to 1⅜" thick wooden frames. All slate joints are doweled with brass dowels.
Cushions	See circular enclosed.
Pocket Irons	No. 6 Pocket Irons furnished on all tables.

Excel

The Lincoln

DESIGN PATENTED APRIL 1st, 1919

A 1919 billiard table supply catalog from the "Excel Billiard and Pocket Table Co." Very good condition, 18 pages, ALL COLOR, great piece, $750+.

A 1928 Brunswick-Balke-Collender Billiard Table AND Supplies catalog, fair condition, 131 pages plus some order blanks, some color images, rare, $550+.

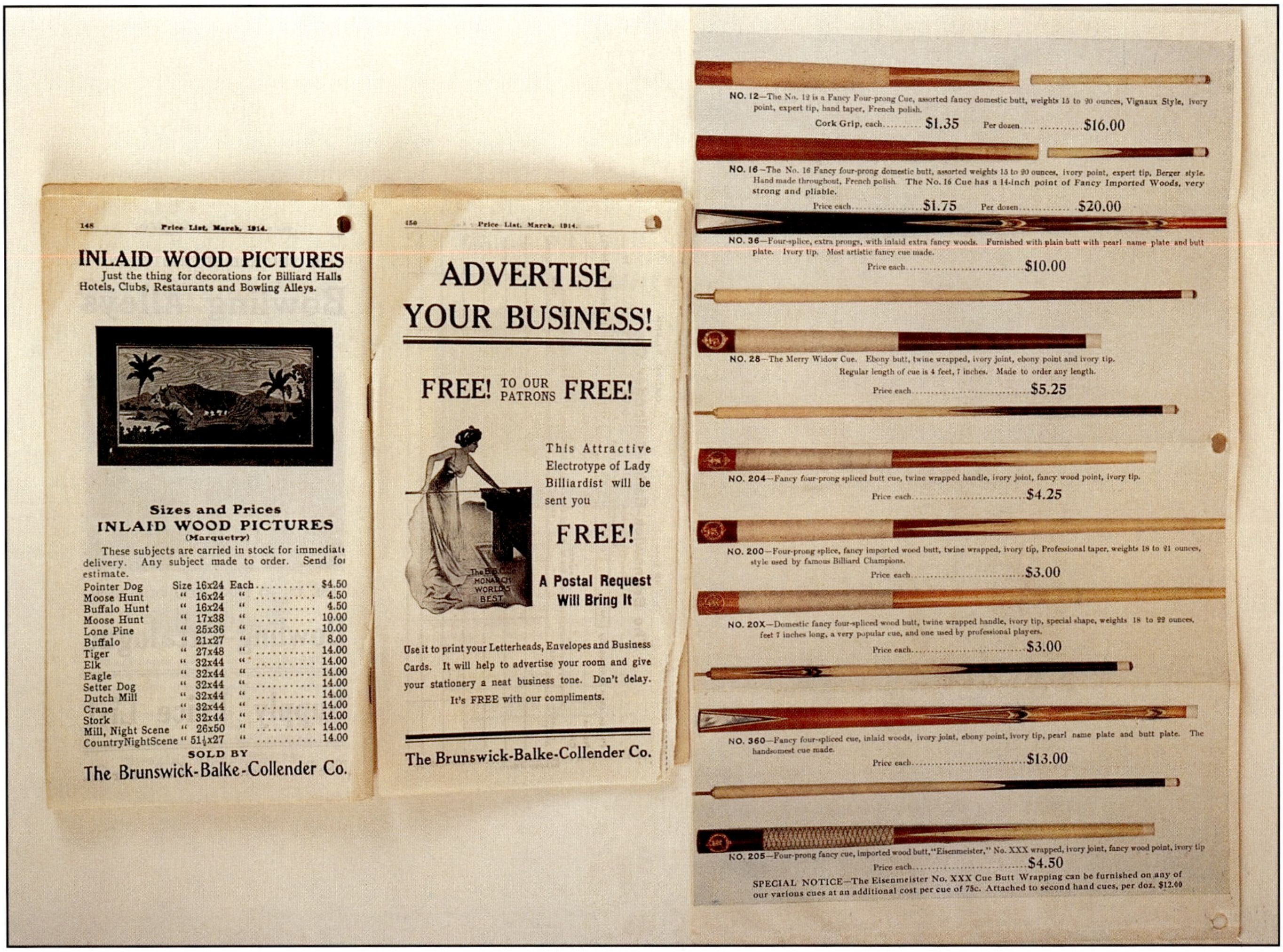

A few pages from a 1914 Brunswick-Balke-Collender supply catalog, advertising their "Inlaid Wood Pictures!!" and their "Archie Gunn" prints for decorating pool rooms in parlors and at home as well. Rare, depending on condition, $350 to $600.

36 THE BRUNSWICK-BALKE-COLLENDER COMPANY.

BILLIARD MARKERS.

Composition, white and black, extra quality, made especially for us, 34 or 50 to side.
Composition, small size, red and white, 34 to side, manufactured for our firm.
Wood, regular size, maple and ebonized finish, 34 or 50 to side.
Wood, large size, maple and ebonized finish, 50 to side.

HARD RUBBER MARKERS. WILL NEVER BREAK. OUR OWN MANUFACTURE. 50 TO SIDE. THE LATEST INVENTION.

These rubber markers, being hollow, are much lighter in weight than other styles of markers, thus preventing the sagging of the wire upon which they are strung. Although they are hollow they are more substantial and durable than any other style on the market. They are adjusted so carefully that they run easily and smoothly upon the wire, and with even ordinary care and attention will scarcely ever get out of order. They do not catch upon the wire, causing the players more or less annoyance, as is the case with other markers. The buttons will not break if struck sharply with the cue, an improvement of great merit. The roomkeeper is thus always confident that his string of markers is full at either end and not "short" any buttons, which is so often the case, much to the disgust of the players and roomkeepers.

Billiard Markers for Private Residences.

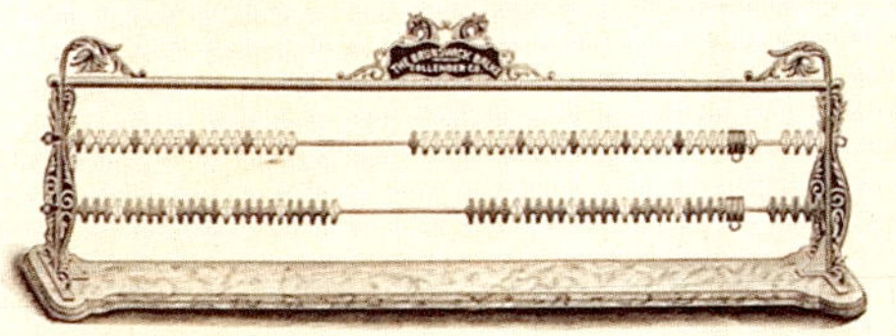

These marker stands are designed for private residences. Ordinarily, we make these stands with a wooden base, the balance of the stand being of metal, in nickel plate, oxydized copper, etc. We furnish the same stand with a marble or onyx base, in place of a wooden base. A combination of onyx and metal makes a very attractive appearance. We can also furnish the entire stand, base and all, of metal. When it is not convenient to use the marker stand on either the mantel, sideboard or table, it can be attached or suspended to the bottom of the cue rack when the latter forms part of the appointments of the room. These stands are also manufactured in oak, walnut or cherry. They are all supplied with composition, wood or rubber markers.

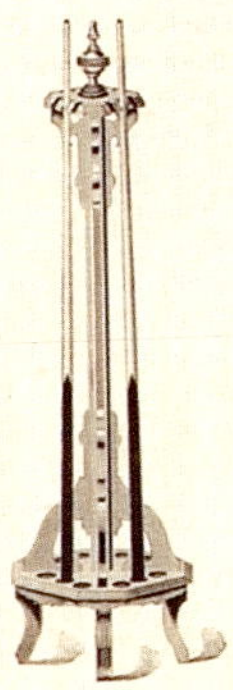

Cue Rack No. 2.

This is a very handsome cue rack, designed for private residences and is arranged for twelve full length cues. These racks are generally made from oak or mahogany, but they can be constructed of any wood to suit the wishes of purchasers. They are made in circular form, so as to occupy the least possible space and at the same time give the greatest amount of accommodation to the players. This rack is desirable when parties do not wish to mar the walls of their billiard rooms by hanging or attaching the ordinary style of rack. It is also an ornamental piece of furniture, and many prefer this style to the ordinary rack.

THE BRUNSWICK-BALKE-COLLENDER COMPANY. 33

BENEDICT PRIVATE LOCK CUE RACK.

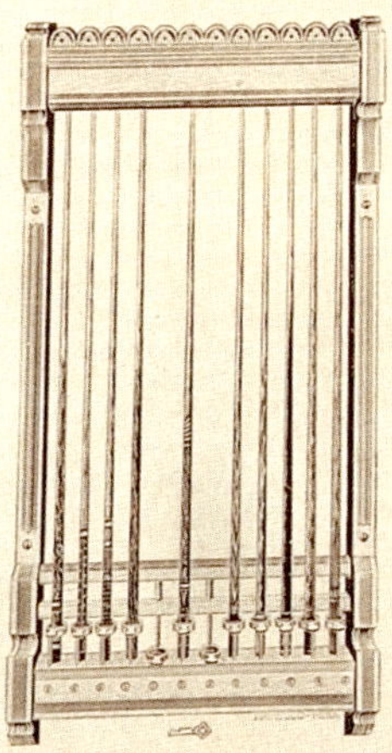

THE Benedict Private Lock Cue Rack is one of the latest and most important additions to the outfit of a billiard room. Its construction is entirely different from all other cue racks, and the mechanism, while of the simplest description, is nevertheless perfect in every particular.

The butts of the cues are held in position by a metal ring fitted at the bottom with rubber, to deaden the sound when it is released from the cue and falls to the base of the rack. When the fastening is unlocked the ring falls down and permits the player to remove the cue. The method of locking the rack is very simple and ingenious. When the cue butt is placed within the metal ring, the latter is raised by the player about six inches, until the mechanism of the lock closes automatically on a small rod welded to the face of the ring and the cue is instantly secured. Each lock is separate and distinct from the other and the owner of the cue is the only person possessing the means to open his particular compartment in the rack.

THE BILLIARD MIRROR.

A NEWSPAPER DEVOTED EXCLUSIVELY TO BILLIARDS.

THE BILLIARD MIRROR is a monthly journal, without a peer in this or any other country. Its mission is to assist in the popularizing and development of "the gentleman's game," and its publishers have gone to enormous expense to make it what it is today, the leading publication in the world of billiards.

Its columns are filled with information of interest to lovers of billiards in every part of the United States. Crisp local news, telegrams, special articles from the great cities of our country, foreign gossip, correspondence, items for roomkeepers and others in the business, the latest and most reliable information concerning prices of billiard goods and other matters of equal importance make

.....THE BILLIARD MIRROR.....

one of the most valuable periodicals published in this or any other country.

The Brunswick-Balke-Collender Company issues this periodical solely for the benefit and advancement of billiards. They want to encourage and stimulate a more general sentiment of admiration for the beautiful science. They are willing to bear the expense if they can produce the result they desire by the expenditure. The people all over the world can receive THE BILLIARD MIRROR regularly, free of charge, by sending their names and addresses to any office or branch of the company.

If you are fond of billiards, send for THE BILLIARD MIRROR.

If you want a really interesting and instructive monthly newspaper, send for it, and above all remember this—you will receive it free.

Excerpt from a VERY rare 1894 "Brunswick Balke Collender Billiard Tables" (and supply) catalog. Front cover is missing, but the following several images show you why they bring what they do, despite the fact that they are almost always found in poor condition. A complete, excellent condition catalog of this vintage from the Brunswick-Balke-Collender Co. will quickly bring well over $3,000. One in this condition currently sells for around $2,500.

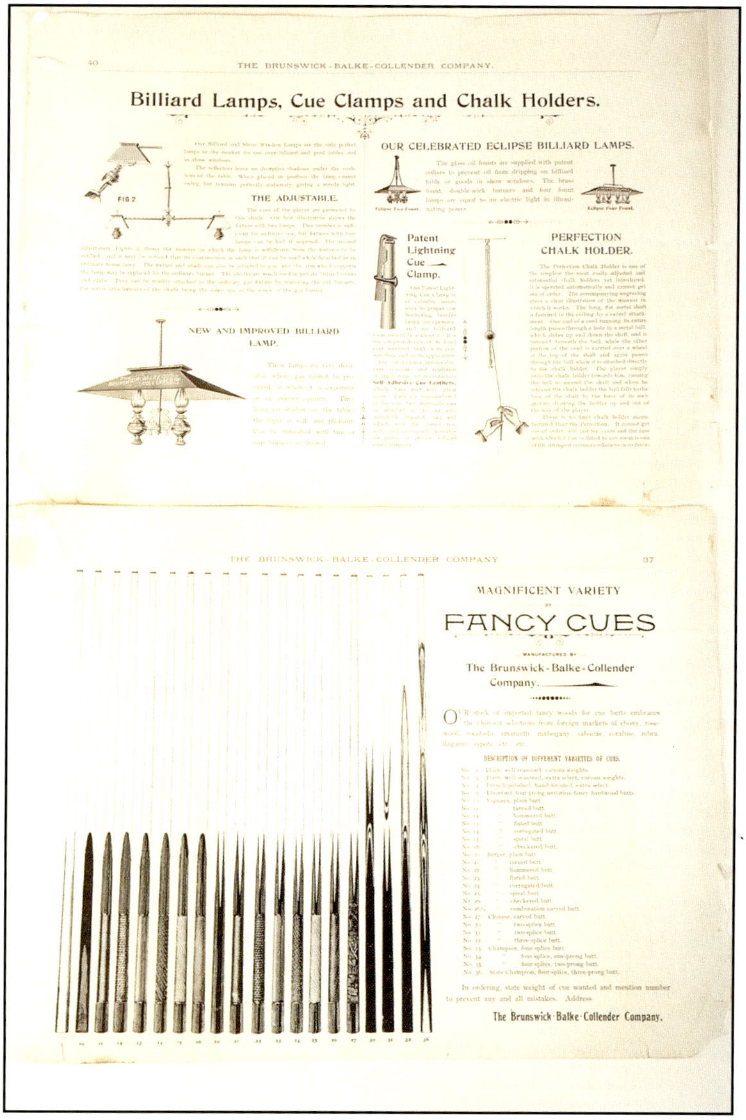
40 THE BRUNSWICK-BALKE-COLLENDER COMPANY.

Billiard Lamps, Cue Clamps and Chalk Holders.

OUR CELEBRATED ECLIPSE BILLIARD LAMPS.

FIG 2

THE ADJUSTABLE.

Patent Lightning Cue Clamp.

PERFECTION CHALK HOLDER.

NEW AND IMPROVED BILLIARD LAMP.

THE BRUNSWICK-BALKE-COLLENDER COMPANY 37

MAGNIFICENT VARIETY OF

FANCY CUES

MANUFACTURED BY

The Brunswick-Balke-Collender Company.

DESCRIPTION OF DIFFERENT VARIETIES OF CUES.

In ordering, state weight of cue wanted and mention number to prevent any and all mistakes. Address

The Brunswick-Balke-Collender Company.

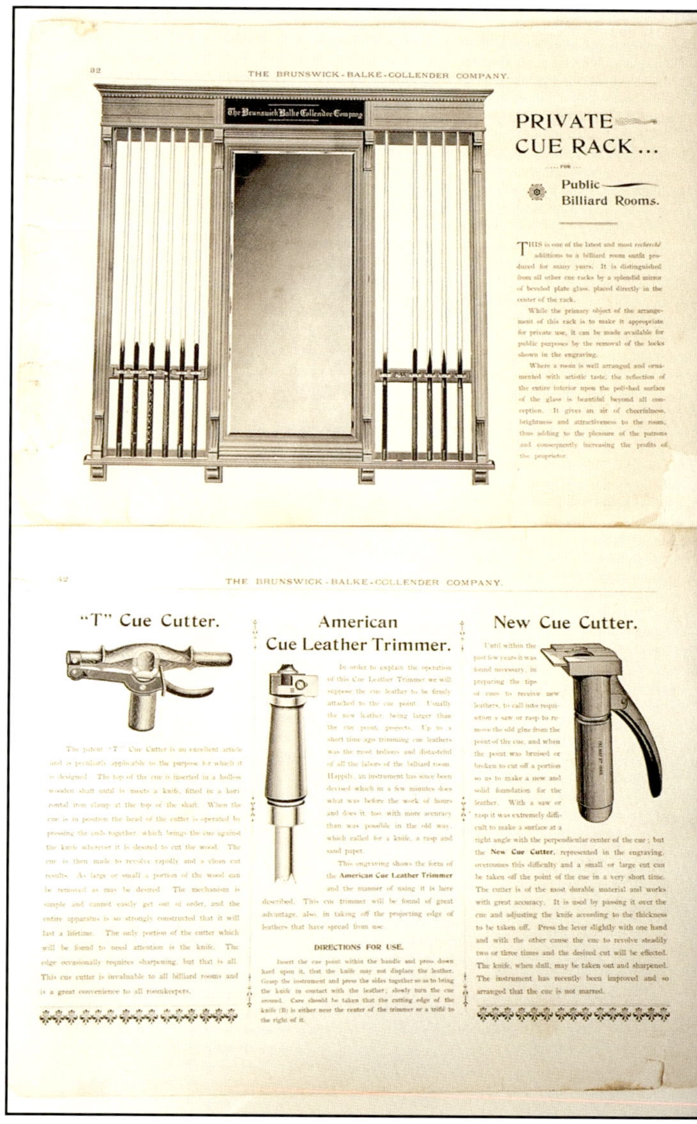
32 THE BRUNSWICK-BALKE-COLLENDER COMPANY.

PRIVATE CUE RACK...

FOR

Public Billiard Rooms.

THIS is one of the latest and most *recherché* additions to a billiard room outfit produced for many years. It is distinguished from all other cue racks by a splendid mirror of beveled plate glass, placed directly in the center of the rack.

While the primary object of the arrangement of this rack is to make it appropriate for private use, it can be made available for public purposes by the removal of the locks shown in the engraving.

Where a room is well arranged and ornamented with artistic taste, the reflection of the entire interior upon the polished surface of the glass is beautiful beyond all conception. It gives an air of cheerfulness, brightness and attractiveness to the room, thus adding to the pleasure of the patrons and consequently increasing the profits of the proprietor.

42 THE BRUNSWICK-BALKE-COLLENDER COMPANY.

"T" Cue Cutter.

American Cue Leather Trimmer.

DIRECTIONS FOR USE.

New Cue Cutter.

Until within the past few years it was found necessary, in preparing the tips of cues to receive new leathers, to call into requisition a saw or rasp to remove the old glue from the point of the cue, and when the point was bruised or broken to cut off a portion so as to make a new and solid foundation for the leather. With a saw or rasp it was extremely difficult to make a surface at a right angle with the perpendicular center of the cue; but the **New Cue Cutter**, represented in the engraving, overcomes this difficulty and a small or large cut can be taken off the point of the cue in a very short time. The cutter is of the most durable material and works with great accuracy. It is used by passing it over the cue and adjusting the knife according to the thickness to be taken off. Press the lever slightly with one hand and with the other cause the cue to revolve steadily two or three times and the desired cut will be effected. The knife, when dull, may be taken out and sharpened. The instrument has recently been improved and so arranged that the cue is not marred.

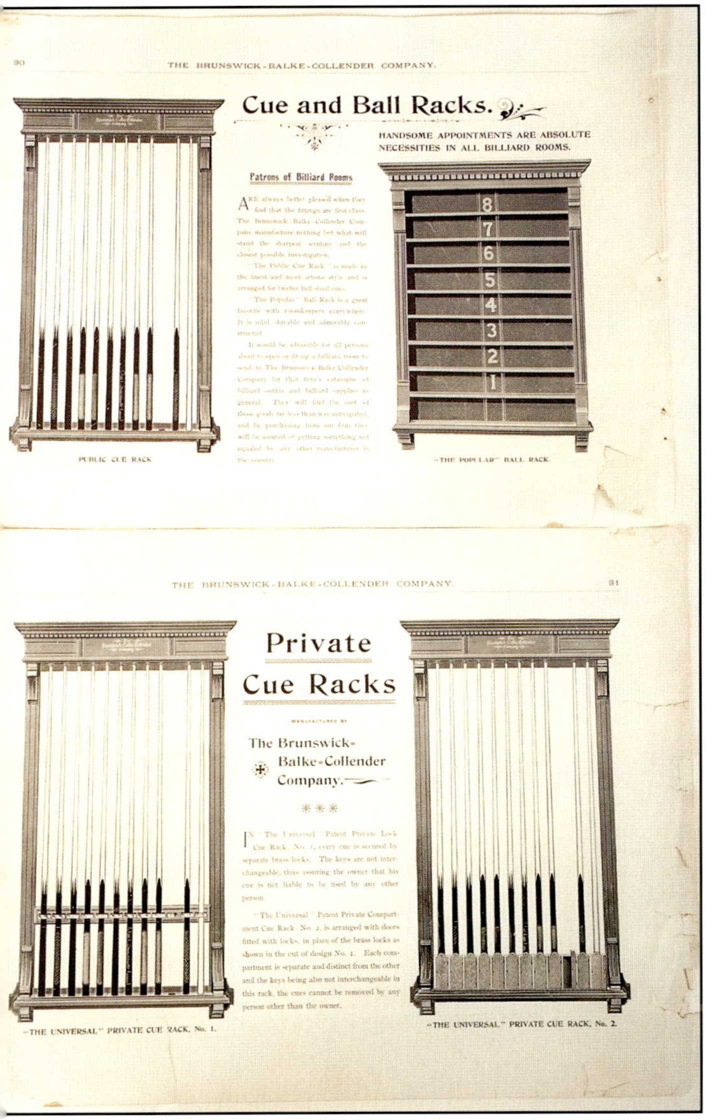

30 THE BRUNSWICK-BALKE-COLLENDER COMPANY.

Cue and Ball Racks.

HANDSOME APPOINTMENTS ARE ABSOLUTE NECESSITIES IN ALL BILLIARD ROOMS.

Patrons of Billiard Rooms

ARE always better pleased when they find that the fittings are first-class. The Brunswick-Balke-Collender Company manufacture nothing but what will stand the sharpest scrutiny and the closest possible investigation.

"The Public Cue Rack" is made in the finest and most artistic style and is arranged for twelve full-sized cues.

"The Popular" Ball Rack is a great favorite with roomkeepers everywhere. It is solid, durable and admirably constructed.

It would be advisable for all persons about to open or fit-up a billiard room to send to The Brunswick-Balke-Collender Company for that firm's catalogue of billiard outfits and billiard supplies in general. They will find the cost of those goods far less than was anticipated, and by purchasing from our firm they will be assured of getting something not equaled by any other manufacturer in the country.

PUBLIC CUE RACK.

"THE POPULAR" BALL RACK.

THE BRUNSWICK-BALKE-COLLENDER COMPANY. 31

Private Cue Racks

MANUFACTURED BY

The Brunswick-Balke-Collender Company.

* * *

IN "The Universal" Patent Private Lock Cue Rack, No. 1, every cue is secured by separate brass locks. The keys are not interchangeable, thus assuring the owner that his cue is not liable to be used by any other person.

"The Universal" Patent Private Compartment Cue Rack, No. 2, is arranged with doors fitted with locks, in place of the brass locks as shown in the cut of design No. 1. Each compartment is separate and distinct from the other and the keys being also not interchangeable in this rack, the cues cannot be removed by any person other than the owner.

"THE UNIVERSAL" PRIVATE CUE RACK, No. 1.

"THE UNIVERSAL" PRIVATE CUE RACK, No. 2.

34 THE BRUNSWICK-BALKE-COLLENDER COMPANY.

PATENT BALL RACK.

A Labor Saving Improvement, Valuable to All Roomkeepers.

THE PATENT BALL RACK

SHOWN here is one of the best produced for years. There have been many alterations in this particular feature of a billiard and pool room outfit, but this Ball Rack, owned and manufactured by The Brunswick-Balke-Collender Company, is unquestionably superior to all others.

In the old style the balls were removed from the different shelves by hand, a slow and laborious process, but our Patent Ball Rack does away with that tedious system altogether. When a game is finished, all the attendant has to do is to pull a spring, which connects with every shelf, causing the latter to fall at each end. The balls roll along the inclined planes formed by the sloping shelves, dropping from shelf to shelf until, reaching the bottom of the rack, they fall through a hole into a basket hanging beneath for the purpose of receiving them.

It is not necessary to touch a single ball with the hand. They roll down the inclined shelves by the sheer force of their own gravity and fall naturally and easily into the basket.

These racks never get out of order, are thoroughly and perfectly finished in the handsomest style and are really one of the greatest improvements ever introduced into a billiard room.

OPEN.

CLOSED.

THE BRUNSWICK-BALKE-COLLENDER COMPANY. 35

COMBINATION CUE STAND.

It is safe to say that no piece of furniture intended for a private billiard parlor or club room has ever been conceived which is so thoroughly adapted to the purpose for which it was designed, as the

COMBINATION CUE STAND.

It is the very essence of convenience, durability and ornamentation, and fills each and every requirement necessary for the proper recording of some of the leading games known to the billiard world. The upper portion has two rows of markers, fifty on each string, for ordinary billiards or pool, while directly beneath the "buttons" or markers is a full-sized pin pool board of the latest and most approved design; under this is a ball rack for use in games of fifteen ball or continuous pool. The lower portion of the stand is inclosed, cabinet style, with two neatly paneled doors fitted with locks and keys. There is a drawer above the cabinet, also furnished with a lock and key, in which such small supplies as chalk, cue tips, sand paper, etc., can be kept. The ingenious manner in which the cue rack is arranged is apparent in the illustration. It is fitted for the reception of six or twelve cues on either side of the stand, as may be desired.

The entire outfit is constructed with particular regard to the requirements of private residences, for which it is specially designed. It is compact, presents a pleasing appearance, and can be made in any wood to harmonize with the fittings of the room. The advantage of the cabinet will be patent to everyone. It can be utilized to store refreshments and serve the purpose of a miniature wine cellar in houses not possessing that accommodation, or it can be made available for other things, as may be considered best by the owner.

The stand can be made, however, without the cabinet or pin pool board. The drawer is, nevertheless, retained in its present position, but where the pin pool board is omitted the markers are considerably lower down. The entire structure does not occupy a space in excess of seven feet by four feet.

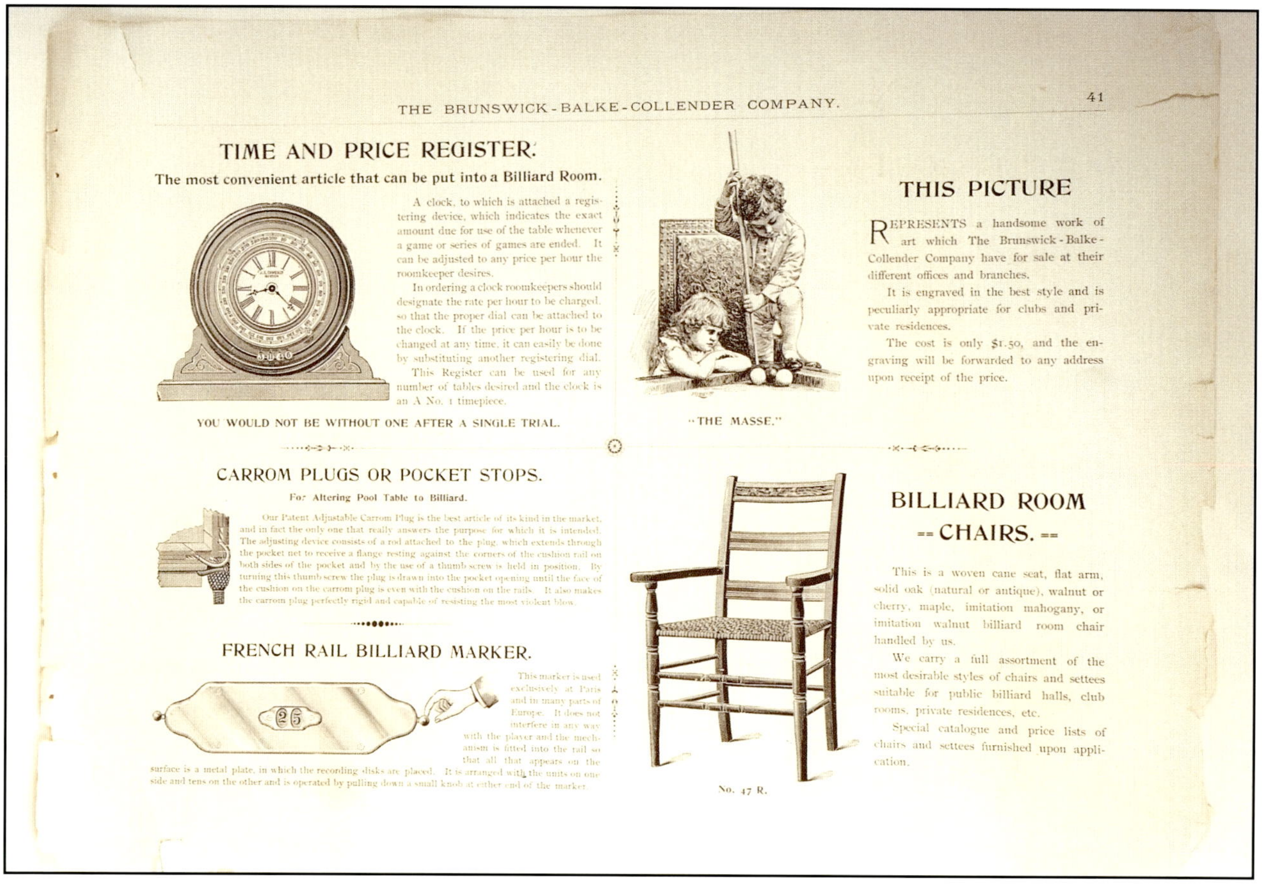
THE BRUNSWICK-BALKE-COLLENDER COMPANY. 41

TIME AND PRICE REGISTER.

The most convenient article that can be put into a Billiard Room.

A clock, to which is attached a registering device, which indicates the exact amount due for use of the table whenever a game or series of games are ended. It can be adjusted to any price per hour the roomkeeper desires.

In ordering a clock roomkeepers should designate the rate per hour to be charged, so that the proper dial can be attached to the clock. If the price per hour is to be changed at any time, it can easily be done by substituting another registering dial.

This Register can be used for any number of tables desired and the clock is an A No. 1 timepiece.

YOU WOULD NOT BE WITHOUT ONE AFTER A SINGLE TRIAL.

"THE MASSE."

THIS PICTURE

REPRESENTS a handsome work of art which The Brunswick-Balke-Collender Company have for sale at their different offices and branches.

It is engraved in the best style and is peculiarly appropriate for clubs and private residences.

The cost is only $1.50, and the engraving will be forwarded to any address upon receipt of the price.

CARROM PLUGS OR POCKET STOPS.

For Altering Pool Table to Billiard.

Our Patent Adjustable Carrom Plug is the best article of its kind in the market, and in fact the only one that really answers the purpose for which it is intended. The adjusting device consists of a rod attached to the plug, which extends through the pocket net to receive a flange resting against the corners of the cushion rail on both sides of the pocket and by the use of a thumb screw is held in position. By turning this thumb screw the plug is drawn into the pocket opening until the face of the cushion on the carrom plug is even with the cushion on the rails. It also makes the carrom plug perfectly rigid and capable of resisting the most violent blow.

FRENCH RAIL BILLIARD MARKER.

This marker is used exclusively at Paris and in many parts of Europe. It does not interfere in any way with the player and the mechanism is fitted into the rail so that all that appears on the surface is a metal plate, in which the recording disks are placed. It is arranged with the units on one side and tens on the other and is operated by pulling down a small knob at either end of the marker.

BILLIARD ROOM
== CHAIRS. ==

This is a woven cane seat, flat arm, solid oak (natural or antique), walnut or cherry, maple, imitation mahogany, or imitation walnut billiard room chair handled by us.

We carry a full assortment of the most desirable styles of chairs and settees suitable for public billiard halls, club rooms, private residences, etc.

Special catalogue and price lists of chairs and settees furnished upon application.

No. 47 R.

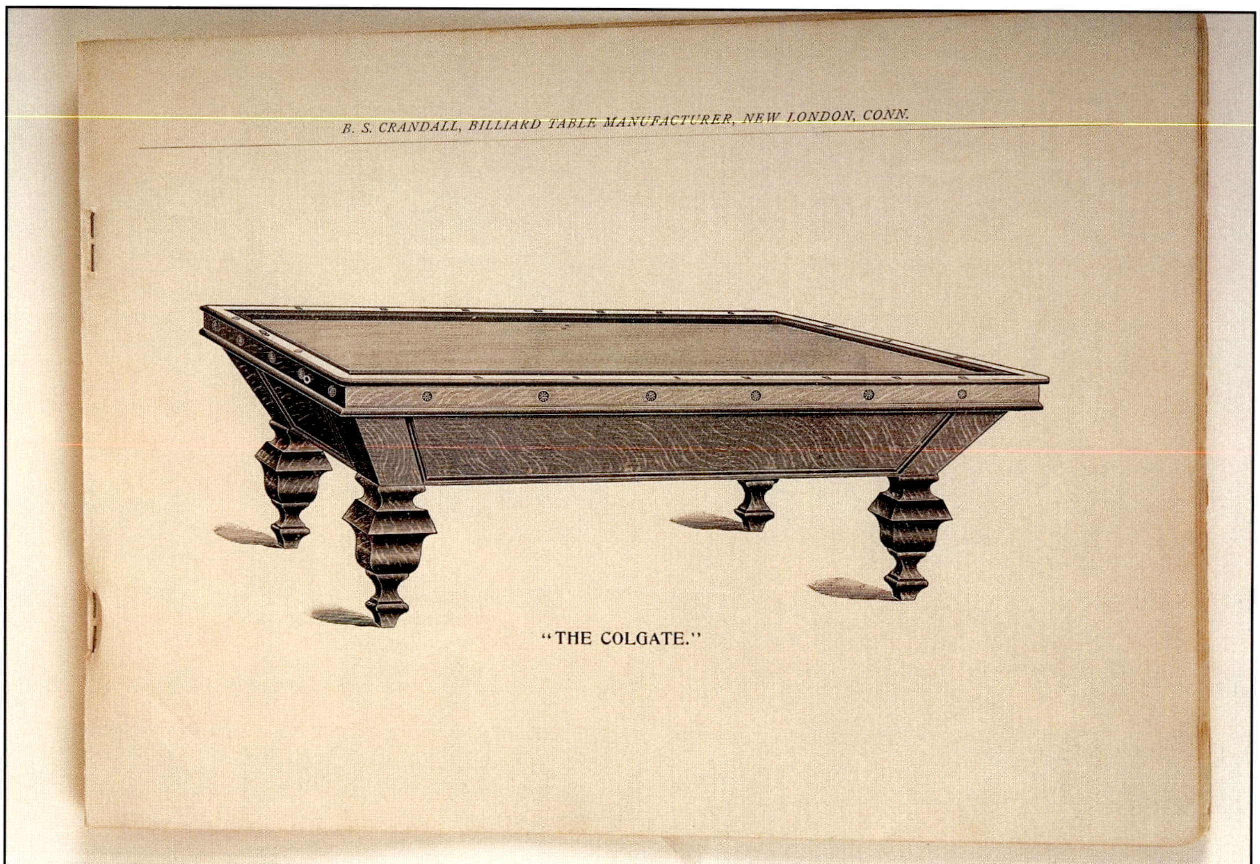
B. S. CRANDALL, BILLIARD TABLE MANUFACTURER, NEW LONDON, CONN.

"THE COLGATE."

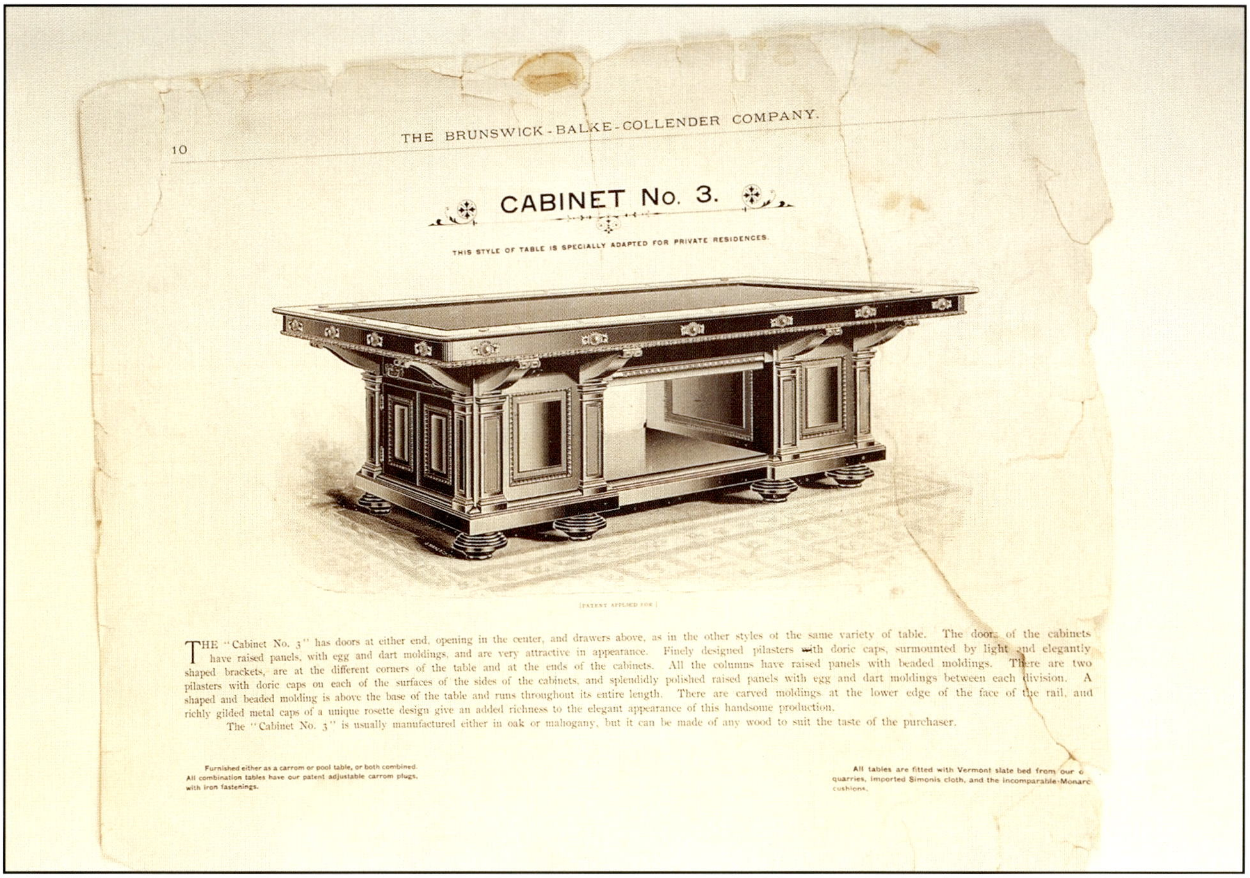

10 THE BRUNSWICK-BALKE-COLLENDER COMPANY.

CABINET No. 3.

THIS STYLE OF TABLE IS SPECIALLY ADAPTED FOR PRIVATE RESIDENCES.

[PATENT APPLIED FOR.]

THE "Cabinet No. 3" has doors at either end, opening in the center, and drawers above, as in the other styles of the same variety of table. The doors of the cabinets have raised panels, with egg and dart moldings, and are very attractive in appearance. Finely designed pilasters with doric caps, surmounted by light and elegantly shaped brackets, are at the different corners of the table and at the ends of the cabinets. All the columns have raised panels with beaded moldings. There are two pilasters with doric caps on each of the surfaces of the sides of the cabinets, and splendidly polished raised panels with egg and dart moldings between each division. A shaped and beaded molding is above the base of the table and runs throughout its entire length. There are carved moldings at the lower edge of the face of the rail, and richly gilded metal caps of a unique rosette design give an added richness to the elegant appearance of this handsome production.

The "Cabinet No. 3" is usually manufactured either in oak or mahogany, but it can be made of any wood to suit the taste of the purchaser.

Furnished either as a carrom or pool table, or both combined. All combination tables have our patent adjustable carrom plugs, with iron fastenings.

All tables are fitted with Vermont slate bed from our o quarries, imported Simonis cloth, and the incomparable Monarc cushions.

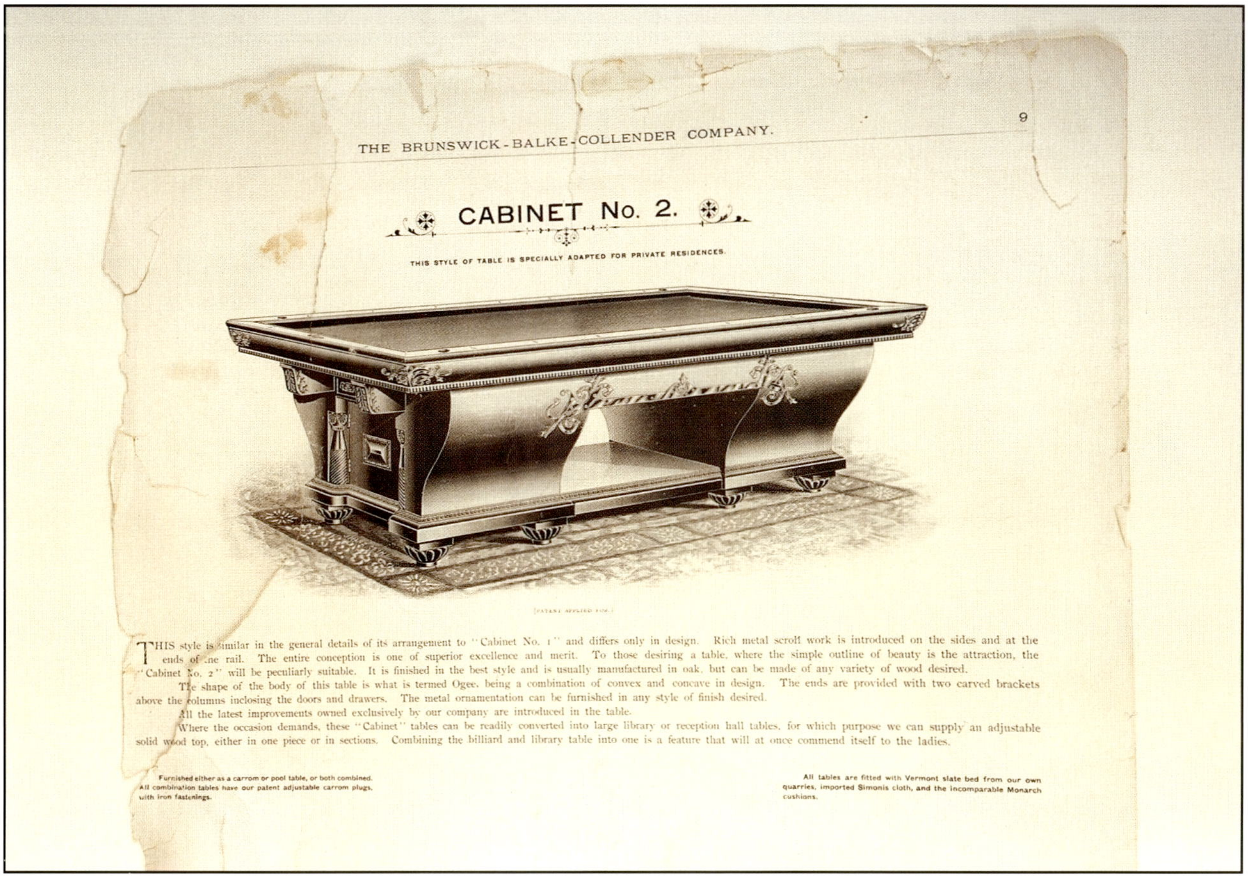

THE BRUNSWICK-BALKE-COLLENDER COMPANY. 9

CABINET No. 2.

THIS STYLE OF TABLE IS SPECIALLY ADAPTED FOR PRIVATE RESIDENCES.

[PATENT APPLIED FOR.]

THIS style is similar in the general details of its arrangement to "Cabinet No. 1" and differs only in design. Rich metal scroll work is introduced on the sides and at the ends of the rail. The entire conception is one of superior excellence and merit. To those desiring a table, where the simple outline of beauty is the attraction, the "Cabinet No. 2" will be peculiarly suitable. It is finished in the best style and is usually manufactured in oak, but can be made of any variety of wood desired.

The shape of the body of this table is what is termed Ogee, being a combination of convex and concave in design. The ends are provided with two carved brackets above the columns inclosing the doors and drawers. The metal ornamentation can be furnished in any style of finish desired.

All the latest improvements owned exclusively by our company are introduced in the table.

Where the occasion demands, these "Cabinet" tables can be readily converted into large library or reception hall tables, for which purpose we can supply an adjustable solid wood top, either in one piece or in sections. Combining the billiard and library table into one is a feature that will at once commend itself to the ladies.

Furnished either as a carrom or pool table, or both combined. All combination tables have our patent adjustable carrom plugs, with iron fastenings.

All tables are fitted with Vermont slate bed from our own quarries, imported Simonis cloth, and the incomparable Monarch cushions.

8 THE BRUNSWICK-BALKE-COLLENDER COMPANY.

CABINET No. 1.

THIS STYLE OF TABLE IS SPECIALLY ADAPTED FOR PRIVATE RESIDENCES.

THE above illustration represents the very latest style of billiard table placed upon the American market and presents features of extraordinary novelty. Hitherto the large open space beneath the bed of a table has been of no use whatever, but in "The Cabinet" every inch of this space is utilized. The bed of the table rests on two cabinets, built at either end and opened by dividing doors, above which are drawers. At one end of the table the drawer runs back far enough to permit of cues being placed within it, thus dispensing with the necessity for a cue rack. The other drawer is smaller in size and may be used to keep balls, tips and all supplies needed for the table. The large spaces in the cabinets beneath the drawers may be made available for the reception of cigars and refreshments. By this clever arrangement everything necessary for the game and the convenience of the players is kept out of sight, and no space is required beyond that devoted to the table itself. This feature alone will recommend "The Cabinet" as the best table ever manufactured for private residences.

Furnished either as a carrom or pool table, or both combined. All combination tables have our patent adjustable carrom plugs, with iron fastenings.

All tables are fitted with Vermont slate bed from our own quarries, imported Simonis cloth, and the incomparable Monarch cushions.

THE BRUNSWICK-BALKE-COLLENDER COMPANY. 19

THE CAMBRIDGE.

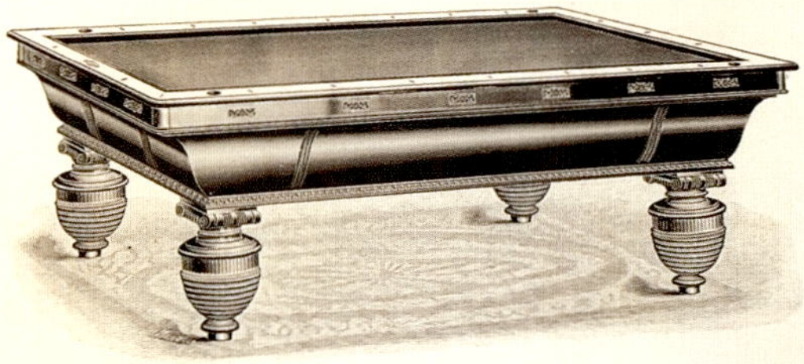

THE "Cambridge" is a counterpart in general design of the "Northern," and will suit the taste of those who desire a table of plain finish in harmony with their room. The metal work, which is a prominent feature of the "Northern," is omitted from the "Cambridge," and the legs of the latter are finished in plainer style. The legs of the "Cambridge" are circular in form with beaded moldings and a fluted band above finished off with Ionic caps. The sides are of Ogee design, furnished with egg and dart moldings at the base of the body of the table. The head blocks and sides are divided by raised moldings. The polished face of the rail has also shaped moldings. The "Cambridge" is made up from the finest quality of quarter-sawed oak in antique finish or in mahogany. It will be made up, however, in any wood desired.

Furnished either as a carrom or pool table, or both combined. All combination tables have our patent adjustable carrom plugs, with iron fastenings.

The legs, besides being joined with wooden dowels, are fastened with a long iron bolt passing through the entire length of the leg to the top of the head block, thus insuring positive solidity.

All tables are fitted with Vermont slate bed from our own quarries, imported Simonis cloth, and the incomparable Monarch cushions.

THE BRUNSWICK-BALKE-COLLENDER COMPANY. 15

THE CHICAGO.

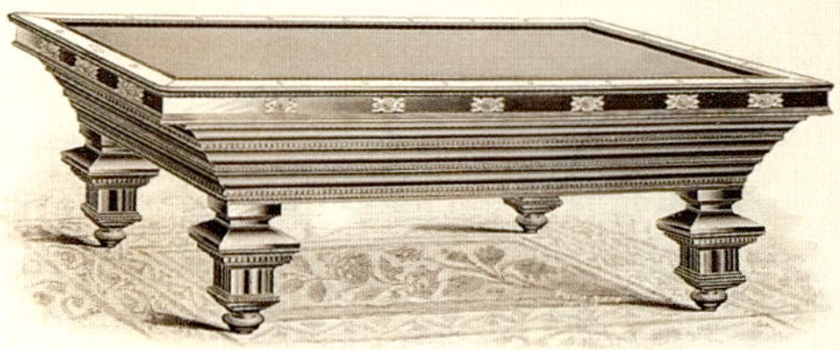

THIS table, which is one of our latest productions, is exceedingly beautiful and pleasing in appearance, and has received unstinted praise wherever introduced. The fine dentil and beaded moldings on the sides, the rich, tasteful carvings, and the general excellence of the workmanship makes the "Chicago" a billiard table second to none. It is usually finished in plain, highly polished mahogany or oak, without inlaid work, but it can be furnished to order of any kind of wood or finish required by purchasers.

Furnished either as a carrom or pool table, or both combined. All combination tables have our patent adjustable carrom plugs, with iron fastenings.

The legs, besides being joined with wooden dowels, are fastened with a long iron bolt passing through the entire length of the leg to the top of the head block, thus insuring positive solidity.

All tables are fitted with Vermont slate bed from our own quarries, imported Simonis cloth, and the incomparable Monarch cushions.

14 THE BRUNSWICK-BALKE-COLLENDER COMPANY.

THE PLAZA.

THE "Plaza" is perfect in outline and finish, and the handsome carved panels and moldings, with which it is ornamented, give it a rich and elegant appearance. usually made in oak, but can be constructed of any kind of wood desired. This elegant and substantial table is of the most chaste design, and is constructed of woods, without inlaid work, depending solely upon the graceful lines of its moldings and exquisite beauty of its carvings for public approval. It is especially suitab private residences, clubs, etc.

Furnished either as a carrom or pool table, or both combined. All combination tables have our patent adjustable carrom plugs, with iron fastenings.

The legs, besides being joined with wooden dowels, are fastened with a long iron bolt passing through the entire length of the leg to the top of the head block, thus insuring positive solidity.

All tables are fitted with Vermont slate bed from o quarries, imported Simonis cloth, and the incomparable M cushions.

THE BRUNSWICK-BALKE-COLLENDER COMPANY. 17

THE JEWEL.

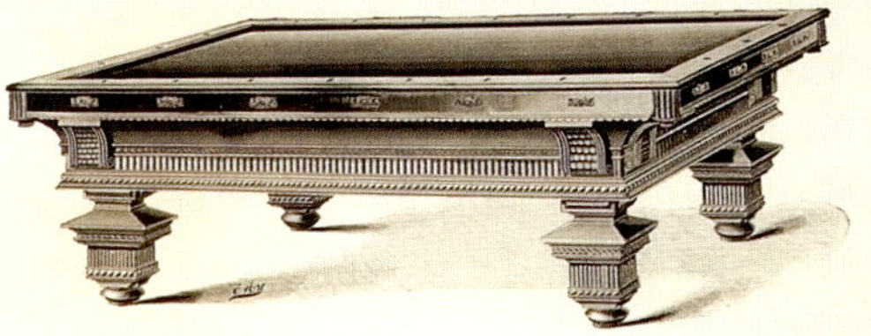

THIS table is entirely new in design and construction, and has been deservedly pronounced one of the most beautiful billiard tables ever produced. Its special advantages are numerous, the principal one being the thickness of the frame on which the slate bed rests. It is no less than seven inches thick, and embodies great strength and solidity with a graceful form. The carved work is highly artistic, chaste and rich, and everything about the table indicates the very perfection of good taste and elegance. The body has a cove form, with brackets at each corner and corrugated moldings on the frame and in center of legs. There are many who prefer the "Jewel" to any other table manufactured by our firm.

Furnished either as a carrom or pool table, or both combined. All combination tables have our patent adjustable carrom plugs, with iron fastenings.

The legs, besides being joined with wooden dowels, are fastened with a long iron bolt passing through the entire length of the leg to the top of the head block, thus insuring positive solidity.

All tables are fitted with Vermont slate bed from our own quarries, imported Simonis cloth, and the Incomparable Monarch cushions.

THE BRUNSWICK-BALKE-COLLENDER COMPANY.

THE PENDENNIS.

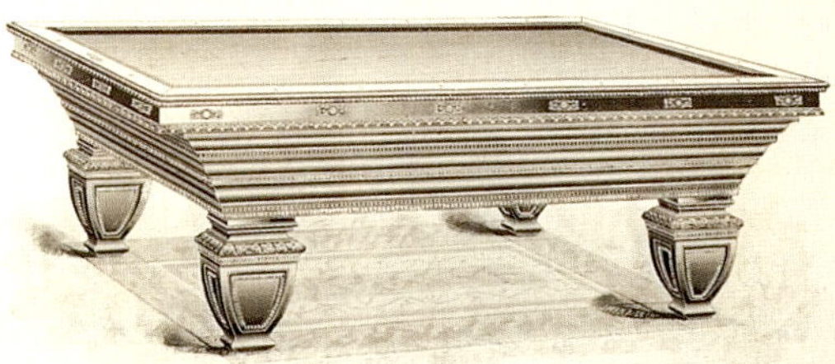

"Pendennis" is a table of great beauty and symmetry of outline, but its chief charm lies in the elegant carving and moldings with which the body and legs are [...]namented. Its rich appearance makes it particularly adaptable for finely furnished billiard rooms in clubs, private residences, hotels, etc.

There are few tables in the fine collection made by our firm which present so many essentials of beauty, solidity and attractiveness as the "Pendennis." The design [...]ly distinct from all others, and is universally admired. It has a singular charm from its very novelty, and the splendid workmanship manifested in every detail of its [...]ion cannot be excelled.

[...]hed either as a carrom or pool table, or both combined. [...]tion tables have our patent adjustable carrom plugs, [...]stenings.

The legs, besides being joined with wooden dowels, are fastened with a long iron bolt passing through the entire length of the leg to the top of the head block, thus insuring positive solidity.

All tables are fitted with Vermont slate bed from our ow[n] quarries, imported Simonis cloth, and the Incomparable Monarch cushions.

18 THE BRUNSWICK-BALKE-COLLENDER COMPANY.

THE AUDITORIUM.

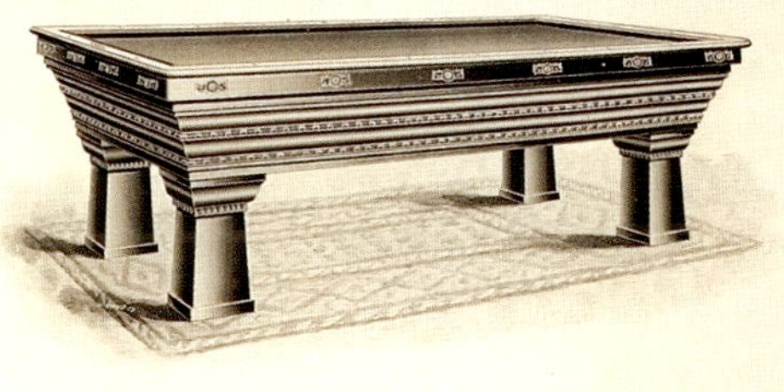

THE "Auditorium" combines richness of design with rare perfection of outline. Exquisite moldings, perfect finish and skillful workmanship are everywhere manifest. This table is usually made in antique oak, but can be constructed of any kind of wood desired. It is very pleasing in appearance. Its general construction at once impresses the beholder with its solidity and substantial character. The tower shaped legs, with Egyptian design of carving beneath the cap directly under the body of the table, produces a very rich and artistic effect, which is greatly heightened by the lines of carvings and fine moldings on the sides.

Furnished either as a carrom or pool table, or both combined. All combination tables have our patent adjustable carrom plugs, with iron fastenings.

The legs, besides being joined with wooden dowels, are fastened with a long iron bolt passing through the entire length of the leg to the top of the head block, thus insuring positive solidity.

All tables are fitted with Vermont slate bed from our own quarries, imported Simonis cloth, and the Incomparable Monarch cushions.

THE BRUNSWICK-BALKE-COLLENDER COMPANY. 13

THE NORTHERN.

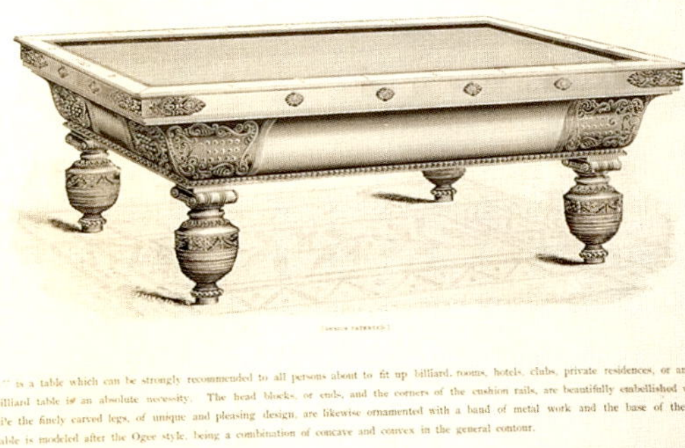

THE "Northern" is a table which can be strongly recommended to all persons about to fit up billiard rooms, hotels, clubs, private residences, or any place, in fact, where a first-class billiard table is an absolute necessity. The head blocks, or ends, and the corners of the cushion rails, are beautifully embellished with metal work of an artistic pattern, while the finely carved legs, of unique and pleasing design, are likewise ornamented with a band of metal work and the base of the legs are also of metal. The frame of the table is modeled after the Ogee style, being a combination of concave and convex in the general contour.

Furnished either as a carrom or pool table, or both combined. All combination tables have our patent adjustable carrom plugs, with iron fastenings.

The legs, besides being joined with wooden dowels, are fastened with a long iron bolt passing through the entire length of the leg to the top of the head block, thus insuring positive solidity.

All tables are fitted with Vermont slate bed from our own quarries, imported Simonis cloth, and the Incomparable Monarch cushions.

THE BRUNSWICK-BALKE-COLLENDER COMPANY. 25

THE POPULAR.

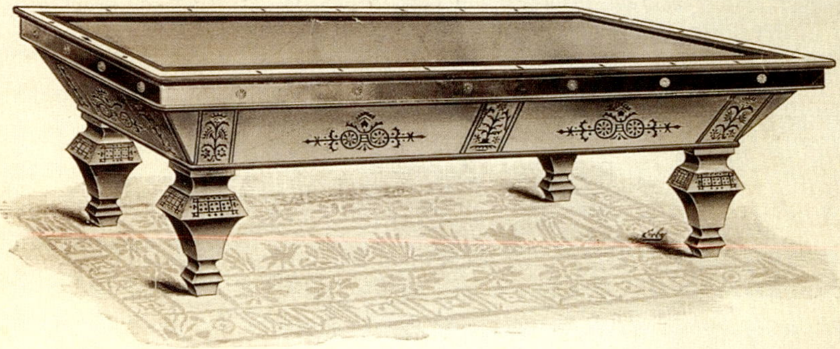

As its name implies, this is a popular table, and possesses merits that entitle it to that position. We furnish this table either in rosewood inlaid with maple, or maple inlaid with rosewood. The "Popular" has long retained a prominent position in all billiard rooms, and in each and every part of its construction is perfect in all particulars.

Furnished either as a carrom or pool table, or both combined. All combination tables have our patent adjustable carrom plugs, with iron fastenings.

The legs, besides being joined with wooden dowels, are fastened with a long iron bolt passing through the entire length of the leg to the top of the head block, thus insuring positive solidity.

All tables are fitted with Vermont slate bed from our own quarries, imported Simonis cloth, and the incomparable Monarch cushions.

22 THE BRUNSWICK-BALKE-COLLENDER COMPANY.

THE MONARCH.

The "Monarch" is indeed most aptly named. Rarely has a finer piece of workmanship been placed before the public in any part of the world. It combines solidity and massiveness with elegance and grace of design. It is highly ornamental, the sides being of wood, tastefully inlaid with different colored mosaics. The body of the table rests upon four splendid iron supports modeled after the king of beasts, finished in black and gold. The inlay work is of California laurel, burl ash, French walnut, rosewood, bird's-eye maple and tulip woods. All the fittings of this magnificent table are of the most elegant description. No expense has been spared in any portion of its construction.

Furnished either as a carrom or pool table, or both combined. All combination tables have our patent adjustable carrom plugs, with iron fastenings.

The legs, besides being joined with wooden dowels, are fastened with a long iron bolt passing through the entire length of the leg to the top of the head block, thus insuring positive solidity.

All tables are fitted with Vermont slate bed from our own quarries, imported Simonis cloth, and the incomparable Monarch cushions.

Three books on the rules of the games of billiards. L to R: Brunswick-Balke-Collender, 1890, 132 pages, good condition, $275; B. B. C. rule book, 1916, 80 pages, fair condition, $65; and J. E. Came, late 1800s, 28 pages, good condition, $100.

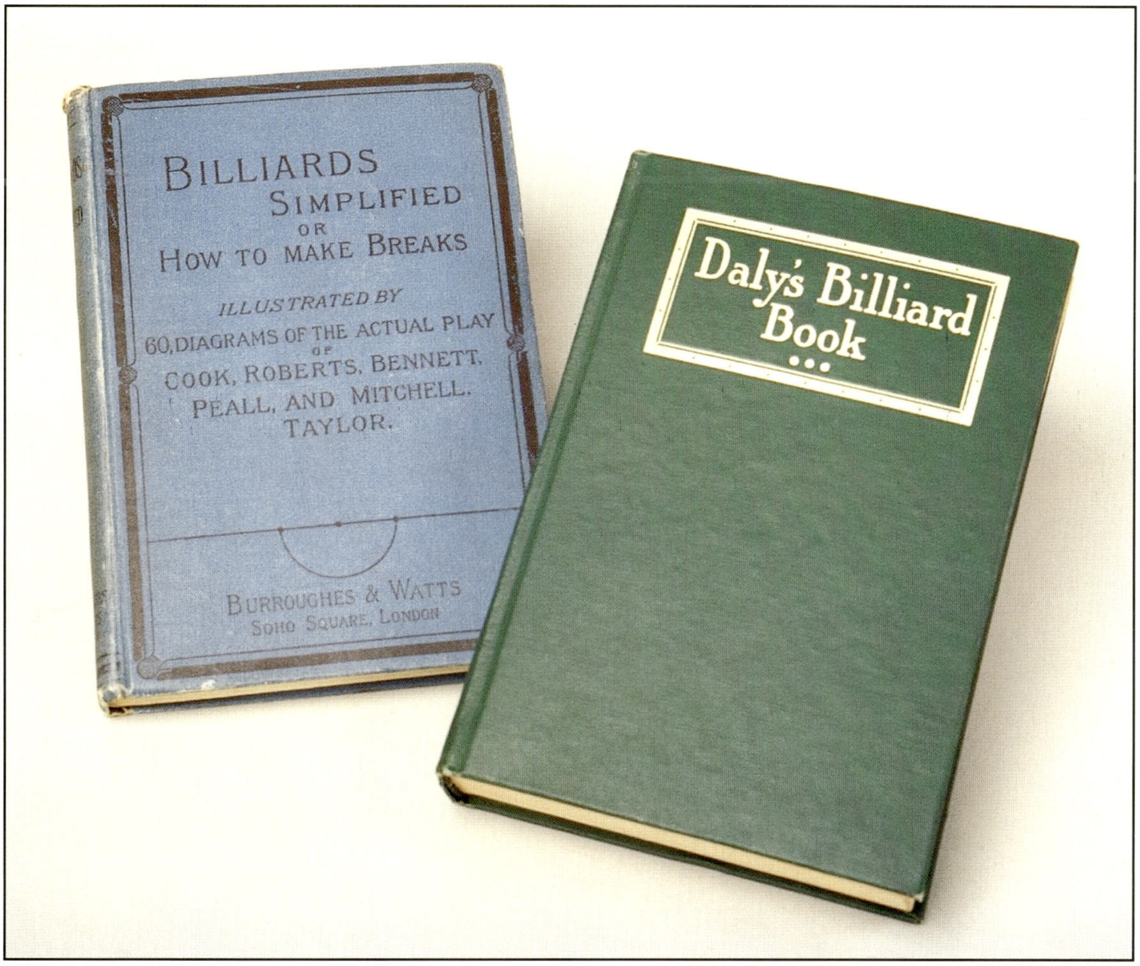

Billiards Simplified, Burroughes & Watts, late 1800s, 300 pages, a rule book, AND a magnificent table and supply catalog in one, super book, very good condition, $225. *Daly's Billiard Book*, 1914, 276 pages, excellent condition, $65.

Modern Billiards by John Roberts, 1902, 334 pages, good condition, $90; *Billiards For Beginners,* again by John Roberts, 1902, 74 pages, fair condition, $55; *Roberts on Billiards*, 1870s, some color, 376 pages, fair condition, $150.

The Badminton Library, by Major W. Broadfoot, R. E., 1896, 491 pages, number 70 from an edition run of 250, good condition, $250; *Garnier's Practice Shots, Scientific Billiards*, all color, 1880, 109 pages, fair condition, $375+.

Left to right: *Modern Billiards*, from the Brunswick-Balke-Collender Co., 1891, 698 pages, fabulous reference guide, very good condition, $375; *Billiards*, by Tom Reece, 1915, 312 pages, good condition, $130; *Modern Billiards*, very rare 1881 second edition, from the "J. M. Brunswick & Balke Co.," some color, 326 pages, $370.

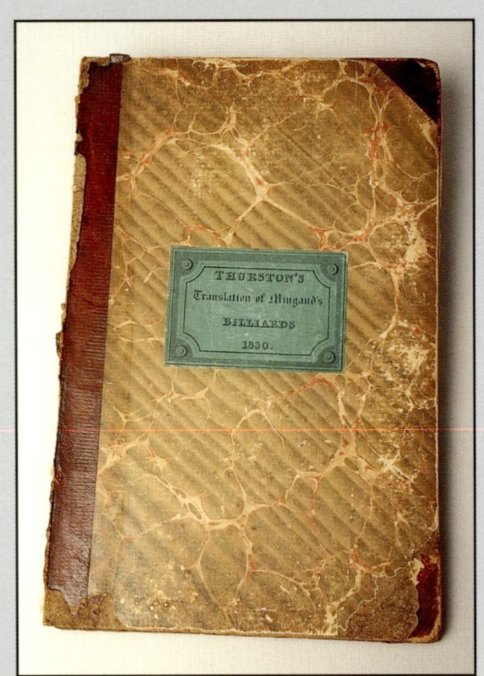

Ultra scarce 1830 example of an extremely coveted billiard book. Authored by Monsieur Mingaud, then translated for the first time into English text by the Thurston Billiard Table firm, this example has a pullout hand colored print at the end of the book. The billiard shots exemplified are also hand colored. 42 pages. Fair but very aged condition, spine needs replaced, otherwise complete. In excellent condition, this is a $2,500 item, in this condition, $2,100+.

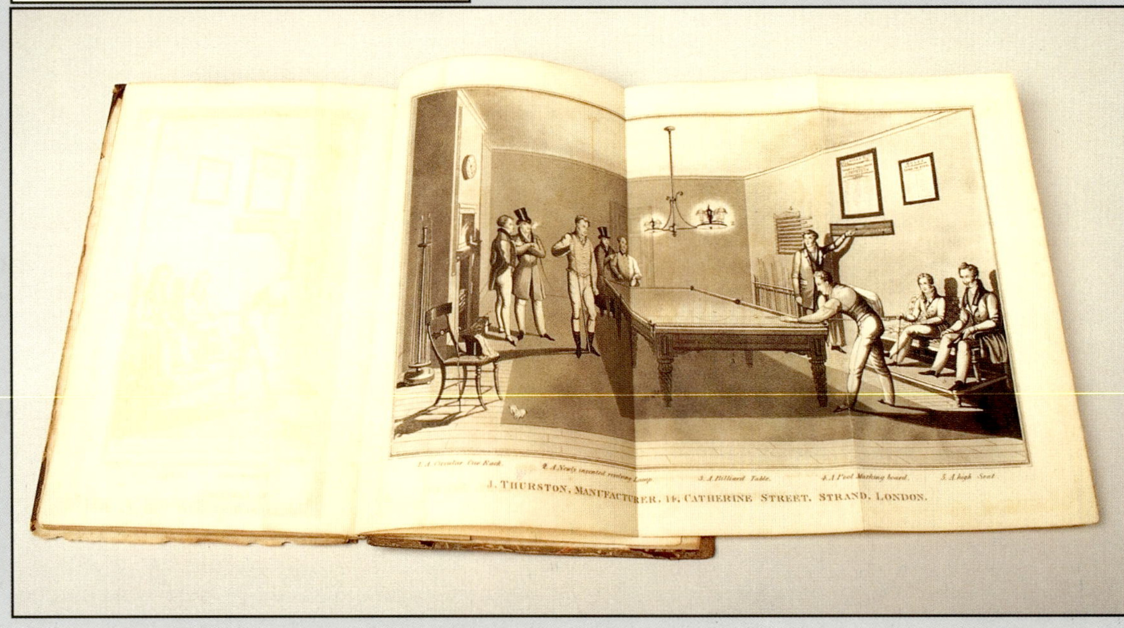

Rare book with a characteristic termed "fore-edge." The faces of the page *edges* are gold leafed on the very tips only. By crisply pressing the full face of the book's edge opposite the spine into a gradual slope, a beautiful color image can be made to appear. This book contains short whimsical stories and poems and the like, and is dated 1864. This is the only connection this book has with billiards. Very good condition, $700+.

Chapter III
Chalk and Related Items

Great category. Amazingly popular. Hard to find some of the rarest pieces. Fairly common otherwise, and relatively affordable. Rare pieces, like with any collectible worth its salt, can get a little pricey, as you'll see.

T: Rare style of "wafer" shaped chalk from the W. A. Spinks Co., c. 1885, excellent condition, $55/piece. B: Earliest chalk was white and is very hard to find, c. 1860s, $45/piece.

Early chalk, condition is critical, these values are for excellent specimens: Top to bottom, left to right: $25; $25; $30; $50 / $55; $20; $25; $30 / Brubacol; rare; $75; "Black label," $15; $30; Brunswick "Monarch," $35.

Top to bottom, left to right, price for excellent specimens: $30; LEXITE, very rare, $100; $35; $15; $20; $30; $25; $65; $25; $45; $40; Saunier Wilhelm, $30.

Top to bottom, left to right, price for excellent specimens: $20; $20; $20; $35; Rosatto Barry Street Co., $20; $35; "Popular," $50; Morescoro, very rare, $100; $15; $45; $35; Kling Tight Expert chalk, $55.

Much more difficult to find, early ROUND chalk, top to bottom, left to right, price for excellent specimen: H & H, very rare, $80; $55; $55; Jacob Schaefer chalk, ultra scarce, $125; Kansas City Billiard Co. "Vignaux" brand, scarce, $125; Eureka, larger sized, $100; Ehrlich, "Dan Patch" series, $95; Powers and Vail, $75; C. B. Liver, Omaha, Neb., $80; $65; $70; $65; $55; Dan Patch by Ehrlich and Son, black label, $90; $60; $55; Brubacol, very scarce, $125; $55.

Top to bottom, left to right, price for excellent piece: Geo. Wright & Co., $90; Draillib, very rare, $65; "Veso" (Czechoslovakian), $65 / $50; "St. Martin," $40; Thurston's, $50.

T: Rare triangular shaped William A. Spinks brand chalk, $150; BL: rare octagonal shaped Eureka brand, $125; BR: very rare "I X L" brand, from Brunswick-Balke-Collender, octagonal, excellent piece would be priced at $150, but in this condition, it would fetch around $75.

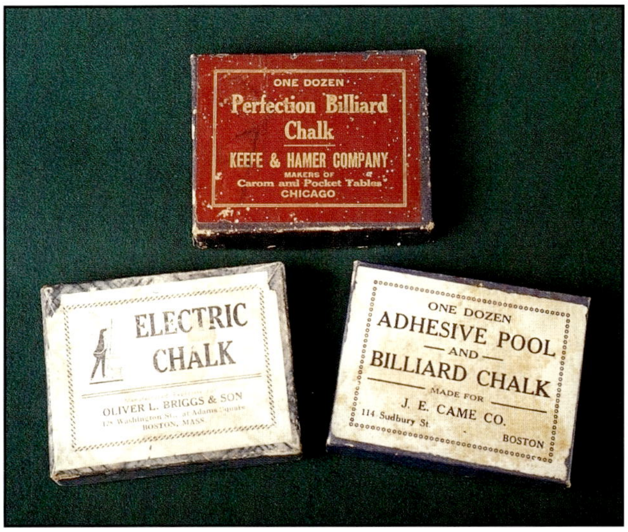

The boxes for chalk are often empty, or close to it. These prices are for good condition examples without any pieces of chalk: T: $100; BL: $75; BR: $95.

TL: Eureka for large round chalk, $175; TR: Spinks' for large round chalk, $150; BL: standard Spinks' box, $95; BR: standard Eureka box, $150.

TL: $65; TR: $75; bottom: very rare, c. 1890s, $175.

T: open box of "Club" brand round chalk, BOX ONLY, $95; BL: $80; BR: $150.

TL: $75; TR: $75; bottom: ultra rare, $250.

Four different "pocket" model chalk holders. Late 1800s vintage, a very difficult collectible to find. Top to bottom, left to right: Celluloid, Burroughes & Watts, $300; sterling plate hinged cube with monogram, $225; aluminum, by W. A. Spinks, $250; celluloid, by Spinks, $295.

Three different sized variations of cast iron "under the rail" chalk receptacles, c. 1870s, many antique tables were adorned with two or four of these. $75 each.

Three much earlier examples of ROUND cast iron chalk cups. Circa 1870s, $110 each.

Three rare examples of c.1870s cast iron chalk cups. T: "The J. M. Brunswick & Balke Co.," very scarce, $250 each; left: vented to avoid build up of chalk residue, $175 each; right: unusual oval design, original gold paint, $175 each.

Rare early wood chalk receptacle, c. 1850s, $300.

Patent model for an "in the rail" chalk holder. All original paperwork, dates to 1876. Excellent original condition, $950.

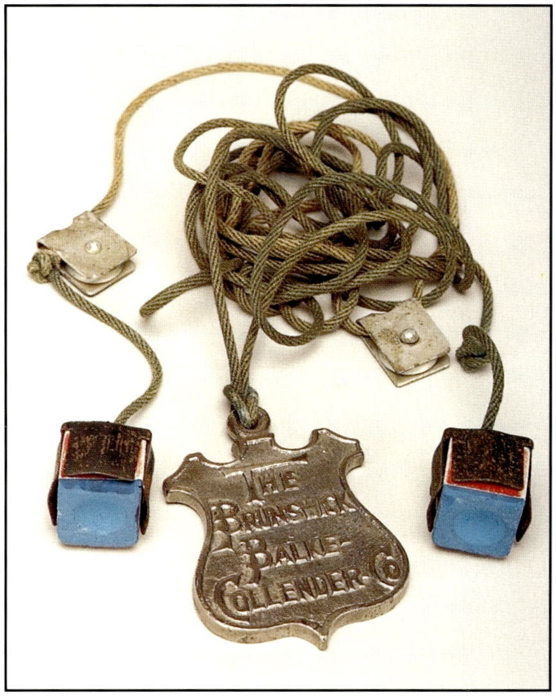

The most sought after variety of "chalk suspension devices" employing the counterweight technique. The Brunswick-Balke-Collender "shield" style, complete unit, rare nickel-plated example (most are either black or raw cast iron), $275.

Mechanical chalk retracting device. Suspended from the ceiling in a pool hall, this piece kept the chalk handily right above the table and, after stroking your cue tip with some chalk, would carry the piece of chalk upwards after it was released. Excellent original condition, c. 1900s, complete unit, $150.

Two examples of the "Williams" brand "recoiling" spring loaded chalk retractor, c. 1890s. L: including rare, square, leather chalk holder and chalk, $275. R: including rare, round, leather, chalk holder for round chalk, $325.

Same principal as the previous device shown, harder to find example, complete and excellent condition, $200.

Chapter IV
Matchbox Holders, Matchsafes, and Pocket Mirrors

Three great individual categories of billiard collectibles. We have placed them all into one category that most dealers call "smalls." These are what are known as *cross collectibles* as they are collected by different people for differing reasons. That, not surprisingly, drives the price up a bit because of the competition to acquire them. All of these types of items advertising billiards are very rare indeed; half a dozen of any of these rarities is considered an "advanced collection"!

Four celluloid matchbox holders: TL: $135; TR: $150; LL: $150; LR: $150.

Four celluloid matchbox holders: TL: $150; TR: $150; LL: $150; LR: $150.

Four celluloid matchbox holders: TL: $150; TR: $150; LL: $175; LR: $150.

Four matchbox holders: TL: $125; TR, litho in tin: $145; LL, celluloid: $150; LR: $125.

Four celluloid matchbox holders: TL, with 1926 calendar: $150; TR: $150; LL: $150; LR, with 1927 calendar: $150.

Three matchbox holders: T: brass, great billiard image engraved into it, $495; LL, celluloid, great pool tables image: $350; LR, celluloid, shows antique table: $325.

Two unique examples of matchbox holders and a great English litho on tin container: TL, litho on tin: $300; TR, porcelain coated holder for the larger sized match boxes, slight damage, hand painted motif: $450; B, tin holder: $135.

Silver-plated brass matchsafe, outstanding image, advertising window on reverse side, with billiard parlor advertisement, dated 1904, excellent condition, $350. Same example, but without original billiard room advertisement, $300.

Same scene, silver plate on brass, slightly different and much rarer shape, complete with advertisement, good condition, dated 1904, $400.

Two very rare celluloid wrapped matchsafes: Left, full color lady bust on obverse side: $495; Right, full color, full bodied nude lady on obverse side, "Love's Repose" dated 1905, graphics show wear: $875.

L: Rare aluminum "compact style" matchsafe, patented 1920: $500. R: Outstanding silver-plated brass "suitcase style" matchsafe, fabulous engraving, excellent condition, very rare: $495.

Rare celluloid Brunswick-Balke-Collender matchsafe, billiard and bowling images on either side, excellent condition, $450. Great brass matchsafe, stippled to simulate leather, from the Brunswick-Balke-Collender Co., fabulous intricate billiard table embossed in plaque, $500+.

Nickel plated brass matchsafe, average condition, $295. Exceptional and rare silver-plated matchsafe with hand painted porcelain cameo in a billiard motif, $1,500+.

Solid sterling silver matchsafe with very handsome monogram engraved on obverse side. Spectacular graphics, best there is: $1,750.

Paper labeled (left) and celluloid wrapped (right) pocket mirrors: L: $235; R: $350.

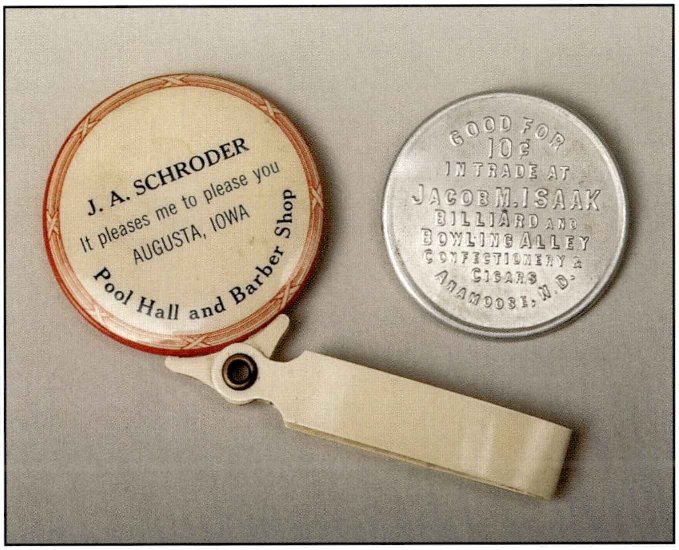

L: Rare combination "barbershop / billiard parlor" pocket mirror, celluloid, c. 1900s, with celluloid foldout handle, $450. R: Early, unusual aluminum pocket mirror, $395.

L: excellent condition celluloid pocket mirror with beautiful, Victorian lady's bust, $650. R: Unique full bodied image of a woman posing in somewhat masculine garb, slight damage to left edge, otherwise excellent, $475.

L: Rare example of an oval, celluloid wrapped pocket mirror, with a 1905 penny captured inside to bring luck and to date it, $495. R: Oval celluloid pocket mirror with gold writing and great color lady's bust, $650.

Two magnificent examples of the rarest celluloid pocket mirrors to be had. Both are what's known as a "good for," as they were exchangeable for merchandise. Same gorgeous scantily dressed lady on each mirror. Both in excellent condition. Circa early 1900s, $900 each.

Chapter V
Triangles, Ball Boxes, and Balls

Early ball-racking triangles have a little niche of their own. Many different sizes, of course, made of different substances and differing woods, and by different companies, help to make up this small, but fun, category. The standard triangle, designed to rack 2 1/4" balls, is relatively common. It's the ODD sizes that rarely surface.

Early billiard and pool balls have been, for a long time, the most asked for collectible in our trade. They command an amazing fascination for novice and seasoned collectors alike. Can't tell you exactly why, but we must confess, our ball collection is very advanced and we, too, really appreciate them. The term "billiard" originally referred to the specific game of "caroms," the game played typically without the use of pockets. A table *with* pockets eventually acquired the nickname of "pool table." Interestingly, the origin of the term "pool room" stems from the fact that most of the billiard parlors were plagued with the disease known as "gambling," and the "office" of the town bookie was, where else, at the "pool room."

Five examples showing most of the different sizes that balls and triangles were offered in. With 2 1/4" being the most common and—if from the late 1800s or early 1900s (as each of these is)—assuming it is in good condition, these typically sell for around $90. You can expect to pay more like $155 each for the rarer sizes.

Three different examples of late 1800s "10 Ball" triangles. One is a signed Brunswick-Balke-Collender and sells for $175, the others, unsigned, good condition, $95 each.

These two are approximately 16" long (O. D.) as they are designed to accommodate twenty-one balls for the game of "baseball pool," c. 1880s, signed example, $225, unsigned $175.

Dovetailed triangle for 2" balls, turn of the twentieth century, $80; c. 1920s nine ball rack, dovetailed corners, rare, $125.

Signed triangles from more obscure companies, Ehrlich & Sons (top) and Oliver Briggs, in good condition, c. 1890s, $125 each.

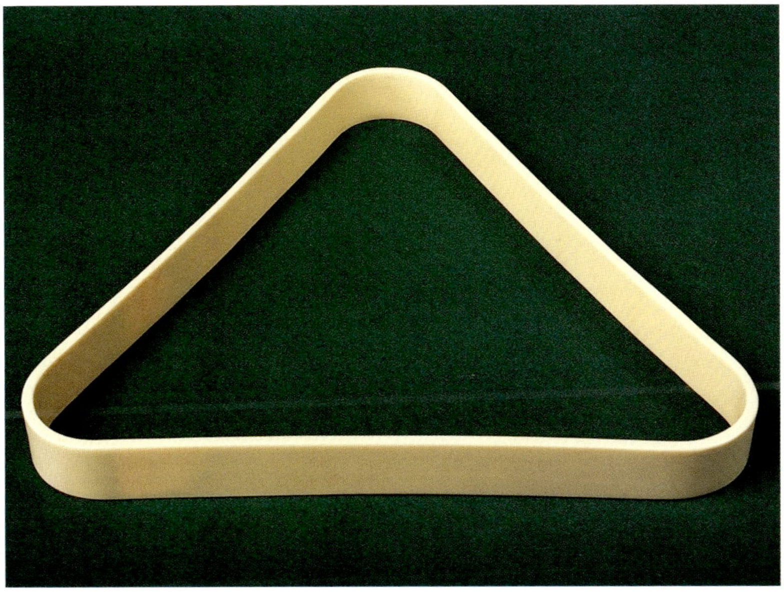

Very rare celluloid triangle. These were intended to look just like ivory, and they do come close, in excellent condition, for 2 1/4" balls, c. 1890s and on through the early 1900s, $250+.

One of a kind "presentation triangle," built from wood and brass from the Spanish cruiser "Reina Mircecles," sunk at the battle of Santiago de Cuba. This piece was presented to "Alfredo De Oro Champion of the World, by Portsmouth N. H. friends" as he served at one time as the American ambassador to Cuba. Beautifully made from mahogany. Because it is a presentation piece to one of the all time greatest billiard champions and is in perfect original condition, $5,500+.

Collapsible triangle, c. late 1800s, maple, in good condition, very rare, $475.

An 1860s primitive, factory, dovetailed maple sixteen ball box with brass hook clasp. Very early and rare example, good condition, $450.

Late 1800s, beautiful book-matched wood sixteen ball box, restored, with unique brass latch, $400.

Early wood box for sixteen balls, typically poor label (labels are rarely even in good condition and are a crucial factor in determining the value of a box), for 2 1/4" balls, unusual ball model, as is, $150+.

Attractive poplar sixteen ball box with unusual label in relatively good condition, fine dovetailing, this style of ball was generally sold by the "Burt" Ball Co. $250+.

Oliver Briggs goes back a long way, but this cardboard sixteen ball box is from the 1920s. Pretty good shape for an early ball box, neat graphics, $200+.

Rare maker for billiard balls, above average condition label, nicely dovetailed, fair condition overall, sixteen ball box, c. 1900s, $250.

Very hard brand of ball box to find, fine dovetailing, good condition, c. 1890s, $300+.

From the "Albany Billiard Ball Co.," this box is for a sixteen ball set of the "Hyatt XXXX" model ball. Labeled "FANCY," and in above average condition, $275 to $300.

Outstanding condition sixteen ball wood box with a fantastic label, sold by "The Brunswick-Balke-Collender Co.," c. 1880s, very rare and early label, $500+.

Late 1800s dovetailed wood sixteen ball box, rare label, tagged "SOLID STRIPE 2 1/4," good condition, $225+.

Cardboard, c. 1900s, sixteen ball box, above average condition with super graphics, from the "Albany Billiard Ball Company," $350+.

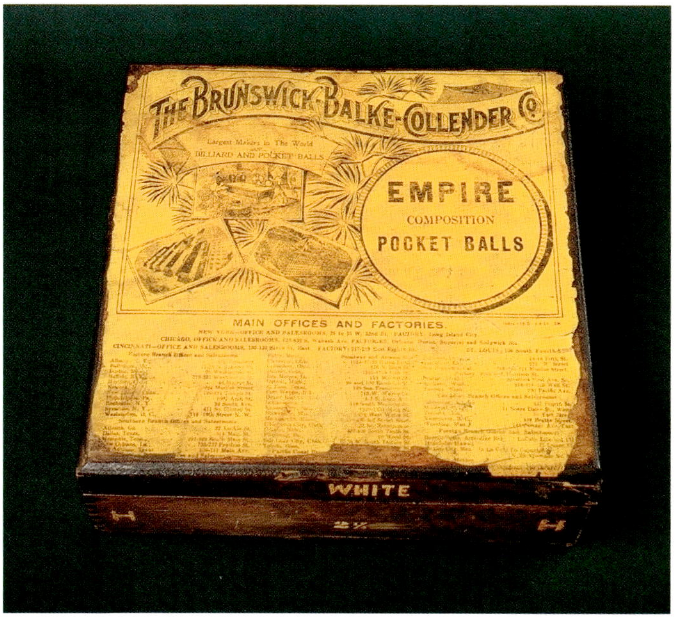

Similar to previous box, but for a different model of ball, the "EMPIRE," c. 1890s, above average condition label, a Brunswick-Balke-Collender sixteen ball wood box, $350+.

Beautiful example of an "Albany Billiard Ball Company" sixteen ball wood box from the 1880s, fine dovetailing, labeled "FANCY," and the "O" refers to the design of the ball itself. Very good condition, great graphics, $375+.

Very rare sixteen ball poplar wood box, tagged with the special label for the sale of ivory numbered ball sets. From the Brunswick-Balke-Collender Co. for 2 1/4" balls, finely dovetailed and in great condition, nearly impossible label to find, $750+.

Outstanding Brunswick-Balke-Collender, c. 1880s, dovetailed wood sixteen ball box. Slight paper loss, spectacular color graphics, structurally excellent, $350+.

"Triangle" model cue ball in original box. This is an early bakelite ball and there were a few different marks (see triangle on this ball) that designated the *hardness* of these break balls. Just the ball, $40; just the box, $75; as a set, $125.

Here are sixteen different cue, or "break balls," showing most of the marks you may see if you collect. All but the ones with the stars or diamonds are $25 to $50; the ones with diamonds (except if the ball is dark brown bakelite) run around $125; a brown bakelite one will bring about $50; and the ones with the stars, the most sought after style, sell for $150 to $200. The vintage for these balls runs from the middle 1800s through the middle 1900s.

A rare TWO BALL SET of ivory billiard balls in the original box. From the Brunswick-Balke-Collender Co., this set sold to the proprietor who understood that the RED ball need not be ivory to satisfy the customer. They only shot with the two white balls, one with a dot and one without. 2 7/16" balls, c. 1890s, good condition, $400+.

Think about it, nearly every pre-1900 three ball set of carom (billiard) balls you'll find are going to be made from ivory. (It's just the OPPOSITE for numbered balls). This set is made from composition (they're usually clay), and is actually quite scarce. No lid for the box, very good condition, c. 1880s, $150.

Very unusual version of composition billiard balls. They are standard bakelite balls, but the design is both unique and great for display, they ARE rare, excellent condition, $300+.

Imported from England, c. 1900, 2 1/8", for snooker tables, parlor tables, and combination dining/billiard tables, composition balls in original box, overall good condition, $250.

Excellent condition set of early 1900s composition carom balls, in the original box, 2 1/8", $300.

A nice ivory set, imported from England, 2 1/8", good original box (missing cotton stuffing), $500+.

A nice set of ivory carom balls, 2 1/4", from a supplier by the name of Phil Jost, Jr., from Chicago, c. 1900s, with original cardboard box, excellent condition, $500+.

Rare full "BAKELITE" set from the "Frank Rosatto" Billiard Supply Co., c. 1900s, poor label, wood box, balls excellent, $325.

Rare J. E. Came set of 2 3/8" ivory carom balls in original box. Box in relatively good condition, balls are excellent, $600+.

Brunswick-Balke-Collender cardboard box, c. 1900s, with excellent set of ivory carom balls, good condition, $550+.

Three ball ivory set in an unusual 1940s vintage wood box in pretty fair condition, with a brass hasp! $500+.

A set of three super ivories from the "Albany Billiard Ball Company." "XX" quality (close to the best), 2 3/8" size, overall excellent condition, $600+.

Rare oak carom ball box with pinned corners, hinges, and lock set. Excellent condition, ivory balls are mint, $650.

Excellent condition ivories in a leather covered wood box, felt lined, with an elaborate hasp set for locking the balls from use. These are tournament quality balls in very fine condition in a presentation style box. Leather showing wear, c. 1890s, $1,000+.

Choice set of ivory balls in a rare mahogany box. Hinged lid with hook clasp, $650.

Top of the line, tournament quality, ivory three ball carom set in a velvet lined leather case. Very rare, cloth hinges, nickel-plated brass hasp lock, $1,500+.

Highest possible quality, mirror finish ivory billiard balls, marked "Match balls," from "Brunswick Balke Collender," in a leather covered, silk lined presentation case. As good as it gets, largest size, 2 7/16", c. 1890s, $2,100+.

A rare four ball set in the elusive "clay" type ball. Large 2 7/16" size, c. 1880s, in wood box, good condition (for ancient clay billiard balls), $300.

A good condition complete set of bakelite 2 3/8" carom (billiard) balls, in a box labeled "Empire Billiard Balls," from the Brunswick-Balke-Collender Co., c. 1890s, $400.

Very scarce four ball set of unusual composition balls. Note the green and blue balls! These sets are sometimes seen in early photographs and lithographs showing them being used in certain games of billiards. Good condition, with box, c.1880s, $500.

A "Sandford Bell & Lahm" four ball set of ivory carom balls. Nice graphics on a cardboard box, above average condition, $600+.

A "J. E. Came & Co." four ball ivory set. Nice graphics, rare, c. 1880s, cardboard box, $650+.

"New Hyatt Patent Billiard Balls" from the "Syracuse Billiard Table Co.," finely dovetailed oak box, c. 1880s, far above average condition, balls excellent, $800+.

Choice set of four ball ivories in a dovetailed wood box, from "The Brunswick-Balke-Collender Co.," c. 1880s, lithograph on wood label, $750+.

Great condition four ball ivory set, in a wood box, from "The Brunswick-Balke-Collender Co.," paper label, c. 1890s, $600+.

From the "A. Hand Billiard Mfg. Co.," this is a hard brand to find, a beautiful four ball ivory set. The box is cardboard and in far above average condition, the balls are outstanding, c. 1890s, $650+.

A set of 2 1/4" clay balls, with "out of the ordinary" sized smaller numbers. Ball collectors will notice this. Excellent condition, c. 1890s, $300+.

A 2 1/8" clay set, again with the smaller style numbers, used on parlor tables and snooker tables, c. 1890s, $400+.

Strange group of eleven balls, (four short of a full set, can anybody help us complete it?), that appear to be made out of every color of clay that was used in ball making. Good condition, these don't have numbers, c. late 1800s, incomplete set, $500.

Manufactured by Brunswick-Balke-Collender, beginning in the late 1800s, these were called "Empire" balls. 2 1/4", excellent condition, very rare, $1,000+.

Turn of the century (1900) celluloid ball set in the rare 2 1/8" parlor table size. Advanced "yellowing" from age, great for display purposes, $400+.

This is a rare, very early, full set from the "Burt Billiard Ball Co.," c. 1880s, called "Solid Red" balls. Clay, no numbers, 2 1/4" size, excellent condition, $500+.

Another rare "red" set from the "Burt" Co., this style sports a white dot on each ball, again, no numbers, clay, excellent condition, c. 1880s, $500+.

"Solid Reds" from the "Burt" Co. again, but this rare version has little yellow stars on it. No numbers, c. 1880s, very good condition, clay, $650+.

Extremely rare 1860s vintage clay pool balls with *ENGRAVED* numbers. This is a 2 1/8" set and one of only two sets we've ever found. Excellent condition, $1,500.

Our other set of 1860s vintage, engraved numbered, clay pool balls; these are 2 1/4" in size, and are also in very good condition, very scarce, $1,500.

A 2 1/4" very early engraved numbered composition (clay) pool ball set. Circa 1880s, very scarce, excellent condition, $1,000+.

This great little set is only 1 7/8" in diameter. These were manufactured for use on the tiny "parlor" tables of the period. This is an early, c. 1890s, example and the standard sized numbers only serve to accentuate the minute stature of this rare "speckled" set. $400+.

Early version of the "bakelite" style of composition balls, c. 1900s. This set is a bit harder to find in this "Dart" style with the tiny points located at the "3 and 9 o'clock" spots on the ring around the number. Very good condition, 2 1/4", $400.

Full set of 2 1/4" composition balls, c. 1900s, numbers in the solid colored half of the set (1-8), match the color of the ball, while the numbers in the rest of the group are set into black circles in white. Excellent condition, $350.

A 2 1/8" set of composition balls, early 1900s, with *paper* number labels! Very good condition, $250.

A 2" "Burt" brand pool ball set. Numbers inside scalloped background, c. 1890s. Excellent condition, rare, $450.

1 7/8" set of turn of the twentieth century parlor table balls. Numbers MATCH the color of the ball! Excellent condition, $300+.

1 7/8" set of speckled, or "agate," balls, c. 1890s, white numbers in black circles, scarce set, excellent condition, $450+.

Unusually tiny 1 3/4" set of "agate" balls, white numbers on black scalloped backgrounds, c. 1890s, very rare, excellent condition, $500+.

Extremely scarce example of a rare style of ball. These are 2" balls that are both "speckled" and are in the version called "Dart" balls. The smaller size, combined with the standard sized inset number in this rare set of clay balls, makes them a great find for the serious ball collector and super to display. The heavy "agate" feature makes them one of our favorite specimens. Circa 1890s, excellent condition, $1,250+.

Beautiful, excellent condition set of finely speckled pool balls. 2", c. 1890s, $600+.

A VERY hard to find set of 2 1/4" clay pool balls with the unique feature (in CLAY), having the numbers for the 9 through 15 balls setting in the "field" rather than in the stripe on the ball. The "Dart" versions of early balls, which became known as the "Centennial" in 1945, all sported the little points at 3 and 9 o'clock around the circle the number was set into. This style of number location in the "field" is still sold today; however, it has been a very elusive example to find in the early clay vintage without the darts! Good condition, c. 1890s, $500+.

ALL of the following sixteen ball sets are priced based on the assumption that they are in very good to near mint condition. The other factors that determine the value of a set of antique pool balls are scarcity and the material the balls are made from. This set is made from clay, is a *standard* 2 1/4" size, and the set is not all that rare. Most sets like this are found in poor condition and sell for around $100. The numbers in these composition style balls were put on by hand, one at a time, way back when, and are rarely exactly consistent in size. A set as pristine as this one now retails for around $200. The cue ball with the star sells separately for $150+.

This is the "Dart" ball set, 2 1/4", clay, sold by Brunswick-Balke-Collender and several other firms and billiard supply houses in the late 1800s and on. Fairly hard set to find—even harder to find in good condition, trust me. This set is in far above average condition, $250+.

The balls in this set measure 2 1/8" in size, that makes the set a bit more rare. They are from the "Burt Billiard Ball Co.," in the original good condition box, balls have the scarce "hand engraved" numbers and are in great shape, c. 1880s, $1,500+.

Rare set of "POKER" balls from the late 1800s. The photo reveals the fact that each ball has a number on one side and a "J," "Q," "K," or "A" on the other. These are an early clay set in great condition, several companies offered them, 2 1/4", $800+.

This set is tough to find. This is a set of "POKER" balls, in the 2 1/4" size, but they are also in the rare "Dart" version! They are clay, from the late 1800s, in very good condition. Because they are "Dart" balls, $1,000+.

Ultra rare clay 2 1/4" set of solid red balls with red numbers in scalloped circles. Excellent condition, c. 1880s, $2,000+.

Another ultra scarce 2 1/4" set of composition balls from the late 1800s. Mint condition, buy 'em when you see 'em, with original red dot cue ball, $2,500+.

This is the pride of the Burt Billiard Ball Co.'s fleet. These 2 1/4" clay balls, c. 1890, were only "surface striped," so they are typically found with a little to a lot of color loss. In addition, the numbers were surrounded by a few different styles of background design. This set is commonly referred to as the "numbers in a gear" style. You can see why. In addition, the numbers were hand-engraved into the balls. They are very scarce and highly sought after. They are called "double striped" balls in the very early catalogs and were offered by most of the leading billiard supply firms. This set is in relatively excellent condition, $2,000+.

A 2 1/4", 1890s set of clay "Burt Double Striped" balls. Numbers in an eleven point "star" background. Some color loss, excellent condition, RARE, $2,000+.

Very rare 2 1/8" sized "Burt Double Striped" balls. These numbers are set into a "daisy" or "scalloped" background, in very good condition with minor color loss, in an original dovetailed box, c. 1890s, $2,500+.

One of the rarest styles of balls, and it is nearly impossible to find a set that does not look as though its been run through a blender. The technique used in making this elusive "Direct site" model ball from clay in the late 1800s apparently must have been flawed. This is one of the nicest examples you may ever see, 2 1/4", WITH very rare original box, labeled "HEXAGONAL," and with its "New Hyatt /Hexagonal / Direct Site Billiard Balls" paper label, $2,500+.

One of the most sought after styles of collectible pool balls. This is the "Zig-Zag" set, 2 1/4", clay, original star cue ball, in its hard to find original box, c. late 1800s, outstanding condition set of balls in a very hard pattern to get. WITH box, $2,500+; without box, $1,500-2,000.

The rarest and most sought after style of antique billiard ball of them all. These are called "Wave-O-Lene" balls. They date from the early 1900s, possibly earlier; we're still researching them. These balls were offered by the Brunswick-Balke-Collender Co. These are also in the rare "Dart" style! 2 1/4". Made from clay. In absolutely superb condition. Not including personal carrying case, $5,000+.

This is an extremely early set of what were called "sand checked" ivory pool balls. They are definitely from the bottom of the barrel and would fall into the "F" grade category, the cheapest ivory balls available. These are a mid-1800s example of 2 1/4" ivory in the most affordable state. They have hand engraved numbers, some are already gone or nearly gone from wear. This is as rare a set as you can find in antique billiard balls. The blue diamond cue ball is not original to the set and is valued separately at $125. Today, this ultra scarce set of ancient ivory balls would sell for $4,000+.

Rare, full set of c. 1880s, all red, ivory numbered pool balls. 2 1/4". IVORY balls of this vintage typically vary slightly in circumference as they were often "turned" to "true them up" as needed. Hand engraved numbers, as on ALL ivory balls, very good condition, $5,500+.

This is an unusual sized set of early ivory numbered balls at 2 3/16"! Note the hand engraved numbers are placed in the stripes on the #9 through #15 balls. They're in very nice condition, c. 1880s, hard to find in this size, $6,000+.

Top two rows are a set of very scarce "Burt" brand ivory pool balls. Engraved numbers, "double striped" style, 2 1/4" size, c. 1890s, excellent condition, $6,500+. Bottom two rows are a set of what was termed the "professional size" (2 5/16") ivory pool balls. Engraved numbers, rare set with numbers in the "field" rather than in the stripe on the #9 through #15, VERY HARD size to find, excellent condition. This set has fractures from exposure to cold temperature, otherwise close to mint, $6,000+.

HUGE, mid-1800s set of ivory numbered balls. This set has the numbers hand dyed into the balls. Inconsistent circumferences from periodic turning of members of the set that went "out-of-round" over the years, most are in the neighborhood of 2 3/4"!! Most sets with dyed numbers are of European origin. This set is in relatively good condition, $5,000+.

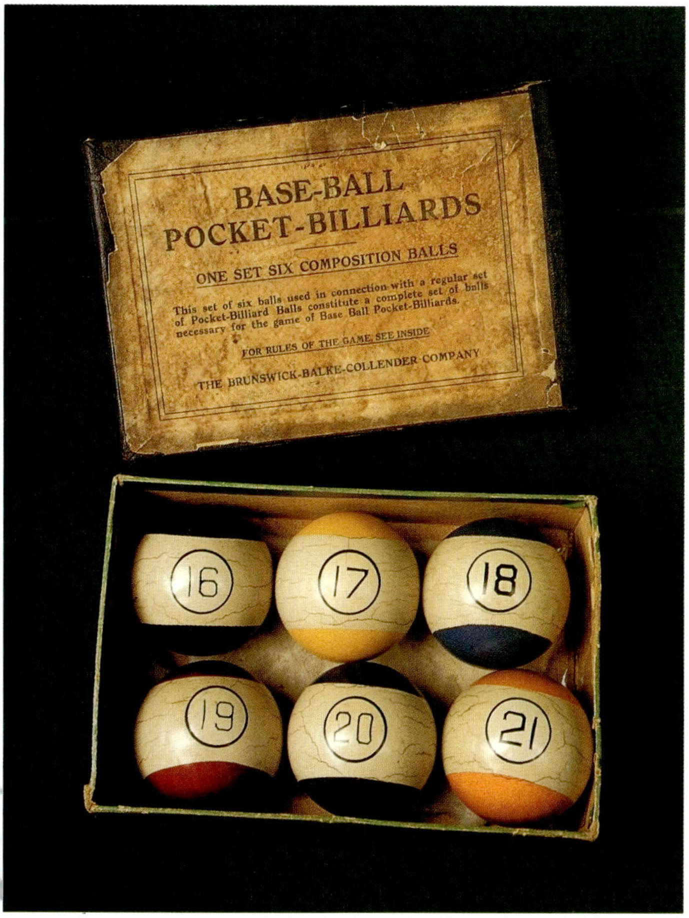

This is a set of balls sold separately with which one would play the game of "baseball pool." The box is hard to find with the balls, and this is only one of seven or eight variations of ball-design that these appear in. 2 1/4", clay, c. 1890s, WITH box, balls in very good condition, and in one of the more unusual designs, $700+.

Very early 2" ivory ball set for the game of "Life Pool"! In original locking, quarter-sawn oak, felt-lined case, excellent condition, c. 1880s, RARE, $2,000+.

Early 1900s set of clay 2 1/8" snooker balls. In original Hyatt cardboard box, these are a little more scarce in that they are in the "Dart" version, very good condition, $450.

Late 1800s ivory snooker set, 2", very nice grain painted locking case, very good condition balls, a rare find, $5,000+.

This photo serves to show *most* of the sizes that ivory billiard and pool balls were offered in over the years. This display starts at 1 1/2" and moves in tiny varying increments until it reaches the 2 7/16" ball. The last set of carom balls are 2 3/4" and are made from celluloid. 2 1/2" ivory balls *were* available in the early, American catalogs, though we have yet to find a set. Ivory 3-ball carom sets in excellent condition, without a box, sell for $225 for the smallest sizes on up to $500+ for the larger sizes. Size and condition are the determining factors.

Here are the only three balls we have to show you from a very rare set of early clay 2 1/4" pool balls. These examples do not have numbers, but rather imbedded "rank" letters and engraved "suit" emblems in them for playing a variation of the game of billiards poker. Early 1900s, excellent condition, $100/ball.

Late 1800s, 2 1/4", clay, poker or, "Court," style balls. These are ultra scarce and we only have these two. Anyone have a set we can buy? They're in very good condition and clearly show an engraved "King" and "Queen" in both "fields" of the balls with corresponding letters, "K" and "Q." There are no numbers on this set, $100/ball.

Chapter VI
Medal, Tokens, and Trophies

Medals are not exceedingly rare, but they do tend to surface more often in the metropolitan areas. This is because most of the billiard tournaments were held in the "big city."

Tokens, on the other hand, though they ARE more readily available, claim one of the most interesting positions in the field of billiard collectibles. There are probably in excess of 2,000 distinctly different tokens related to billiards to be found! Here are just a very few unusual shapes and denominations. Those distributed by billiard table manufacturers typically fetch higher prices, with the "Good For" examples and those with a "town and state" being the most sought after.

"Silver dealers" and "trophy collectors" will quickly tell you, examples of billiard trophies are surprisingly difficult to locate. We've averaged less than one per year for the past twenty-six years. Bear in mind, we look only for trophies from the 1800s and early 1900s. Later examples are more readily available and, of course, sell for a little less.

Three early billiard medals, left to right: copper on spelter: $75; sterling, 1936: $125; sterling, 1938: $125.

Three more nice billiard medals, left: sterling with gold plate, $150; center: sterling, $125; right: sterling with gold plate center, 1931-2, $150.

L: Beautiful brass watch fob (YMCA), with chain and watch clasp, $225. R: "Wheatley's 3 in 1" (Barbering, Bowling, Billiards) 1913 watch fob, pewter, $225.

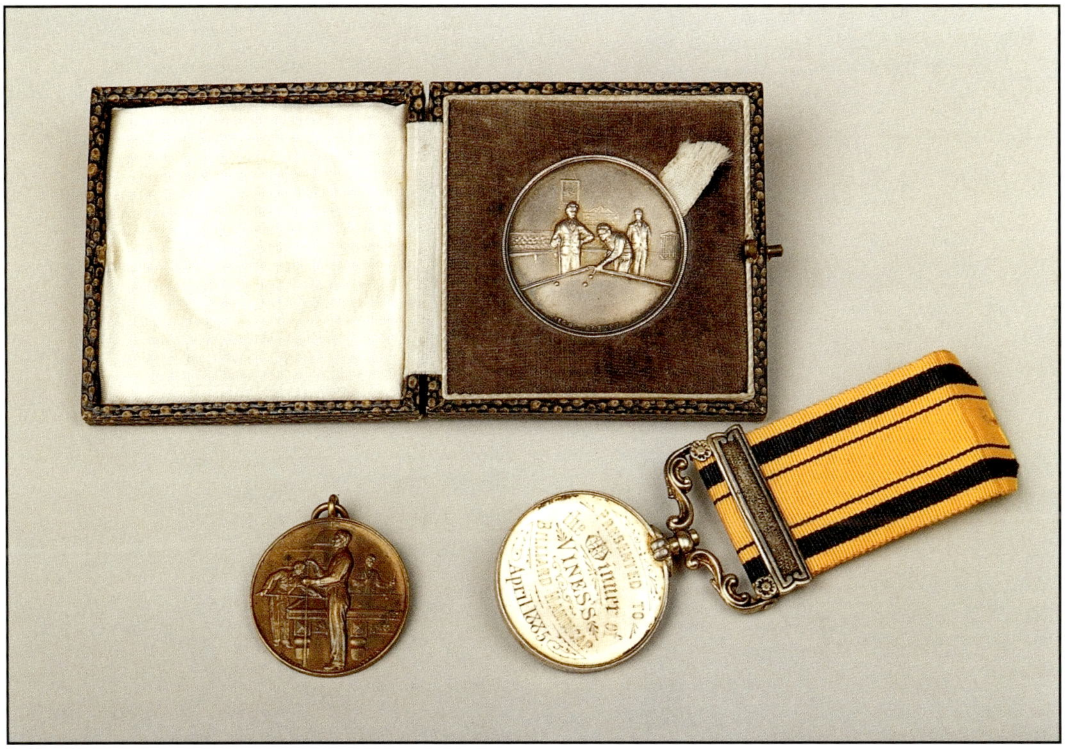

T: beautiful sterling billiards and cards medal, dated 1928-29, in presentation box, $350. LL: half dollar sized copper medal, very good condition, great detail, great image, $180. Lower right: 1885 first prize medal for the "Viness Billiard Handicap," sterling, $450.

Billiard tokens: left to right, top to bottom: $10; from Tucson, Arizona, $30; rare table depicted, $250; / $15; $18; $15.

Tokens: left to right, top to bottom: $15; $15; $15; / Superior Billiard Supply, $50; $15; $15.

Some rare shapes in the billiard token field: left to right, top to bottom: $75; $50; $23; / very rare shape, $95; $65; very rare shape, $85.

Unusual cutouts in billiard examples, left to right, top to bottom: $20; $40; $20; / $50; $40; $40.

Some more very hard to find billiard examples, left to right, top to bottom: $65; $75; $325; / $125; $165; $95.

More scarce tokens, left to right, top to bottom: $110; odd table design, $155; rare manufacturer's example, $195; / $145; rare manufacturer's example, $250; $85.

Some more rare ones, Brunswick distributed, left to right, top to bottom: $95; $115; $125; / $110; rare shape, $145; $225.

VERY hard to find combination billiard and barbershop tokens, left to right: $90; $95; $80.

Sterling silver-plated trophy, "Century Motor Club Billiards," 6" tall, 1910, $225.

Identical, but 10" tall, sterling silver-plated trophy, 1911, "Century Motor Club Billiard Championship, " $275.

Sterling silver trophy, delicate design, for a "Pyramids Championship," 1934, 8 1/2" tall, $975.

Greater Pittsburgh Lyceum, 1912-13, silver-plated, 17" tall, $325.

Beautiful sterling silver trophy, "Toronto Cup Billiards H" cap, 1933, 8 1/2" tall, $950.

Halifax Junior Billiard League Championship Trophy, worn silver-plating, 1933 –1934, 12" tall, $225.

The Peninsular Club Championship Consolation Billiard Tournament, sterling silver, 1914, 8" tall, $895.

Pittsburgh Courier "Two Leg Trophy," 1931 – 1933, 15" tall, sterling plated with gold wash interior, $550.

Exceptionally ornate sterling silver-plated 1902 trophy for the North Carolina Billiard Association, with notation for highest score (run) for billiards of "95," some interior pitting, 10 1/2" tall, $1,500.

The Amidon Cup, 1917 trophy, made from pewter, 7" tall, $245.

1903 3rd prize for the Republican Club Billiard Tournament, sterling silver-plated, triple handled, 5 1/4" tall, $375.

Spectacular triple handled ten year span "passed on" silver-plated billiard trophy. Runs from 1904 to 1914, 9" tall, handles designed to simulate stag horns, "Cananea Club Pool Tournament," outstanding example, some silver loss, $1,250.

Never presented silver-plated "Brunswick Balke Collender" trophy in a spectacular art nouveau motif, 17" tall, substantial silver loss, otherwise excellent condition, c. 1890s, $1,500+.

"Chicago Pool Tournament," 1910, 4 1/4" tall, glass bottomed, copper plated pewter tankard, $650.

Three handled porcelain trophy, "Crescent Athletic Club," 1906, 5 5/8" tall, $850.

A 6 1/4" tall, triple handled, glass bottomed, pewter tankard, "Junior Bottle Pool Tournament, First Prize, Won by G. G. Hall, 1899," $900.

"Intermediate Cowboy Pool Tournament, Second Prize, 1900 – 1901, E. H. Drew," 6 1/4", glass bottomed, pewter tankard, with hinged lid, excellent condition, $795.

RARE 9" tall, pewter, glass bottomed, lift lid tankard, "Mount Pleasant Field Club Pool Championship, 1899, Won by Nathaniel S. Hyatt" (possibly related to the Hyatts of billiard ball manufacturing fame?), $975, assuming no relation; if he is a descendant, considerably more.

"1898, Tavern Club Consolation Pool Tournament, First Prize, Class D," 2" tall, sterling silver-plated match holder, $350.

Pewter candlestick trophy, nearly devoid of silver plating, 6" tall, "Highland Club of West Roxbury, Handicap Billiards, First Prize, 1907-8, " $235.

Sterling silver ashtray with great billiard theme, 3" by 4", $495.

Bronze and marble billiard trophy (this guy looks exactly like Willie Hoppe), 9" tall, excellent condition, early 1900s, never presented, $450.

Fabulous cut glass cigar humidor, solid sterling silver lid with imbedded partial ivory billiard ball, 7" tall, "Hamilton Club Billiard Tournament, 1905," mint condition, outstanding piece, $2,800.

Pewter figured billiard trophy, "Ray Neimer, Billiard Champ., Raven A. C. [athletic club]," 7 1/2" tall, 1929, bakelite base, $250.

L: Photocopy from an early billiard book showing one of the many trophies won by Jacob Schaefer Sr., c. 1880s, and, R: one of the actual miniature "look alike" figures cast from solid silver to proudly stand atop them. A trophy like this one would be an expensive item indeed, (at least $5,000), and we feel the highly detailed Jacob "the Wizard" Schaefer effigy in sterling, at only 3 3/8" tall, is worth at least $450.

"Wesley Schools Shield, Presented by Harold Roebuck, Esq. of China, 1923," all buttons are sterling and the dates for the consecutive winners run from 1923 to 1936. Ebonized backboard, hangs on wall, $1,800.

"The Aberdare & District Billiards League, Presented by Burroughes & Watts, Billiard Table Manufacturers, London & Cardiff," silver-plated copper on oak backboard, individual buttons commemorate winners from the years 1931 to 1935, hangs on wall, $1,500.

The silver plating is all but gone on this superior grade trophy. Pressed from solid copper and mounted on solid oak, this impressive piece reads, "Birkenhead & District Snooker League," and sports the facilities coat of arms in genuine porcelain. A truly spectacular specimen, $2,500+.

Chapter VII
Photos, Prints, and Posters

Very rare stuff! We've owned just a handful of duplicate items from this category. Again, buy it when you see it if you genuinely want to display this type of early billiard paraphernalia. In this category, it might be a good idea to take what you find when it is available and upgrade, if possible, later on. Great billiard images are definitely a rare commodity.

An 8" x 10" photo advertising another product that Brunswick-Balke-Collender manufactured, excellent original photo, $95.

This Delightful Billiard-room at "Treddinnock," a Suburban Philadelphia House, is Adjacent to all the Living Apartments. Simplicity is the Keynote in the Decorative Treatment, the Sway of the Colonial Being Apparent in Every Detail

The Billiard-Room of a Country House

Mural Paintings, Marked by Colorful Charm, Adorn the Walls Above a High Paneled Wainscoting in the Billiard-room in an Abington, Pa., Home

These six images from *Suburban Life* magazine, 1914, comprise an article portraying some of the nicer home billiard rooms in the country. Full article, $65.

In a Germantown, Pa., House, Beautifully Tooled Leather Hall Panels Form a Distinctive Feature of the Billiard-room

Wood Paneling has Been Used with Excellent Effect Here, and the Fireplace Adds to the Coziness of the Room

A Billiard-room of Great Attraction at Bryn Mawr, Pa., is Paneled with Quartered Oak Stained to a Brownish Gray. The Fireplace, in an Alcove, is of Moravian Tile

In This Room of a Portland, Maine, Residence, Facilities for Luxurious Lounging are not Lacking

Early 3" x 5" original photo showing an inlaid "Eclipse" model pool table, $75.

Another original photo taken in the same billiard room, a couple of different players, "mates" of photos are fairly scarce, $75.

7" x 9" spectacular Victorian original photo, ornate, brilliant novelty table shown, $195.

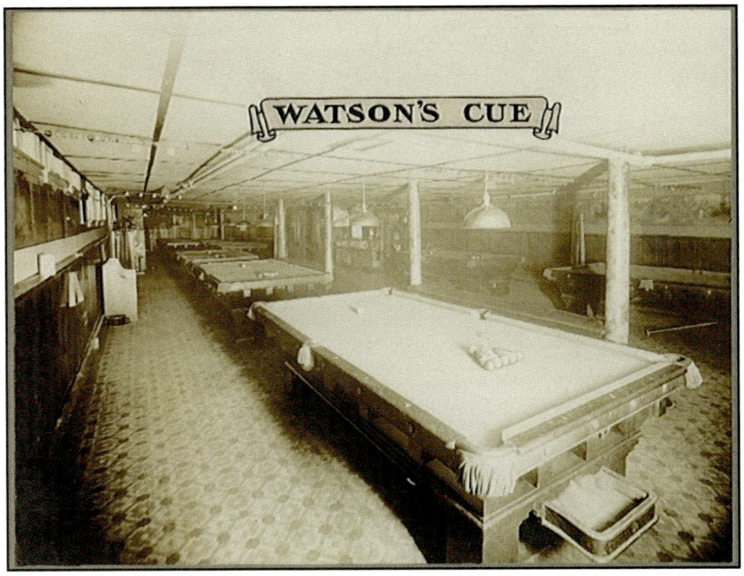

Three 6" x 8" images from "Watson's Cue" billiard room, in Reading, Pennsylvania. All three images are from the same building and would strongly suggest that there were three floors of tables, with the upstairs room apparently being called "The Roundup Billiard Parlor," also operated by Cole W. Watson! The last photo shows a "Billiard Experts" poster on the wall. A RARE set of three "mate" photos, $675+.

3.5" x 7" early image of a pool room; the top has been trimmed slightly, $55.

An important 4" x 5" image of two "Eclipse" pool tables, a very rare view of a Monarch cue rack, a Non-Pariel cue and ball rack, two very early kerosene billiard lights, and ALL the pool balls are white! This photo has creases, so, $195.

5" x 7", early room, $125.

7" x 9", shows three cue/coat closets, and all the goodies in a typical early 1900s pool hall. The back of the photo says, "The Club Pool Parlor, Waco, Texas," excellent condition, $225.

A 7" x 9" photograph showing an Eclipse billiard table and a great gas light. Note: the fellas are playing FOUR ball carom billiards. $180.

Two billiard and three pool tables, the Narragansett model, four cue racks, several spectator chairs, gas lights, and a whole slew of ceiling mounted scorekeeping bead sets and Brunswick-Balke-Collender shield shaped chalk counterweights. This photo also shows two celluloid headed bridges. 6" x 8", $225.

8" x 10" photo of the "Dobbs Libby House" billiard room. "Union League" model pool table, by B. A. Stevens, c. 1880s, mounted with convertible rails to play "carom" billiards, while pockets (visible) are blocked by cushions. $250.

Two ornately inlaid tables, one billiard (no pockets), and one pool, and two super Eastlake cue racks, 6" x 8", a little faded, $225.

4" x 4" photo, two "Southern" model tables, great gas lights, nice condition, $80.

Large 12" x 14" original print from an architectural manual dated 1903, showing an octagonal floor model cue rack in front of a mantle top style scorekeeper and the top of the room's pool table with unusual worsted wool pockets, $95.

7" x 9" print from *The Inland Architect and News Record* magazine, 1892, Narragansett model table, fancy ball rack and pin pool scoreboard pictured, and very rare model of billiard cue, along with a fantastic light, $150.

Early 5" x 7" 1900s pool hall photo showing a group of very rare ceiling hung mechanical "game counters" in a very nicely equipped room, good condition, $75.

A great image of what was probably the entire membership of the "Gentlemen's Club"! A 1923 date, nice equipment displayed, 5" x 9", very nice condition, $80.

An 11" x 14" reproduction of an original photo of the incredible billiard room from one of the two homes that were built for the Baer brothers, who founded the city of Bettendorf, Iowa, early 1900s. $45.

A 14" x 19" original photo, about as big as you'll ever see, of a room with York model tables, a great mirrored cue rack, and neat gas lights. They are playing with sets of ALL white and ALL red composition balls and the wall is lined with spectator chairs, $450+.

A 14" x 16" image that's hard to beat; a very rare photo, $600+.

A 16" x 18" image, from 1891, depicting the champions and the "EMBLEM" of the tournament, which is a highly detailed, very ornately carved, pocketed model pool table, complete with a bridge and miniscule pool balls!! The cues look like trees compared to today's sleek designs. One heck of a photograph. $1,000+.

A 1976 original "signed" photograph of one of Europe's all time greatest players, Claude Falkiner. The image area is 6" x 8", shows slight creasing, and is housed in a new frame, $300.

An original 8" x 10" print from the Brunswick-Balke-Collender Co., c. 1900. Excellent condition, $750+.

A turn of the twentieth century set of three 8" x 10" photos from Brunswick-Balke-Collender, in the original frame, outstanding original condition, 1,500+.

A fabulous photo of a fabulous billiard player, Jerome R. Keogh; the image size is 7" x 9", shooting on a Narragansett model table, c. 1890s, a period in which he was one of the champions of the world. Very rare image, obviously, $650+.

Nov. 13, 1915

THE NATIONAL POLICE GAZETTE, NEW YORK. 13

ALFRED DE ORO.

DEFEATED FORMER CHAMPION GEORGE SLOSSON RECENTLY IN A THREE-CUSHION CARROM MATCH.

A 9" x 13" image of Alfredo De Oro, another one of the world champions, taken from an issue of *The National Police Gazette*, which covered many major sports events of the period. The image is dated 1915 and is a nice piece, although the magazine misspelled his name, $25.

Set of six large (approx. 22" x 28") sepia tone photographs of six legendary pool players. Excellent condition, rare, set of six, $1,800. Individually, $300+.

8" x 10", sepia tone photograph, taken by a Butte, Montana, art studio, c. 1900, with the legendary Willie Hoppe demonstrating a *masse* shot for George Butler Sutton (right), and someone I have yet to positively identify. Any tips? Great, rare image, $650+.

Original 3" x 5" photograph of Michael Phelan, considered by most to be the "father of billiards" in America, late 1800s, good condition, $500.

Imposing, excellent condition, 4" x 6" original photograph of George Sutton posing proudly with two of his many championship medals and one of those elusive, miniature pool table tournament "emblems," or "trophies"! Circa 1890s, $475.

Original 1890s photograph, 4" x 5.5", of the amazing, world champion "Finger Billiardist," Yank Adams, posing with an actual advertisement proclaiming his field of expertise. Excellent condition, extremely scarce image of a very important player, $750+.

Attractive, color, original sales flier from the 1920s. 8" x 10", nice condition, $90.

Highly coveted original photograph of possibly the greatest billiard player of all time. Many times world champion. Shown demonstrating a *masse* shot, this image is as good as it gets. 4" x 6", c. 1880s, Jacob Schaefer, known as "The Wizard," $1,000+.

Rare print distributed by the W. A. Spinks Billiard Supply Co. featuring "Miss Cue," a clever play on words, in one of the promiscuous poses typically displayed in her series of fun images. Good condition, 7" x 13", copyright 1911, $495+.

Circa 1910 offering from Brunswick-Balke-Collender, these three prints are from an original series of watercolors done by Archie Gunn, a renowned artist of the period. Although this IS an image that has been reproduced (so you need to be careful), an original in good condition ordinarily sells for around $1,250 to $1,500.

ARCHIE GUNN
1910

ARCHIE GUNN
The Brunswick-Balke-Collender Company
"A Graceful Stroke"

This is a beautiful 15" x 20" color image of the fairer sex at play. Entitled "Billiards at Home," and distributed by Brunswick-Balke-Collender, c. 1900. Replaced antique frame, excellent condition, $750.

Circa 1900, this is another special color print showing how the gals favored the game of billiards as well. 10" x 13", original frame, $650.

Very early image of two elegantly dressed ladies playing billiards. Color, 8" x 10", late 1800s, museum matted, rare image, $350.

In a restored antique frame, this large 17" x 21" hand colored image is a very striking piece indeed. This shows how magnificent the billiard furnishings were at a very early stage of the game, c. late 1800s, $1,500.

Late 1800s "valentine" print, from a series, with a cute poem. 8" x 14" image, rare, $175.

Early original watercolor, German, note cues on outer edges, 19" x 25", perhaps one of a kind, $795.

Original 1892-93 French print, 5" x 6", excellent condition, $175.

This image was issued by The Burrowes Billiard Table Co. at the end of the 1800s. Exceptionally nice original oak frame with gesso balls and cue sticks. The image is 7.5" x 9". This version is a rare hand colored example, $450.

Circa 1900, Bernhardt Wall color image, original frame, gesso balls, and title "Kiss," extensive soiling, $150. If found in excellent condition, $275.

Rare double-framed version of a twin set of early 1900s Bernhardt Wall images, gesso balls, cue, and scoring beads displayed, excellent condition, each print is 9.5" x 13.5", $550+.

This is the full set of "Vanity Fair" prints addressing the world of billiards in the late 1800s. Each image is 9" x 14". All are in excellent condition, reframed, $200 each.

Rare, relatively small picture woven from *SILK*, c. 1890s. 5" x 7", excellent condition, beautiful image, $400+.

This image is also woven from pure SILK. These are from the 1890s. This image is 7.5" x 14"; it also appears in a diminutive version at 3" x 5" and a "biggest" size at 12" x 23". It was also created in color (see next photo), excellent condition. This size and the larger one, $400+; the smallest one, $225.

This is the rarest version of the 1890s SILK print. I believe it is only available in this 7.5" x 14" size, mint condition, $650+.

One of the hardest to find turn of the twentieth century images ever issued by Brunswick-Balke-Collender Co. At 12.5" x 13.5", in color, original frame, if in excellent condition, $975.

Rare, outstanding, stained glass, Victorian image depicting two children playing billiards. This is the only one we've ever seen, 15" x 20", $1,000+.

Incredible reverse painted GLASS door insert. This glass was in a door on Wabash Ave. in Chicago at the turn of the twentieth century. 23" x 32", outstanding condition, framed to display, $3,250.

Offered in a choice of different sizes, this being the biggest size available. Brunswick-Balke-Collender created these magnificent and highly detailed pictures to exemplify their incomparable wood-inlaying skills. There was a nice selection of subject matter offered, and they also solicited photographs from clients to create replicas of their favorite images. This version is 22" x 40". Extremely rare and highly sought after, c. 1900. Smaller sizes, $1,500+; this largest size, $3,600+.

One more largest available example of an "Elk" in *inlaid woods* from the Brunswick-Balke-Collender Co. Some of these are found with a Brunswick paper sticker on the reverse, some are not, and some have another slip of paper denoting the often exotic combinations of woods used in its creation. 22" x 34.5", excellent condition. Smaller sizes of this image, $1,500+; this largest size, $4,000+.

Unusual cardboard poster that was tacked to the underside of the late 1800s Brunswick-Balke-Collender billiard tables showing a customer how he should assemble his new piece of furniture. 9" x 17.5", good condition considering where it "lived," a neat, scarce item, framed to display, $495.

Some water staining to this c. 1900s color version of a hard to find poster, 14" x 22". In this condition, $500+.

Large window display flier advertising the upcoming February through March 1925 World 18.2 Balkline Billiards Championship to be played in Chicago. 22" x 32", excellent condition, framed to display, from the Brunswick-Balke-Collender Co., $500.

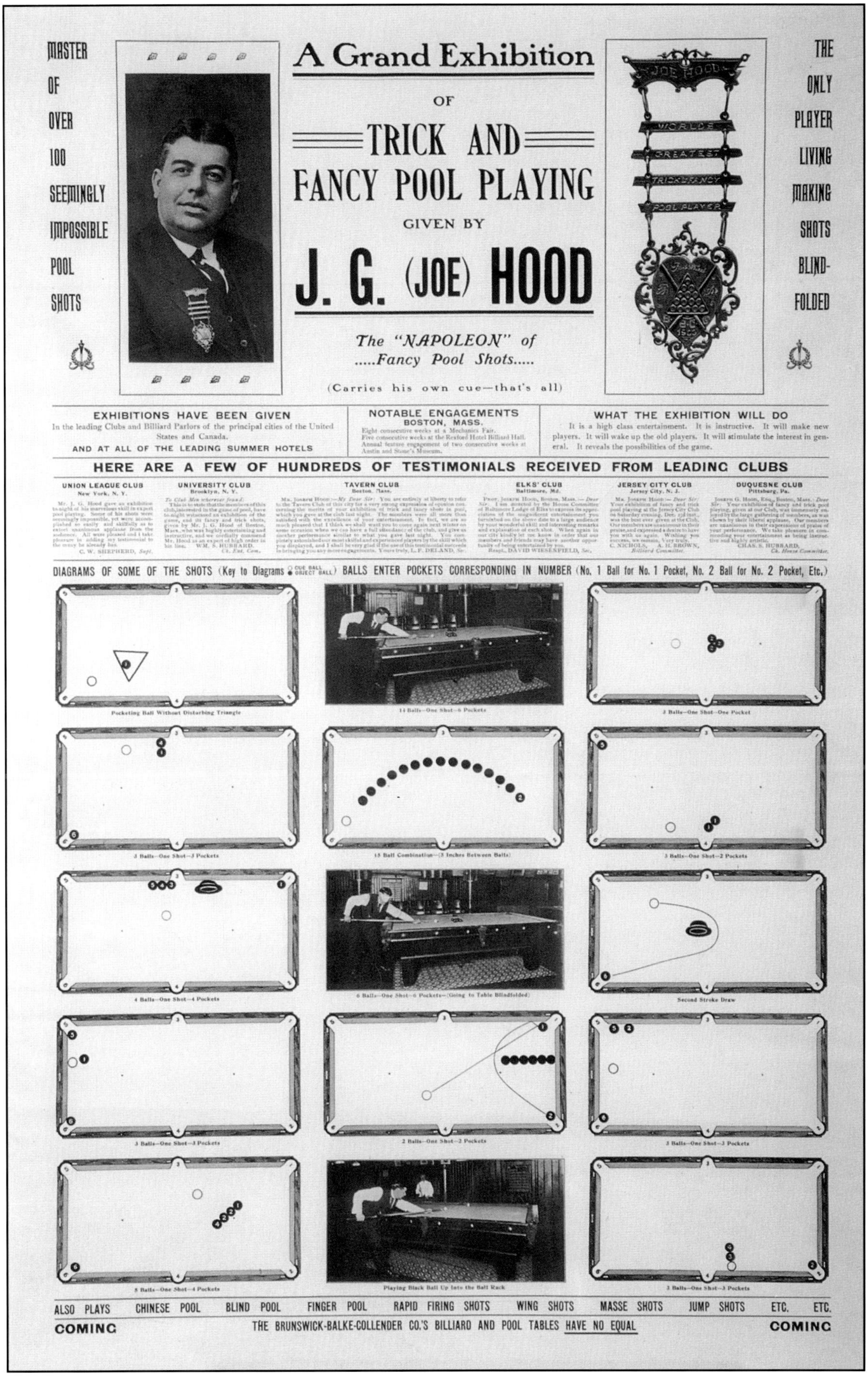

Outstanding condition 14.5" x 22.5" original poster advertising "A Grand Exhibition" by the famous trick and fancy pool shot performer, Joe Hood, c. 1900s, issued by the Brunswick-Balke-Collender Co. An extremely scarce and coveted piece of ephemera, $1,000+.

Early 1900s color poster of rules from the "Draillib" (billiard spelled backwards) Billiard Cloth Co. Neat graphics on left and right edges (advertising Hyatt brand balls), hard to find, 21" x 27", super condition, original frame, $950+.

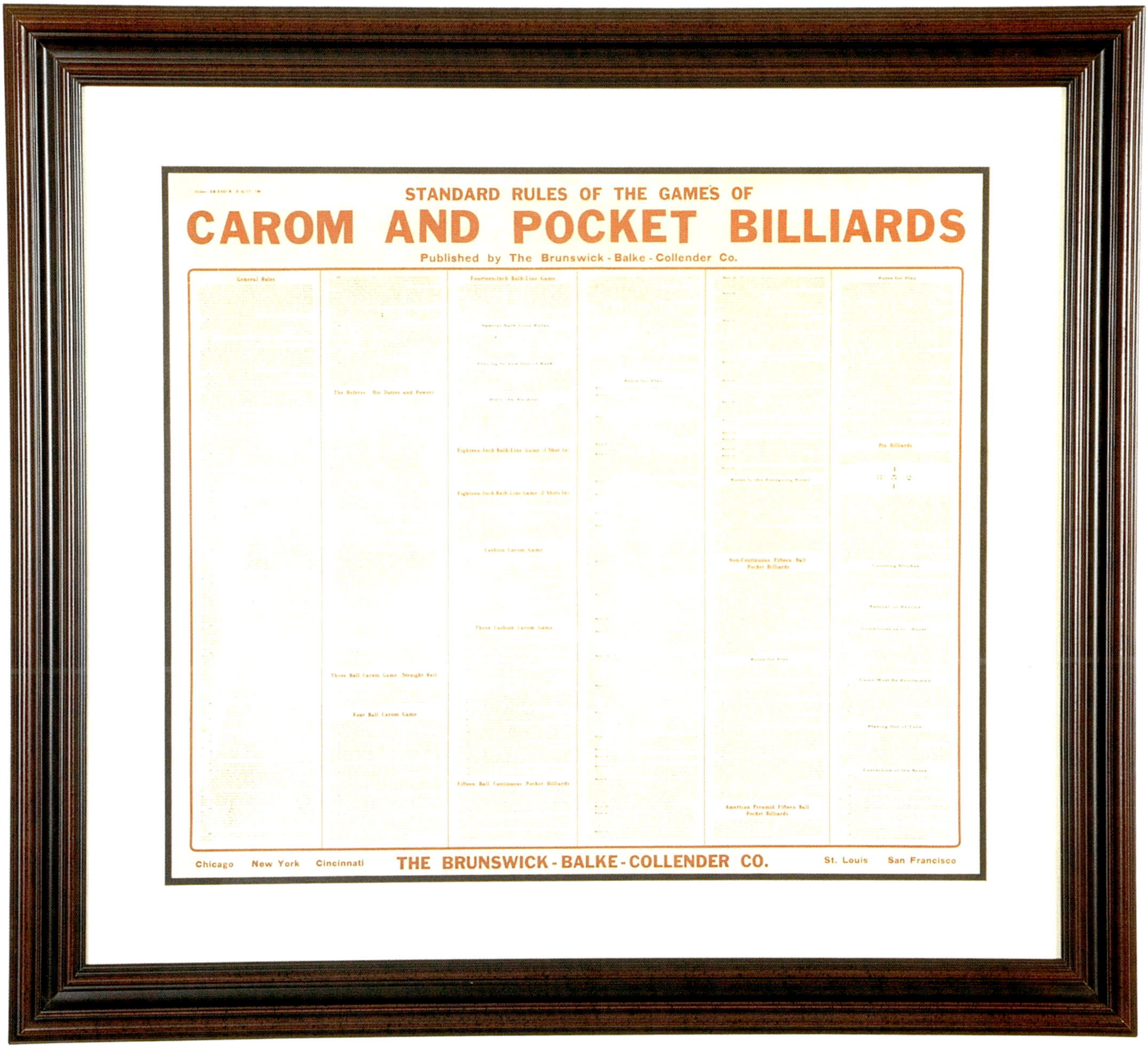

This was one of Brunswick-Balke-Collender's offerings of a rules poster, exceptional condition, 20" x 24", dated 1917, reframed, in this condition, $1,000+.

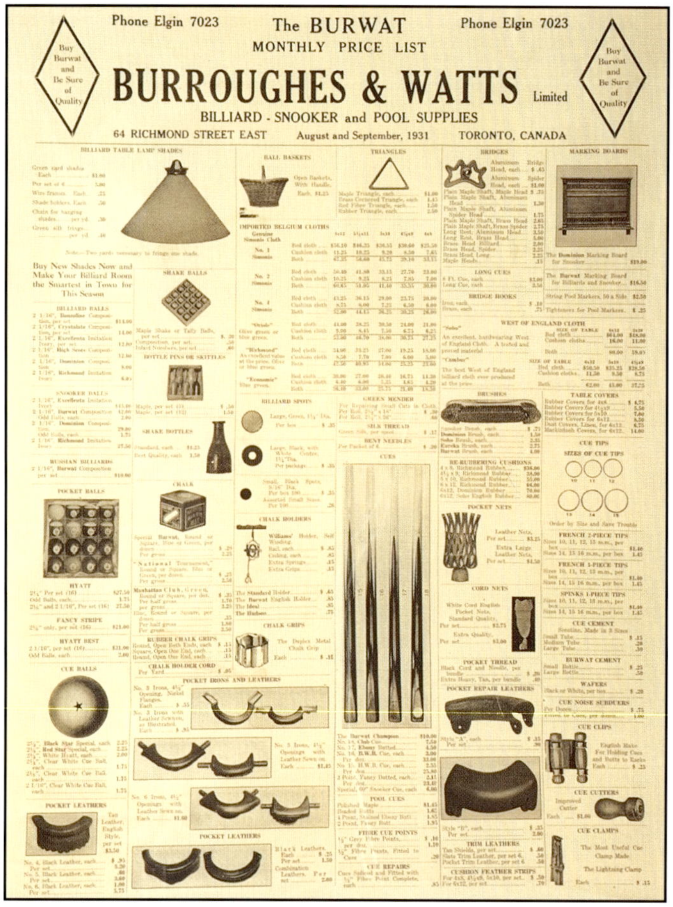

Phone Elgin 7023 | The BURWAT | Phone Elgin 7023

MONTHLY PRICE LIST

Buy Burwat and Be Sure of Quality

BURROUGHES & WATTS Limited

BILLIARD - SNOOKER and POOL SUPPLIES

64 RICHMOND STREET EAST | August and September, 1931 | TORONTO, CANADA

Buy Burwat and Be Sure of Quality

Two sided, four page, fold-open flier , 16" x 22", from Burroughes & Watts, 1931. This one is from Toronto, Canada, excellent condition, of a quality suitable for framing, $675.

Print from an early watercolor, artist unknown, estimated vintage late 1800s, original appears in an 1850s periodical, reframed, 12" x 18", excellent condition, $750+.

Early 1800s color print, 6" x 8", rematted and framed, excellent condition, outstanding image, $695.

An 1882 original Currier & Ives color print; this is an ultra rare example issued by "The Brunswick-Balke-Collender Co." Good condition, reframed, 12" x 16", $2,000+

An 1889 original Currier & Ives color print, very good condition, reframed, 10" x 14", $950+.

An 1871 original Currier & Ives color print, excellent condition, reframed; one of the hardest C & I images to find, even rarer considering it was issued by a very early billiard table manufacturing company known as "O. D. Benjamin"! 13" x 16", $3,250+.

Copyrighted 1882, this fabulous color lithograph advertises "Falk's Milwaukee Beer," "A. Werner & Co. Champagne," and "The Brunswick& Balke Co."! The spectacular table is an Exposition Novelty model and is virtually never seen in early advertisements. 10" x 14", excellent condition, $2,250+.

An 1869 color lithographed sales banner, 19" x 24", fair condition, reframed, very rare, early advertisement, $900+.

Circa 1860s color advertising flier from "E. Brunswick & Co.," very good condition, reframed, 7" x 9", $550.

Fabulous 1860s color lithograph from the "Kavanagh & Decker" Co., 16" x 22", outstanding condition, reframed, very scarce image, $3,600.

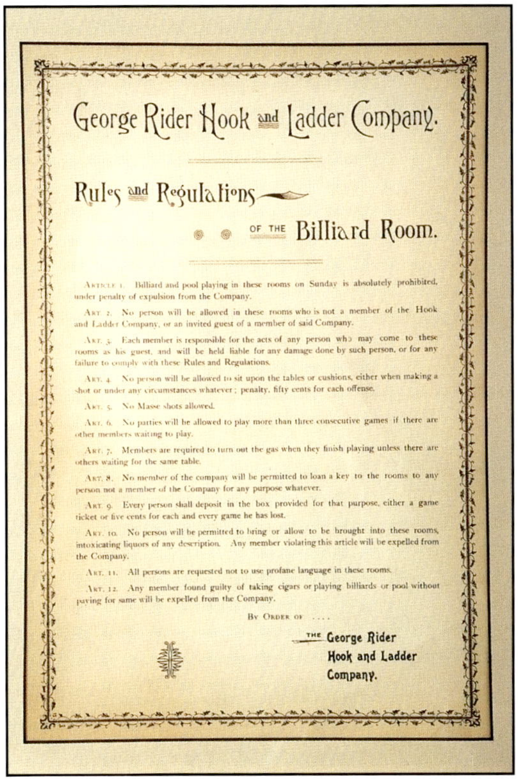

George Rider Hook and Ladder Company.

Rules and Regulations of the Billiard Room.

Article 1. Billiard and pool playing in these rooms on Sunday is absolutely prohibited, under penalty of expulsion from the Company.

Art. 2. No person will be allowed in these rooms who is not a member of the Hook and Ladder Company, or an invited guest of a member of said Company.

Art. 3. Each member is responsible for the acts of any person who may come to these rooms as his guest, and will be held liable for any damage done by such person, or for any failure to comply with these Rules and Regulations.

Art. 4. No person will be allowed to sit upon the tables or cushions, either when making a shot or under any circumstances whatever; penalty, fifty cents for each offense.

Art. 5. No Masse shots allowed.

Art. 6. No parties will be allowed to play more than three consecutive games if there are other members waiting to play.

Art. 7. Members are required to turn out the gas when they finish playing unless there are others waiting for the same table.

Art. 8. No member of the company will be permitted to loan a key to the rooms to any person not a member of the Company for any purpose whatever.

Art. 9. Every person shall deposit in the box provided for that purpose, either a game ticket or five cents for each and every game he has lost.

Art. 10. No person will be permitted to bring or allow to be brought into these rooms, intoxicating liquors of any description. Any member violating this article will be expelled from the Company.

Art. 11. All persons are requested not to use profane language in these rooms.

Art. 12. Any member found guilty of taking cigars or playing billiards or pool without paying for same will be expelled from the Company.

By Order of ....

The George Rider Hook and Ladder Company.

Neat, unique, c. 1860s piece of early ephemera. List of rules for the billiard enthusiasts of the "George Rider Hook & Ladder Co. [fire fighters]," 8.5" x 12.5", excellent condition, new matting, $495+.

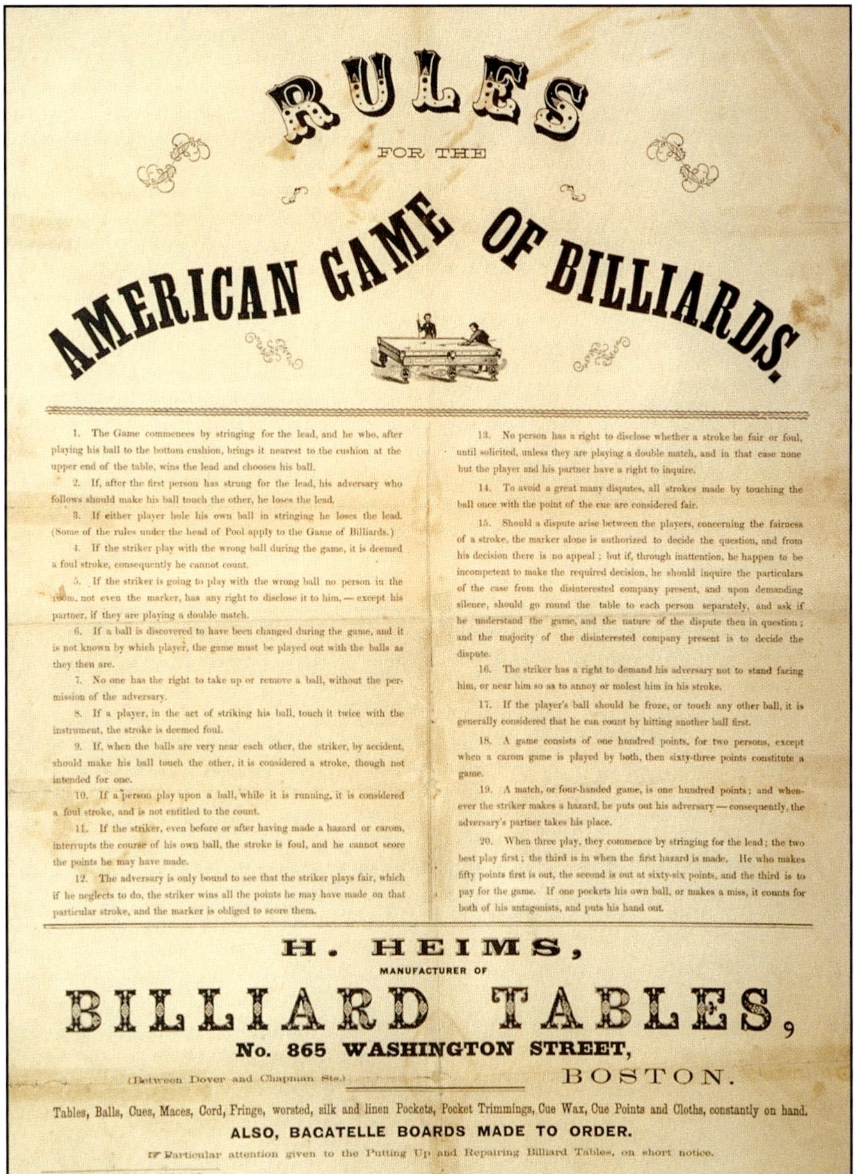

RULES FOR THE AMERICAN GAME OF BILLIARDS.

1. The Game commences by stringing for the lead, and he who, after playing his ball to the bottom cushion, brings it nearest to the cushion at the upper end of the table, wins the lead and chooses his ball.

2. If, after the first person has strung for the lead, his adversary who follows should make his ball touch the other, he loses the lead.

3. If either player hole his own ball in stringing he loses the lead. (Some of the rules under the head of Pool apply to the Game of Billiards.)

4. If the striker play with the wrong ball during the game, it is deemed a foul stroke, consequently he cannot count.

5. If the striker is going to play with the wrong ball no person in the room, not even the marker, has any right to disclose it to him, — except his partner, if they are playing a double match.

6. If a ball is discovered to have been changed during the game, and it is not known by which player, the game must be played out with the balls as they then are.

7. No one has the right to take up or remove a ball, without the permission of the adversary.

8. If a player, in the act of striking his ball, touch it twice with the instrument, the stroke is deemed foul.

9. If, when the balls are very near each other, the striker, by accident, should make his ball touch the other, it is considered a stroke, though not intended for one.

10. If a person play upon a ball, while it is running, it is considered a foul stroke, and is not entitled to the count.

11. If the striker, even before or after having made a hazard or carom, interrupts the course of his own ball, the stroke is foul, and he cannot score the points he may have made.

12. The adversary is only bound to see that the striker plays fair, which if he neglects to do, the striker wins all the points he may have made on that particular stroke, and the marker is obliged to score them.

13. No person has a right to disclose whether a stroke be fair or foul, until solicited, unless they are playing a double match, and in that case none but the player and his partner have a right to inquire.

14. To avoid a great many disputes, all strokes made by touching the ball once with the point of the cue are considered fair.

15. Should a dispute arise between the players, concerning the fairness of a stroke, the marker alone is authorized to decide the question, and from his decision there is no appeal; but if, through inattention, he happen to be incompetent to make the required decision, he should inquire the particulars of the case from the disinterested company present, and upon demanding silence, should go round the table to each person separately, and ask if he understand the game, and the nature of the dispute then in question; and the majority of the disinterested company present is to decide the dispute.

16. The striker has a right to demand his adversary not to stand facing him, or near him so as to annoy or molest him in his stroke.

17. If the player's ball should be froze, or touch any other ball, it is generally considered that he can count by hitting another ball first.

18. A game consists of one hundred points, for two persons, except when a carom game is played by both, then sixty-three points constitute a game.

19. A match, or four-handed game, is one hundred points; and whenever the striker makes a hazard, he puts out his adversary — consequently, the adversary's partner takes his place.

20. When three play, they commence by stringing for the lead; the two best play first; the third is in when the first hazard is made. He who makes fifty points first is out, the second is out at sixty-six points, and the third is to pay for the game. If one pockets his own ball, or makes a miss, it counts for both of his antagonists, and puts his hand out.

H. HEIMS,
MANUFACTURER OF
BILLIARD TABLES,
No. 865 WASHINGTON STREET,
(Between Dover and Chapman Sts.) BOSTON.

Tables, Balls, Cues, Maces, Cord, Fringe, worsted, silk and linen Pockets, Pocket Trimmings, Cue Wax, Cue Points and Cloths, constantly on hand.

ALSO, BAGATELLE BOARDS MADE TO ORDER.

☞ Particular attention given to the Putting Up and Repairing Billiard Tables, on short notice.

Alfred Mudge & Son, Printers, 34 School Street.

Another 1860s period print, or poster, of the rules of the games. Fair condition, 13.5" x 18.5", rematted, certainly one of the oldest rules posters still in existence, $1,500.

An 1880s billiard rules poster from "The Merle & Heaney Manufacturing Co." Extremely rare, original frame, nice table depicted, fair condition, 24" x 24", $2,350.

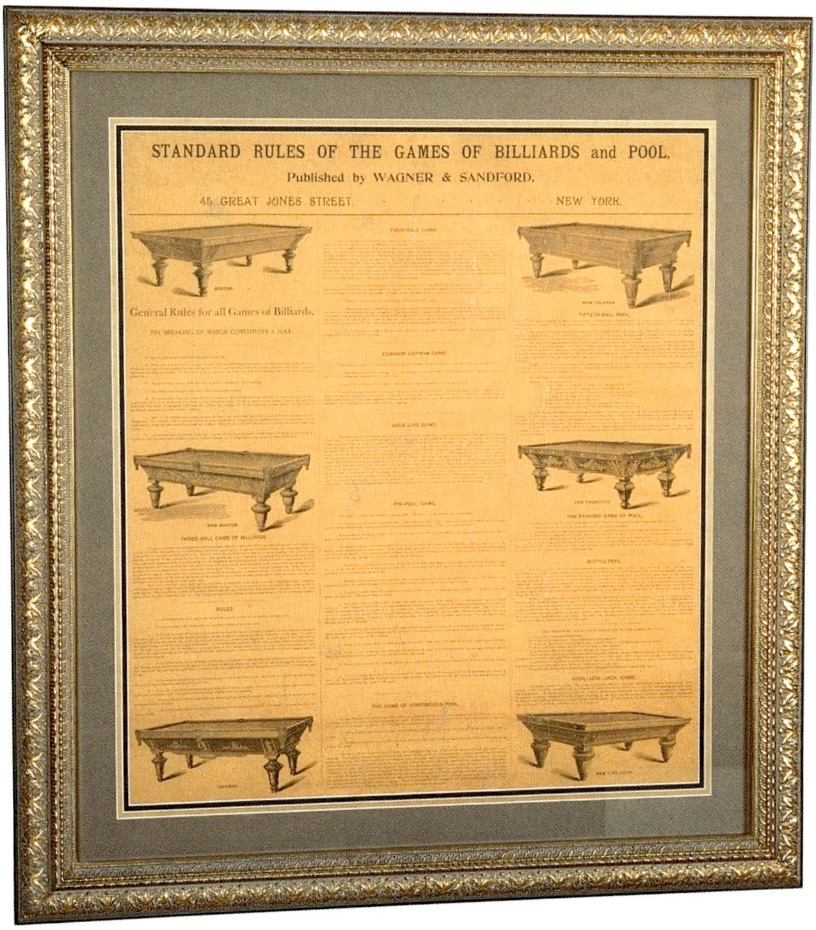

An 1880s billiard rules poster from the "Wagner & Sandford" Co. SIX tables shown, colossal 24" x 27", good condition, reframed, $3,000+.

An 1870s "The Decker Co." rules poster, spectacular graphics, good condition, reframed, ultra scarce image, 20" x 23", $3,250+.

Tournament poster, 1925, Brunswick-Balke-Collender issued. These are quite rare and highly sought after, 19.5" x 25.5". There are reproductions. This is an original, reframed, very good condition, $1,500+.

Early 1900s "Billiard Experts of the World" poster. Watch for reproductions. Issued by Brunswick-Balke-Collender, very good condition, reframed, 26" x 38". This is an original, $2,500+.

Late 1800s original example of another rare Brunswick-Balke-Collender "Billiard Experts of the World" poster. This one sports a red background and shows some different players. 26" x 36", very nice condition, reframed. Again, watch for reproductions. $2,500+.

Another version of the Brunswick-Balke-Collender issued "Billiard Experts of the World" poster, green background (sometimes the players are different). This version was sold by Brunswick's Canadian branch company. Rare, $2,750+.

Fabulous, and highly sought after, self-framed tin sign of "Stars of the Billiard World," issued by Brunswick-Balke-Collender in the early 1900s. In excellent original condition, 31" x 41" (whole sign). This piece will easily bring $5, 000+.

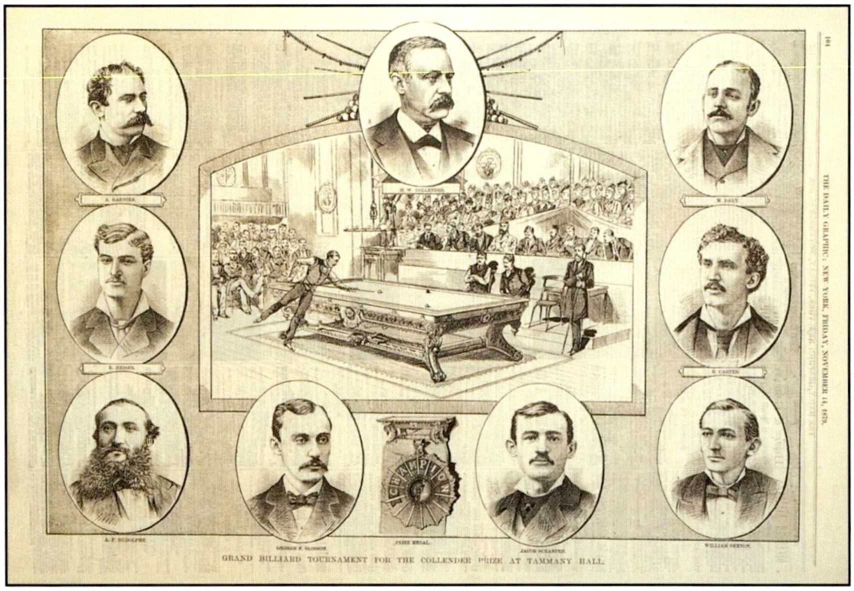

From the *Daily Graphic*, November 14, 1879, a full page newspaper advertisement depicting the national billiard tournament contestants and illustrating the tournament medal to be won. Fabulous table image, 13.5" x 20", excellent original piece, $155.

Greatest billiard color lithograph we've ever seen. This piece commemorates the April 17, 1883, outcome of the world's championship match in Chicago, hosted by "The Brunswick-Balke-Collender Co." These were called "souvenirs" of the events. The piece in the center of the image is actually the "emblem" of the tournament, testifying to the quality of the first prize trophies that were created for the winner. This miniature table has more detail in it than most of the finest tables ever built. This book's cover photo is an example of the actual full sized table one would win for being the champion of one of these worlds class events. 20" x 26", outstanding condition, ultra rare, reframed, $9,000+.

Chapter VIII
Miscellaneous Billiard Collectibles

This chapter deals with a large assortment of unusual, early collectibles that don't really fit well into a category of their own, but are nevertheless interesting and worth the investment if the price is right.

Unless otherwise stated, ALL containers shown in this chapter are priced as though they are empty. Four chalk boxes, all in pretty good shape. TL: from an obscure company from New York, $55; top right and BL: from the renowned firm of Sydney Laner, $45 for either example; BR: Des Moines Billiard Table Co., hard to find, $55.

Five different containers for spots for pool tables. All are from the late 1800s to the early 1900s. TL: $65; TR: obscure brand, $75; LL: $60: LC: $55; LR: $15.

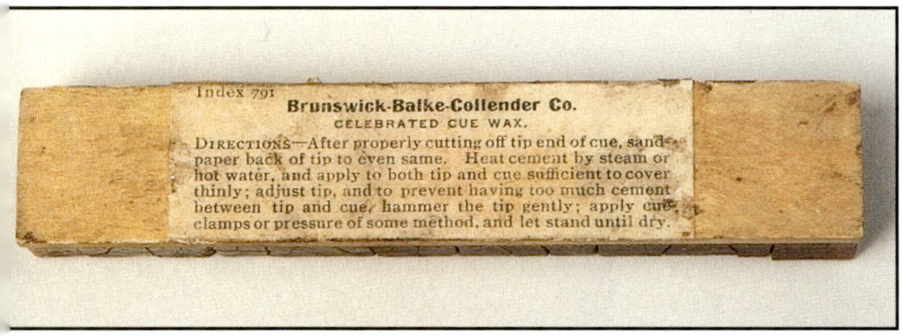

A dried up stick of cue "wax" (or glue), for attaching leather cue tips, from the Brunswick-Balke-Collender Co., c. 1900, hard to find, good condition, $95.

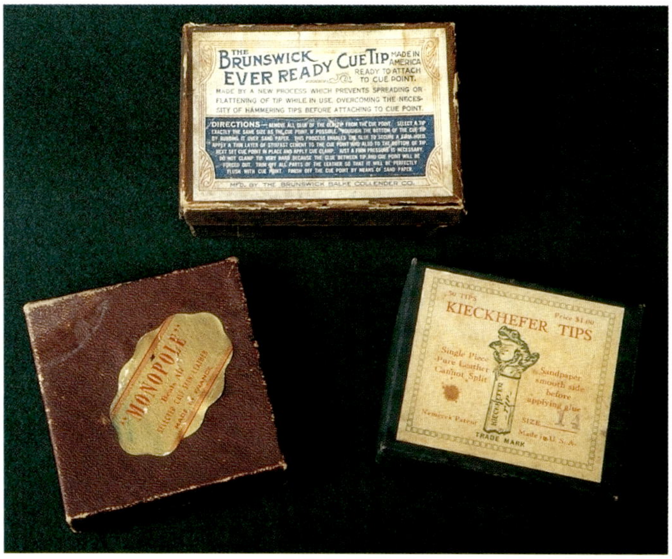

Three early 1900s boxes for leather cue tips. All are in fair to good condition T: $50; BL: $20; BR: $85.

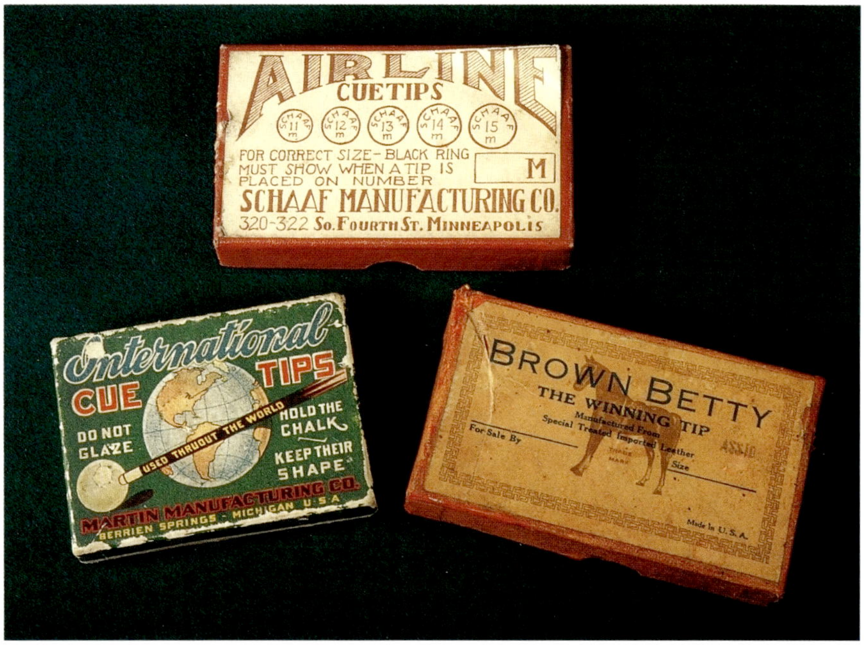

Three more early 1900s cue tip boxes. T: $45; BL: $40; BR: very rare, $125.

Three more cue tip boxes. Early 1900s examples. L to R: Silver King, common, $15; Champion, $25; Diamond, $30.

Three more late 1800s cue tip boxes. L to R: $85; $45; $55.

T: Box for a "Lightning Cue Tip Fastener," from Brunswick-Balke-Collender, late 1800s, rare (this was one of Brunswick's cast iron devices for attaching tips to cues), good condition, $95. B: "Wafers" were little circular gluing tabs for attaching cue tips. From Australia, good condition, $35.

Approximately 5" tall container for "PLAS-CO-CEMENT" from the "KIECKHEFER MFG. CO, Inc. / Chicago," good condition, $40.

Five containers for billiard cloth-mending products. TL: cardboard, $40; center left: lithograph on tin, $85; BL: paper label on tin, $65; TR: early tin, $110; BR: $30.

T: rare nail file, $75; LL: celluloid hone, $35; LR: oval celluloid hone, poor condition, $85.

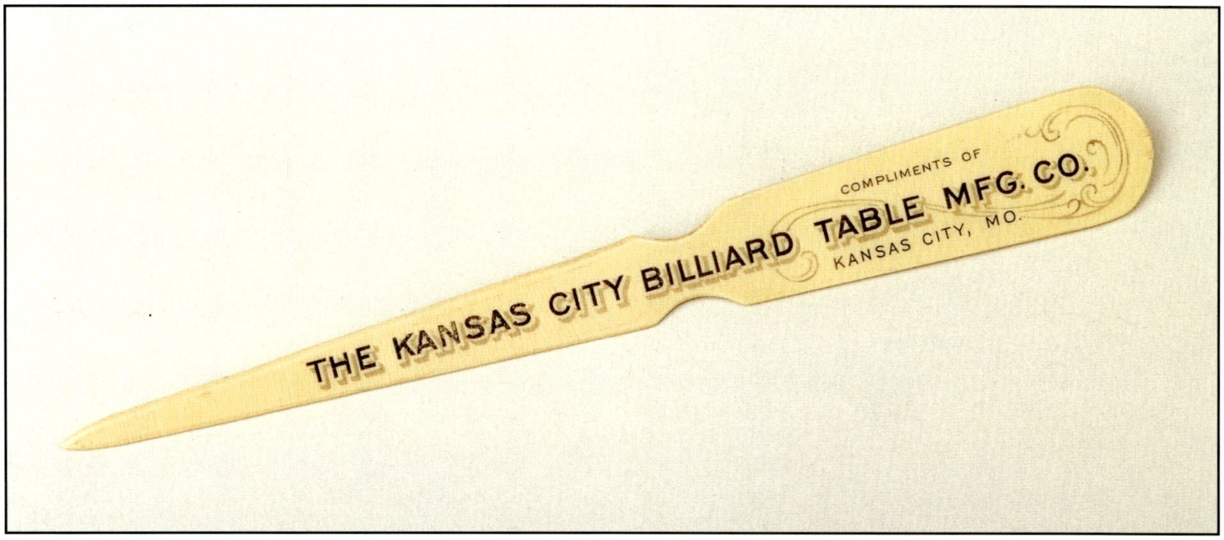

A 6" celluloid letter opener, the other side shows an antique pool table, mint condition, rare, $295.

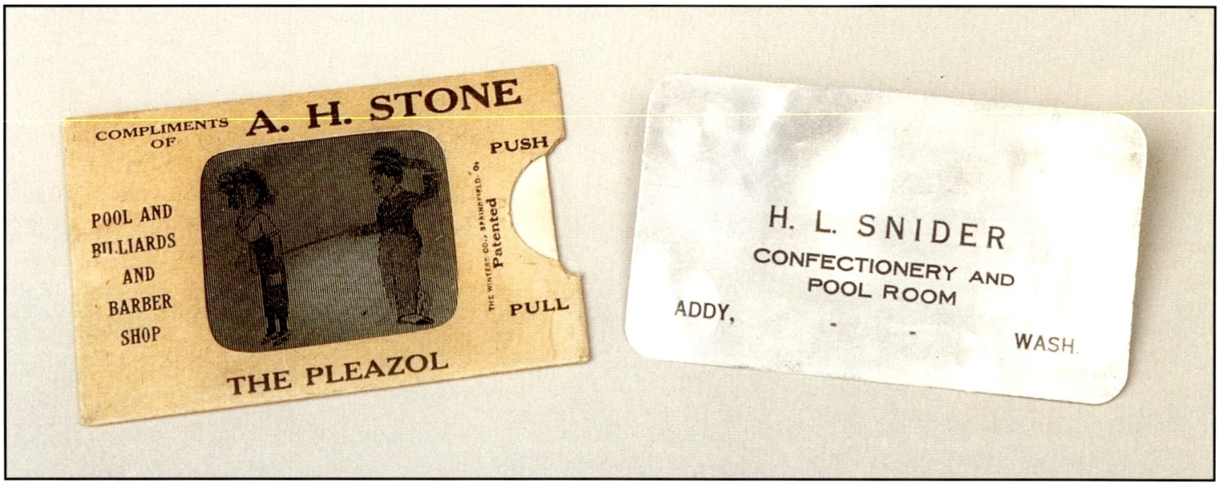

L: More evidence of the tight ties between billiard rooms and barbershops, this is a comical "flicker" novelty piece. Pushing and pulling on the tab on the right causes the man's leg to kick, he tips his hat, and his walking stick gently taps the pretty lady's backside. In addition, her arms swing back and forth and her head revolves to see who's doing it. Great animated gadget, very good condition, $175. R: Rare aluminum trade card, other side shows a cute cartoon image, good condition, $70.

Left to right: All of these items are from the early 1900s. Monkey image "dexterity" toy and pocket mirror, tin (the idea is to get all the little balls in all of the little holes, all at the same time), good condition, $165. Rare dice-shaker toy, celluloid, five die inside, excellent condition, $295. Rare celluloid dexterity toy, "William A. Spinks & Co.," excellent condition, $250.

Heavy tin and porcelain ashtray, 6", very unusual billiard item, early 1900s, very good condition, $195.

Rare lithograph on tin ashtray, outstanding graphics, early 1900s, good condition, 4 1/4", $235.

Two interesting late 1800s items. L: nickel-plated brass cigar cutter, rare, $230. R: with a nude depicted on the obverse side, this nickel bottle opener is a neat item, and it's hard to find one with billiard advertising on it, very good condition, $155.

Large tobacco tin with great color lithography. Same scene on top of lid, showing a man playing billiards in the background, good condition, $425.

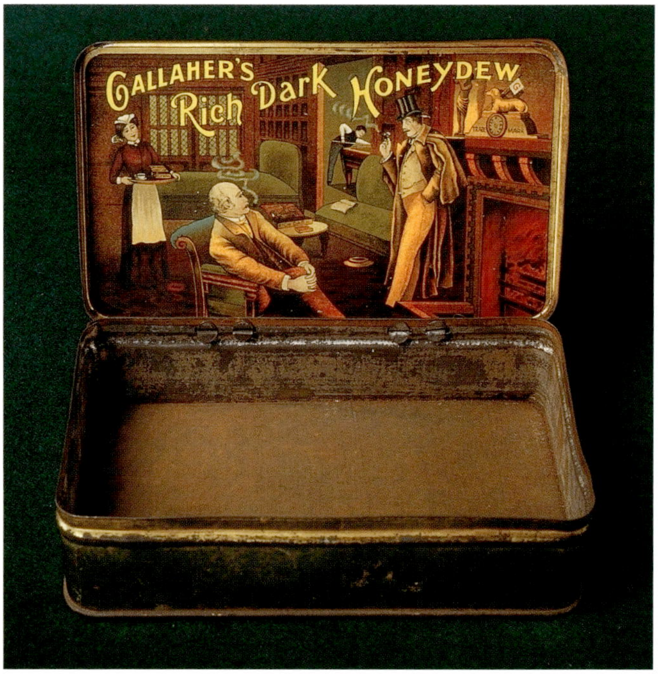

Large tin tobacco canister with fabulous Currier & Ives images lithographed all over it, very good condition, rare, $795.

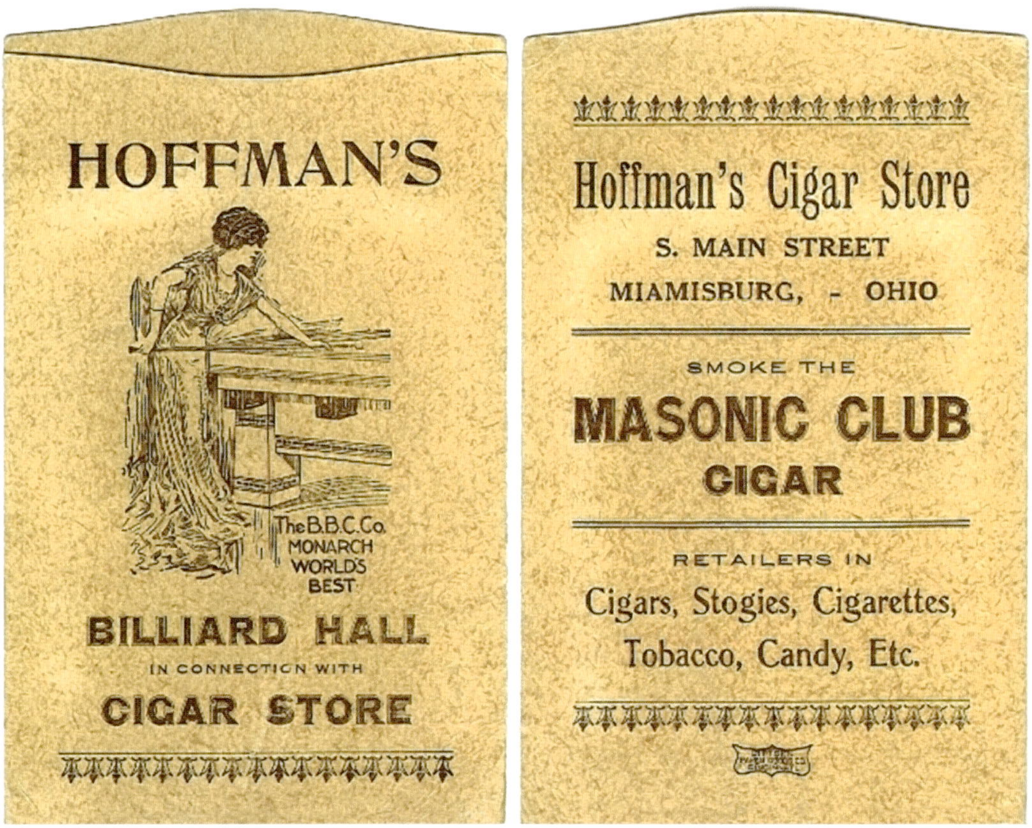

Circa 1910 to 1920 shirt pocket cigar pouch. Advertisement for the Brunswick-Balke-Collender Co., a billiard parlor, and a brand of cigar. Excellent condition, very rare item, $230.

Late 1800s cigar box sample label, great color lithography, 5" x 8". Excellent condition, rare, $400+.

Late 1800s cigar box sample label, another great image, 6" x 9", good condition, $500+.

Extremely rare "wood lithograph," in color, from the 1870s. This is a cigar box sample image, some moisture staining, super billiard scene, $1,000+.

An actual cigar box, as opposed to only a "sample label," showing one of the previous scenes in use, but with a different cigar manufacturer. Good condition, $375.

Two late 1800s cigar boxes. These two particular images are extremely scarce. They show "Jacob Schaefer, The Wizard," with great billiard scenes in the background. Color lithography at its best. Both are in very good condition. L: $1,250+. R: $1,500+.

T: Pool table felt brush from the "J. L. HOLCOMB MFG. CO. INDIANAPOLIS," early 1900s, good condition, $150. B: Table brush from the "SCHAAF" billiard table company, early 1900s, $95.

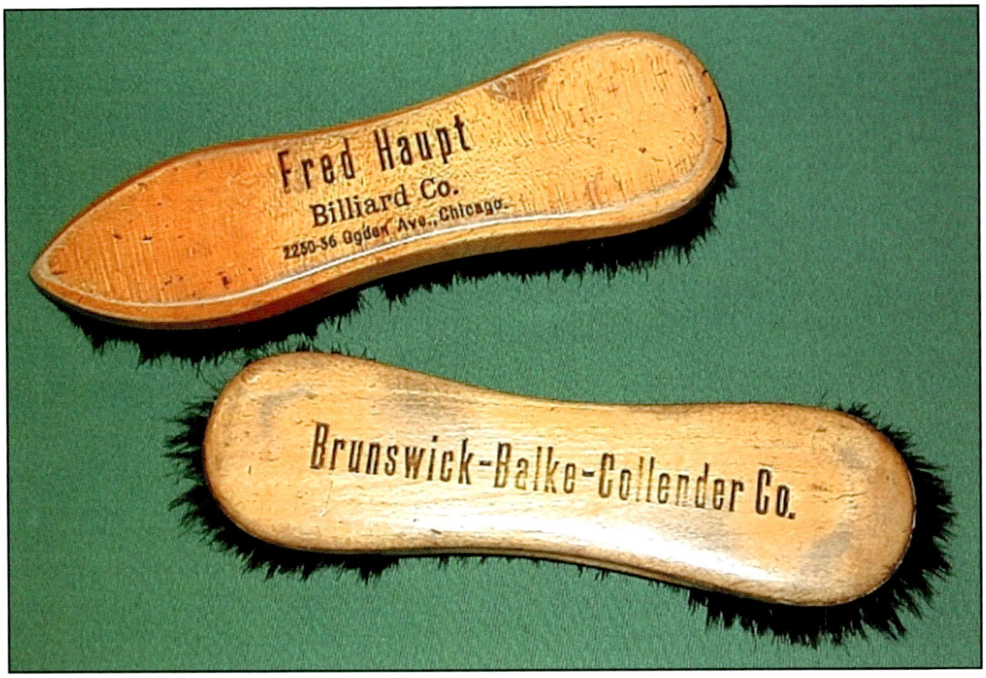

T: Rare bullet-shaped billiard felt brush from the "Fred Haupt Billiard Co.," late 1800s, excellent condition, $200+. B: Nice example of a c. 1890s table brush from the Brunswick-Balke-Collender Co., $225+.

T: Late 1800s, very unusual pool table felt brush designed for use on the large 10 ft. and bigger pool tables. Neat piece, good condition, $300+. B: Exceptionally fine quality billiard table felt brush from an English manufacturer, c. late 1800s. The green velvet top is there for protecting the table when cleaning under the rails with the fan of bristles on the end. Nice, early and rare item, very nice condition, $450.

A pair of late 1800s style wicker "ball baskets" for catching pool balls as they dropped from either wall mounted ball racks, or the ball return type tables. L: Rare *helmet* shaped example, very good condition, $375+. R: More typical style basket, very good condition, $250+.

Handsome, late 1800s, wicker ball "barrel," English made, sold by Brunswick-Balke-Collender and a few other American billiard suppliers, for handling snooker balls, 14" tall, very good condition, $400+.

Beautiful graphics make this classic Victorian 1901 calendar a real nice find (part of a set of four, with different sporting images on each example), excellent condition, approximately 15" x 21". For just this image alone, $250.

Early 1800s fine porcelain figurine. This is a rare "nodder," as the lady's head will rock back and forth when the piece is shaken. Unfortunately, the butt of her cue stick and her right wrist (which held it), are missing. Though a scarce item, in a very rare medium, with this damage this piece will only fetch around $250.

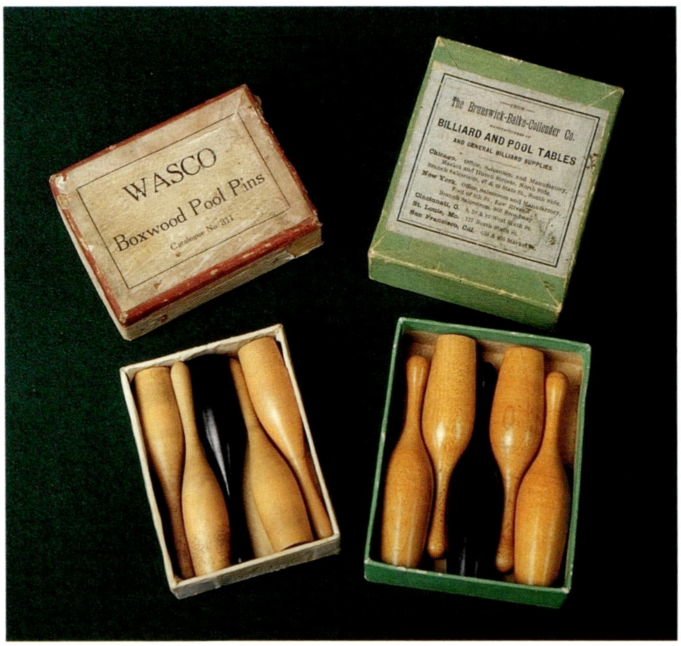

Two late 1800s examples of "Pin Pool" pins in their original boxes. Each set contains four maple pins and one ebony pin. L: "WASCO" brand set, good condition, smaller size, $275. R: Brunswick-Balke-Collender brand set, larger size, very good condition, $350+.

Two Brunswick-Balke-Collender brand leather "Pea Pool" or "shake bottles." Some models have boxwood or ivory tops, which raise their value. These both have leather tops. Peas, or pills, are shown only to exemplify what went into them. L: RARE "Bulldog" version showing bulldog's face (signed Brunswick-Balke-Collender on the other side), very good condition, $200+. R: Standard version, with Brunswick-Balke-Collender logo inscribed into leather, excellent condition, $150+.

Early 1900s set of super tiny pool balls for early children's tables. Composition, with paper labels, complete with cue ball and original box, only 3/4" in size, very good condition, $75.

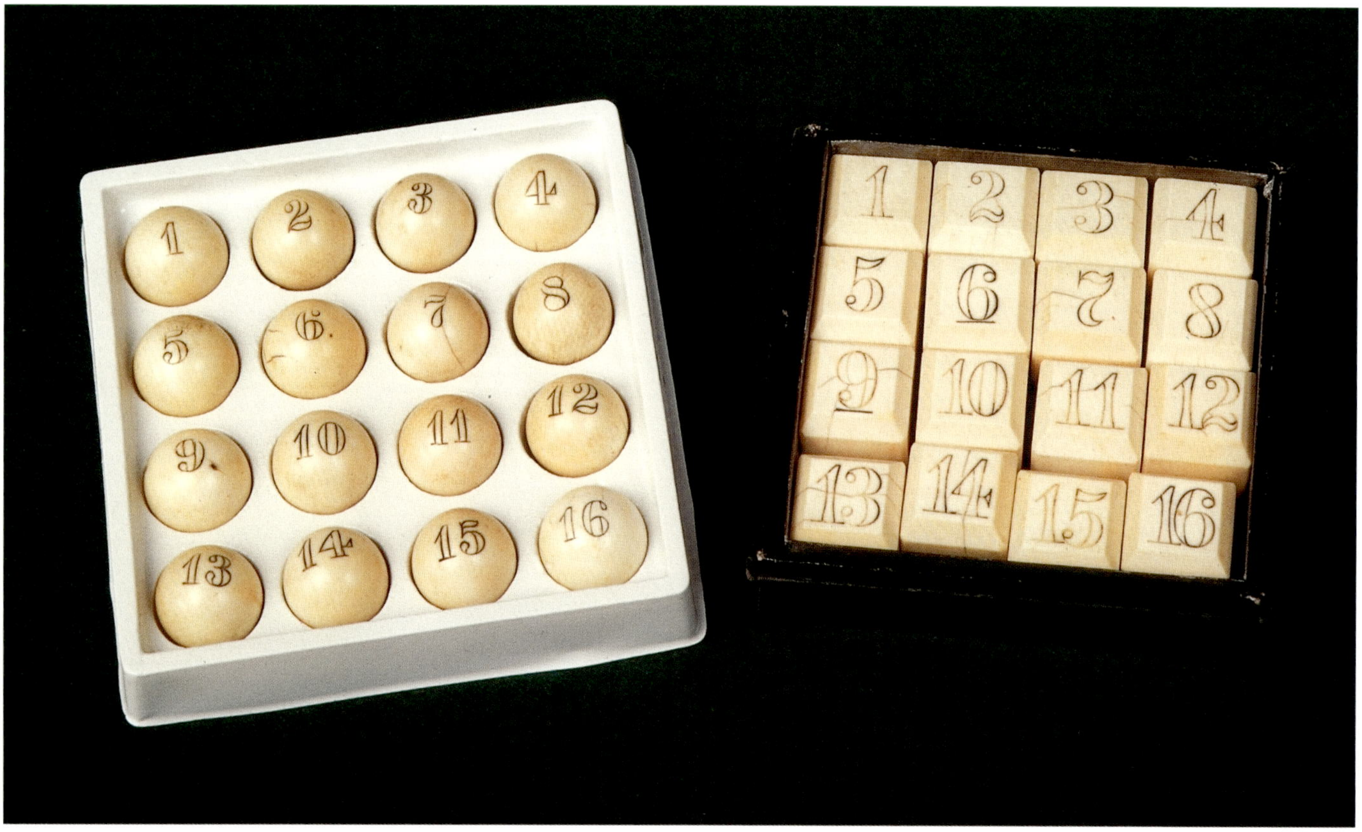

L: Extremely rare full set of scrimshawed ivory peas, c. 1880s, 11/16" in size, excellent condition, $1,500+. R: Ultra scarce set of *square* scrimshawed ivory cubes, also 11/16" in size, in original box, c. 1860s, excellent condition, $2,500+.

Rare "bowling game" set for playing the game on a pool table. The 3 1/2" pins are ebony and the 1 1/2" balls are ivory. An 1880s vintage collectible, excellent condition, $650+.

Maple Brunswick-Balke-Collender billiard cue "leather tip shaping" tool. 6", late 1800s, fairly hard to find, very good condition, $175+.

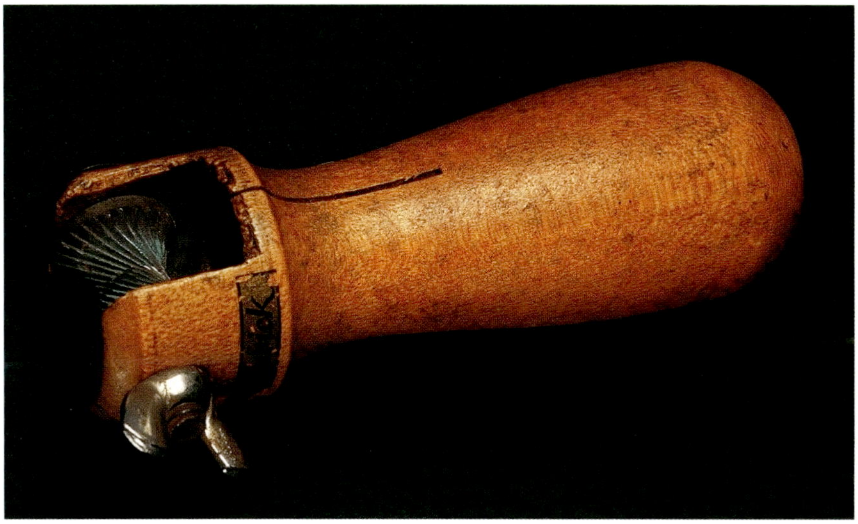

Maple and brass late 1800s "tenon cutter" for a pool cue, good condition, unusual example, $150+.

This tool was for "dressing" the end of the cue, whether it was broken or just had glue residue on it, to prepare it for tenon installation or tip replacement. Made of maple, c. late 1800s, in original box, from the "William A. Spinks Co.," (WASCO), good condition, also a hard to find piece, $350+.

The "T Cue Cutter" from Brunswick-Balke-Collender, c. late 1800s, for preparing cues with broken shafts for new ferrules or tips. Maple, fairly rare, good condition, $250+.

Early billiard cue shaft resurfacing tool with an English ancestry. These are also used for clamping the new glued on tips. The file has a fine side and a coarse side. Made of boxwood and cast iron; beware of contemporary examples. It could be hung on a hook while the cue tip glue dried. Sold by many American billiard supply firms since the late 1800s, this is an "old" one with a boxwood "slide" for tightening the grip on the cue when clamping on a new tip, very good condition, $175+.

Another version of an English style cue shaft resurfacer and tip clamp; also made of boxwood, this example has a brass "tightener" and a brass "hook" for hanging it on the wall when fitted on a cue being repaired. First seen in the late 1800s, very good condition, $175+.

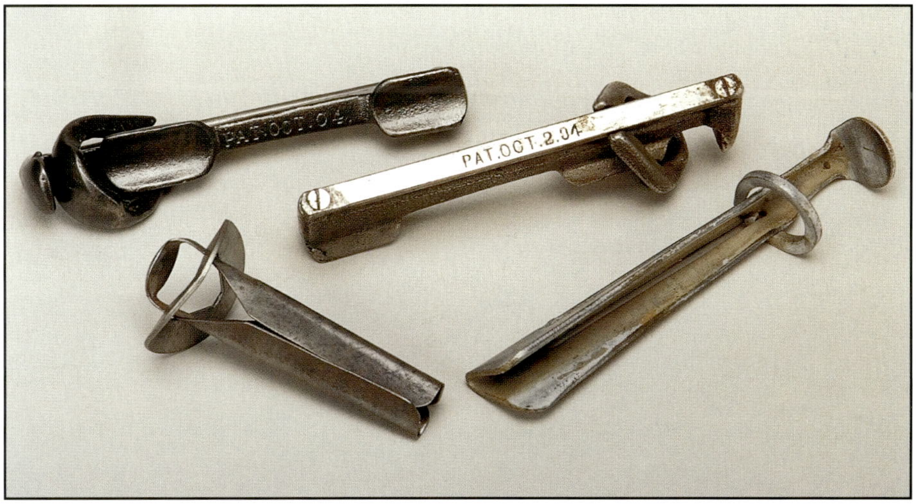

Four late 1800s examples of billiard cue tip "fasteners." These were designed to keep the new tips on straight and tight when they were being replaced. The three cast iron examples facing right are valued at approximately $15 to $30 each; the higher price being paid for the specimens with the patent dates cast into them. The example on the lower left is made of light metal and Brunswick called it the "Jiffy Clamp." It is in good condition and sells for approximately $20.

Here are three more examples of late 1800s vintage cue tip fasteners. All three are made of cast iron. Fasteners appear with and without nickel plating. The top two specimens pictured are dated to 1884, while the lower one's stamp clearly indicates that their patent had only been applied for when it was manufactured. That makes it a little older. It was called "The Perfection" clamp and has a small hook on top to enable the repairman to hang the cue up while it was being worked on. All are in nice, original condition, $30+ each.

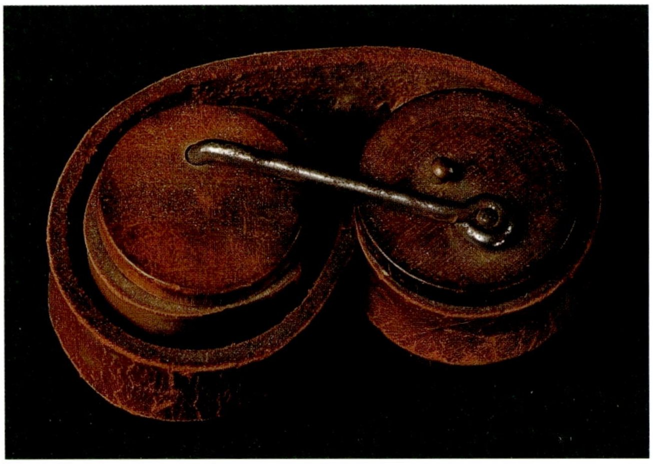

This neat little do-dad was called "The Safety Cue Clamp" and was from Brunswick-Balke-Collender, c. late 1800s, and was made of leather and wood. Good condition, RARE, $250.

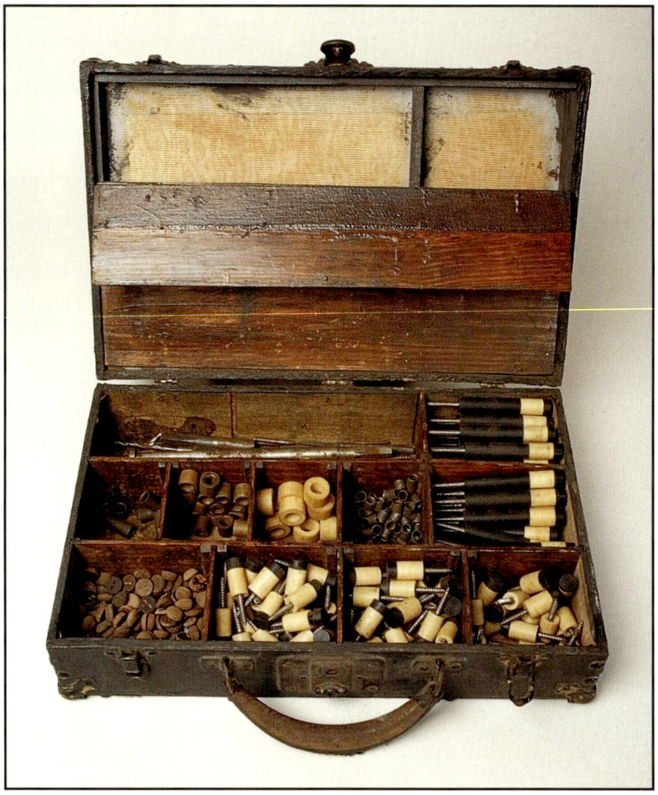

Probably the only one like it, this is a billiard cue repairman's traveling repair kit. Completely stocked with screw on ivory ferrules, ebony and ivory extension/ferrule combination pieces for cues shortened by breakage, tenon bushings, fiber ferrules, ivory collars for joint replacement, leather tips and all the necessary tools for performing the work. The compartment in the lid of the case probably held repair manuals and more drill bits and hack saw blades. It appears to be of late 1800s vintage and in well used condition. In our opinion, this is a very exciting collectible item, $800+.

This is a "Brunswick Strip Puller," c. late 1800s, for removing the wood feather strips that held the felt into the cushion edge channel on the rails of a pool table. 11" blade, wood handle, quite rare, great early billiard tool, good condition, $425+.

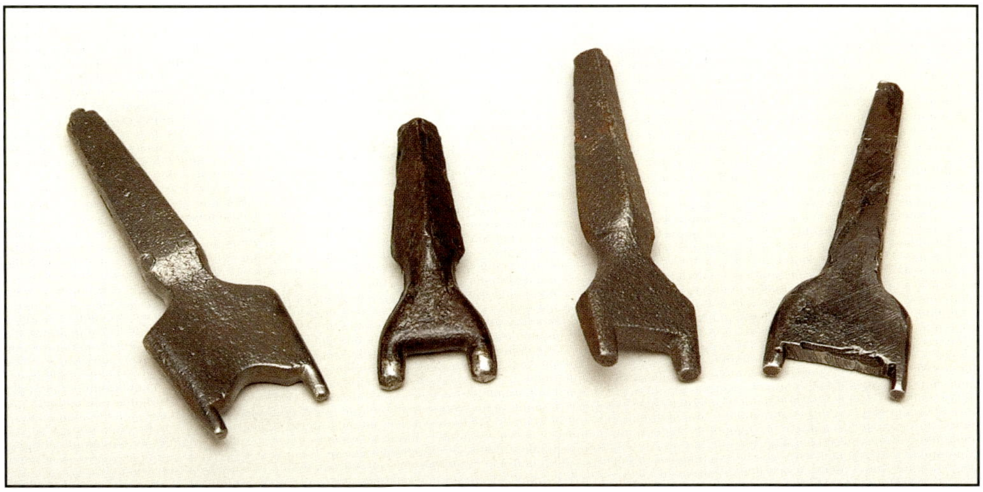

These are 1800s period examples of cast iron billiard table "rail bolt" bits. They were used in a "brace" (old hand drill), and testify, by their differing "spans," to the lack of standardization in the billiard manufacturing business in its early years. $40 each.

Three more late 1800s cast iron pool table tools, all used in a brace. L to R: standard screwdriver bit, relatively common, $20; square cushion, or rail, bolt tool, rare, $90; cabinet and leg bolt tool, fairly rare, $75.

Middle to late 1800s European style billiard cue "keepers." Attached to the wall at around four feet from the floor, these were used to stand a cue at rest with the butt of the cue resting on the floor. T: Ornate cast iron example, for six cues, good condition, $250. B: Stunning nickel-plated cast iron example with tiny rubber wheels on the "keepers" to protect the cue, for three cues, RARE, $400+.

This is another example of an early cue "keeper," made of brass, for six cues, no moving parts, good condition, $300.

These are "sleeve retaining" arm bands, sold by a few different billiard supply businesses in the early 1900s, designed to keep the sleeves of a player's shirt or blouse from interfering with the lay of the balls. Fairly hard to find, there are both brass and nickel-plated brass examples shown here. The box is for the nickel-plated specimens. The bands alone sell for around $50 each and the original box by itself is worth approximately $125.

A neat milk glass example of a talc dispenser. Early 1900s piece right out of a Watertown, South Dakota pool hall, in very good condition, rare, $325+.

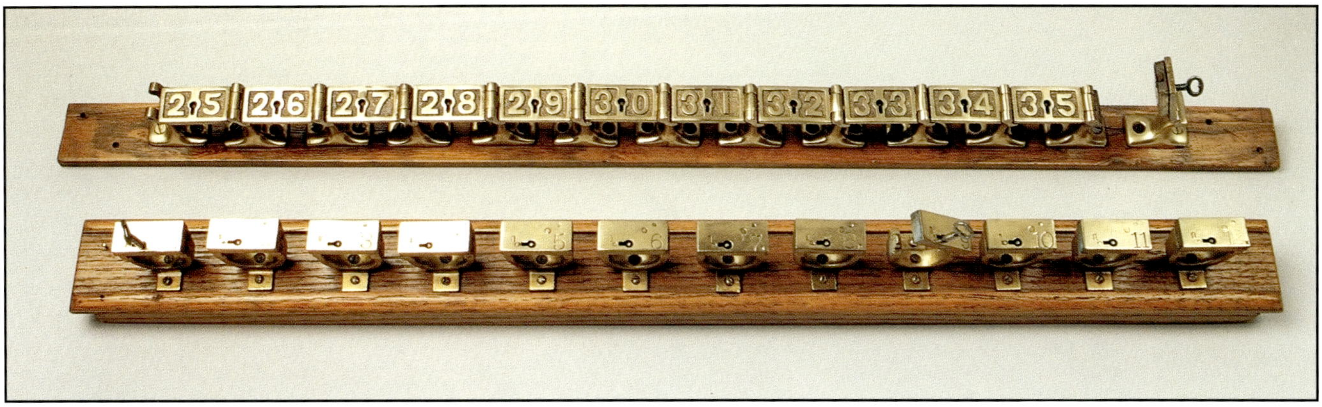

Still mounted on their cue rack cross members, this is a pair of 1880s vintage brass billiard cue locks. Individual locks have been bringing around $50 each. T: Fancier twelve lock set (with only one key), $600+. B: Standard set of twelve brass locks, missing some keys, $600+.

Late 1800s, nickel-plated brass "Brunswick Balke Collender Co. N.Y.," "French Rail Billiard Marker." These were typically attached to the rail "tops," or, sometimes, actually imbedded into the rail top. These were for keeping score in a billiard match, one marker per player, and therefore are usually found in pairs. Beware of reproductions. Fair condition, rare, early original, $250+.

Middle 1800s walnut and brass E. J. Riley Co. billiard table level. Very rare, early piece, very good condition, $400+.

Late 1800s flat iron for drying out damp pool table felt. This very rare example is from the "Kansas City Billiard Table Co.," 5" x 10", good condition, $600+.

This is a Brunswick-Balke-Collender example of flat iron for felt drying and is also 5" x 10". Good condition, $400+.

Another version of the Brunswick-Balke-Collender felt iron, also 5" x 10", and this example has its original trivet. Good condition, $650+.

Four middle to late 1800s examples of bridge hooks. These were purchased by those who elected to display a bridge underneath their tables. All of these shown are made of cast iron. Three are of Victorian design, while the gold painted specimen is the generic style of the day. L to R: $50 each; $25 each; $125 each; $75 each.

These are called "Carom Plugs" or "Pocket Blocks" depending on which catalog you are reading. They were offered by several billiard table manufacturers as far back as the middle 1800s. This full set of six is from the early 1900s and is in excellent original condition, $600+.

Another carom plug set. This set, dated 1881, was handled by both the Brunswick-Balke-Collender Co. and the Benedict Billiard Table Co. This beautiful nickel-plated set has been completely restored and is valued at $900.

This is an 1870s vintage carom plug set, in all brass and brass plated cast iron, that has also been totally restored, and is also valued at $900.

This is a very unusual, old, brass cash register! It is actually capable of registering for THREE different businesses simultaneously. Looking closely, you will notice that it will service a barbershop, a pool hall, and a merchant of cigars and newspapers, all with one machine! Not actually a "billiard collectible," but we thought it deserved a place in our book. RARE, $3,500+.

C. Liebeck
Barber
Pool
Cigars & Papers

Rare early 1900s cut glass billiard sign. Metal frame, hung by chains inside a billiard parlor front window to attract customers. Bulb color determines color when lit. Shown with appropriate green bulb. Restored, 9" x 26", $1,750.

Early pool hall game called "Klik Ball." This is a very unusual version of this game in that it can accommodate three players at the same time. Excellent original condition, 8" x 37", $200+.

Middle 1800s mahogany "Bagatelle" billiard table. Fold-up examples like this one are quite rare. Typically found with four red, four white, and one black ball of approximately 2" each, and child's sized cues. The contraption in the middle with the arches is for yet another type of bagatelle style game. These were designed with children in mind, but are beautifully made and can be a lot of fun. In this "open for play" state, it measures 30" x 72". Closed, it's 30" x 36". Restored, $2,000+.

Early 1900s "Keeno" board game. This gadget was placed on the end of a pool table and then the players shot toward the opposite end and attempted to bank their ball into the small holes. This unusual example actually has THREE different versions of games that can be played on it! Lithograph on wood, very good condition, quite rare, early specimen, 30" x 50", $550+.

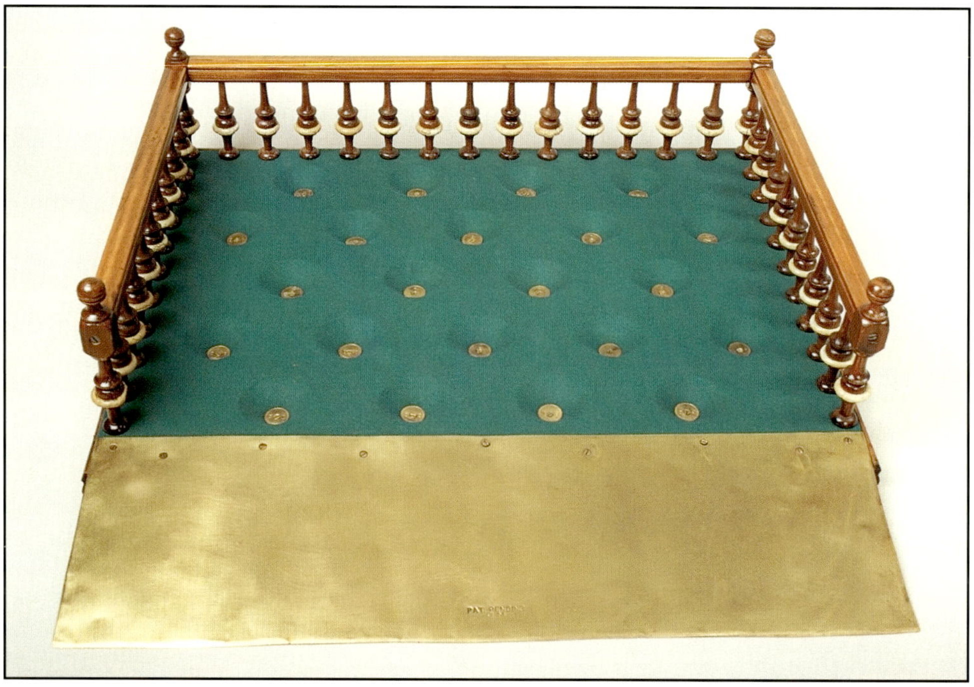

Extremely early (1870s) example of a Keeno Board. This example sat on just one side of one end of a billiard table, which made it a bit harder to "pot" shots on. 24" x 24", very scarce, restored, $1,500+.

Beautiful walnut and brass, excellent all original Keeno board, from the Brunswick-Balke-Collender Co., patent stencil dated on the bottom "1884." Folds in half, 14" x 50" when open, designed for a 9' table, extremely rare, $2,000+.

This is a time keeping clock designed for billiard parlors. Several suppliers handled them. It's called a "Calculagraph." This key wound example is from the late 1800s. The pre-electric examples are relatively hard to come by. Very good condition, $750+.

This is not actually a billiard collectible, but we feel it does belong in the book. This is an early 1900s mantle clock, reworked and equipped with an ingenious device to turn it into what is known as a "trade stimulator." A slot was added on the top and a catch-trough added on the right side. When a coin was dropped in, the clock would chime with each token it distributed. In addition, the mechanism was designed to occasionally award TWO tokens for just the one coin, and, in rare instances, it would even award THREE tokens for only the one coin. This, of course, was quite a temptation, and it obviously DID stimulate trade as the tokens issued were only redeemable at the business the clock was in. The clocks could be filled with tokens for any kind of merchandise, but this clock happens to be loaded with red fiber tokens that read "HINZ POOL HALL / AMIRET, MINN. / GOOD FOR 5¢ IN TRADE"! Excellent condition, $1,500+.

F. E. Welker "game counter." With patents back to the very early 1900s, this ingenious device was designed to be attached to the ceiling above a pool table with the racking triangle attached to it on a thin cord. (see photo). Every time a customer pulled the triangle down to "rack" the balls, the pointer would be advanced one number. The players AND the proprietor were thereby able to keep track of the number of games the gentlemen had actually played. In these instances, players were charged by the game rather than by the hour. Excellent original condition, extremely rare item, $1,250+.

Late 1800s mechanical "price register." This very rare gadget, cleverly tethered through a series of pulleys to a triangle suspended over the pool table, gave a proprietor the ability to accurately tally the amount his customer(s) would owe per table by simply moving around the periphery of the device, in this instance, one nickel at a time. There was no argument when you were ready to check out. 12" x 12", good working condition, $1,500+.

This style of "Time and Price Register" first appeared in the middle 1800s. This one, encased in beautiful oak and trimmed in brass, features ten rosewood "pointers," with scrimshawed ivory numbers on them, which were placed on the outer ring in the location that would mark the time that each individual player checked out the table to commence playing pool. The counter-clockwise rotation of the outer dial would then serve to indicate the amount the customer owed when he or she was through playing by means of an ingenious graduated chart on the face of the dial. This chart was interchangeable to coincide with the price per hour of the proprietor's choice. This particularly early and very rare example, patent dated 1868, is equipped with a price per hour scale that reflects the cost down to the PENNY, and was offered by the J. E. Came Co. $5,000+.

A scarce "admission ticket" to an 1884 pool tournament! This is the only one of these we've ever found, and it's in very nice condition, so we have valued it at $300.

The following several photos are of early billiard table nameplates. They range in age from the 1850s to the early 1900s. Most are made from brass, some from pewter, and one is actually a section of a rosewood rail top with inlaid lead script. Some are solid brass, some are nickel-plated, and many of the early ones are silver-plated. One rare example is actually made from mother of pearl. The scarcity and desirability of each piece is readily evident based on the price that has been assigned to each one. T: Cut from an early 1900s rosewood table rail, $100. BL: Solid lead with the letters surrounded by real rosewood veneer, $100. BR: $150.

T: $25. BL: $35. BR: $40.

L: $75. R: $95.

L: $85. R: $90.

T: $150. B: $150.

T: $175. B: $150.

TL: $225+. TR: $250.
BL: $165. BR: $155.

TL: $175+. TR: $155.
BL: $450+. BR: $450+.

TL: $165. TR: $250. BL: $225.
BR: scarce, $650+.

TL: $200+. TR: $250+. BL: $225+.
BR: $200+.

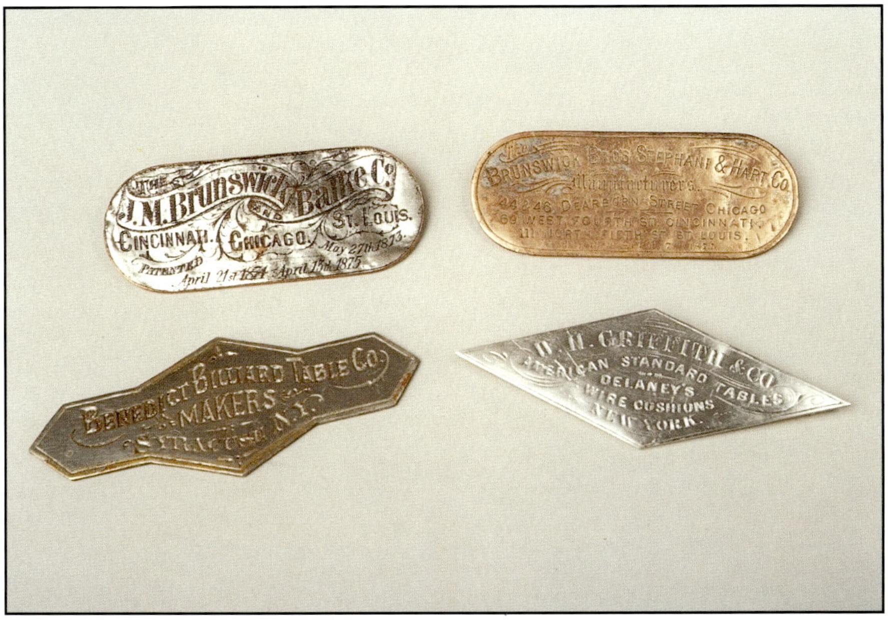

These are extremely rare examples in very good condition. TL: $650+. TR: $750+. BL: $450+. BR: $500+.

TL (mother of pearl, 1880s): $500+. TR: $115. C: $500+. BL (only example like this we've ever seen): $900+. BR: $650+.

These are original 1850s silver-plated spelter nameplates. T: $800+. B: $800+.

Dated 1859, these are extremely rare nameplates. T: $800+. B: $800+.

The following few photos are of what was actually one of the earliest styles of "pockets" for pool tables. They date from the late 1700s and were found on both European and American made tables well into the 1800s. They are made from brass and are "mechanical" by reason that each has a "receiver" which, when invaded by a billiard ball, tilts down to reveal it. Here we show only a few of the many intriguing examples that have found their way through the world of antique collectibles. This is a pair comprised of a "corner" and a "side" pocket specimen. In very good original condition, $500+ each.

On this example, the pretty face drops down when a ball has entered it after being pocketed, excellent condition, $500+.

This handsome gentleman represents a particularly difficult example to locate, $500+.

Another beautiful brass lady corner pocket, $500+.

An ultra scarce specimen, Lady Justice??, $750+.

A lovely French lady corner pocket, $500+.

A French fella with his beret, $500+.

A unique nickel-plated example, $750+.

The very rare lion style, shown with an ivory ball in his mouth waiting to be retrieved and placed back on the table, $800+.

Billiard parlors and barbershops were practically joined at the hip from the middle 1800s to well into the 1900s. It was not all that unusual for a true lover of the sport to advertise his prowess by having a billiard theme applied (hand painted) on his own personalized shaving mug by the barbershop supply houses. Most often, his mug was kept at the local barbershop in the shaving mug rack. Again, a cross collectible (with the barbershop folks), these are very hard to locate and get quite expensive. Condition is ultra important in shaving mugs, so always look them over very carefully. Here are some exquisite examples. L: $950+. R: $800+.

Tables only, no players on these two specimens. L: $850+. R: $1,000+.

Very special models of tables are depicted on this pair. L: $2,000+. R: $1,800+.

L: $1,250+. R: $1,000+.

Left : $1,100+. R: $1,300+.

This is almost a matched pair. Each features the same basic scene because it was a standard image offered by the barber supply houses from their mug decorating departments. A very "busy" image, with great detail, excellent condition, $1,500+ each.

One of the nicest examples you'll see, this image depicts the beautiful "Brilliant Novelty" model pool table by Brunswick-Balke-Collender. Outstanding condition, $1,000+.

The ultimate "billiard" shaving mug. This example obviously belonged to the world renowned super star, Alfredo De Oro. It's in excellent original condition, has phenomenal detail in the image. With this highly patriotic theme and because of who's it was, this mug will easily bring $5,000+.

This is the only authentic salesman's sample billiard table we've ever seen in our twenty-six years in the business. The rails are genuine rosewood with actual imbedded diamonds sights. The table is oak. It has a mission style cabinet, a detailed underside, and is made to factory specifications in every respect. We did replace its original Simonis cloth, both on the table and in the carrying case. Circa late 1800s, ULTRA RARE, $10,000+.

Chapter IX
Scorekeepers

This is an interesting category to say the least. At some point in time, whittling a notch in the rail of the pool table every time you won a game fell out of favor with the billiard parlor proprietor. The need for a device for keeping score was apparent from the get-go and many varieties were introduced over the years. Attached to the cue racks either at the top or the bottom, running from pocket to pocket under the rail, IN the rail, on the wall, incorporated into the wall ball rack, on the counter freestanding, suspended across the ceiling, and even actual floor models are some of the types that have surfaced over the years. Here are a few typical and a few rare examples.

Brunswick Balke Collender slate chalk board for scorekeeping. Oak framed with a shelf for the chalk, c. 1900, restored, rare item, $1,250.

An 1870s "acorn tab" style scoring bead set. Very rare style, excellent condition, $400+.

An 1880s "oval tab" style scoring bead set, stretched above tables across the ceiling with beads being moved by using the cues. Mint condition, very early example, $250+.

An 1890s, pink and brown, rare, celluloid scoring bead set. Very desirable example, $450+.

This unusual set is made with copper and aluminum beads. Hard to find, complete with five extra beads on each set of fifty to allow for playing games to 300 points. $450+.

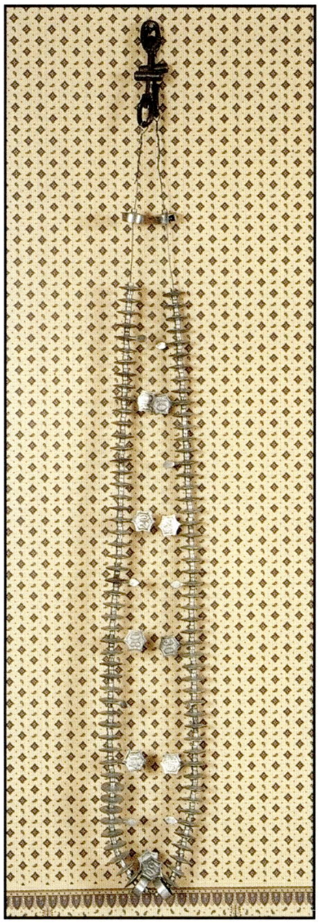

Dated 1912, this set is made entirely from aluminum and was relatively expensive in its time. Hard set to find, perfect original condition, $450+.

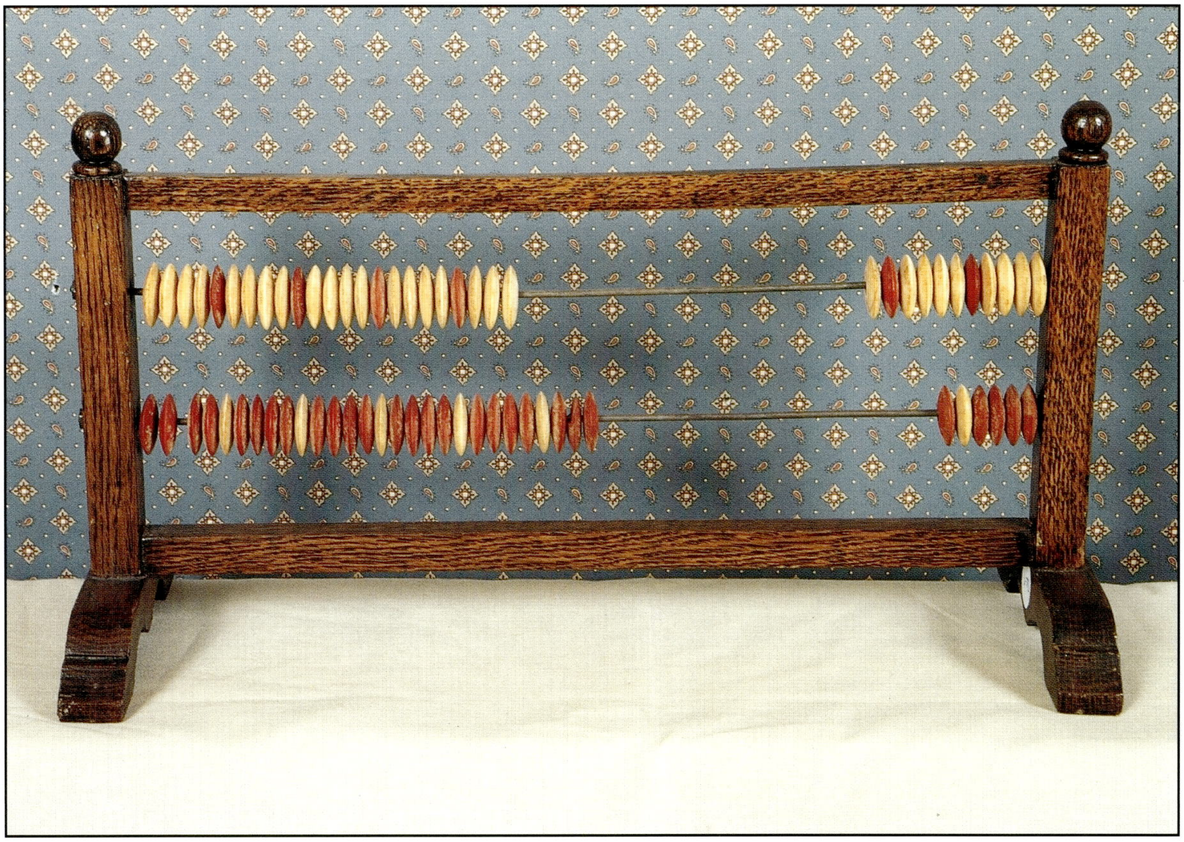

Oak framed "mantle top" style scorekeeper with thirty-five red and thirty-five white celluloid beads total on the two rods, early 1900s, unusual example, $575.

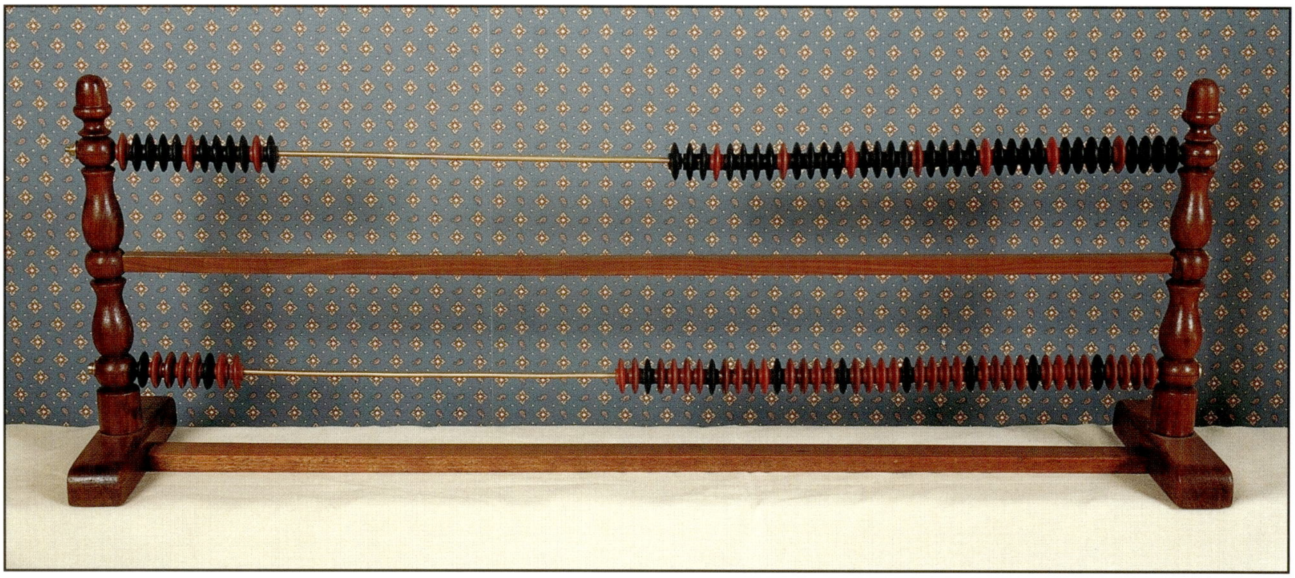

Early version of a mantle top style scorekeeper. Walnut with brass rods and burgundy and black composition beads. Rare model, c. 1870, restored, $750.

Signed "Brunswick Balke Collender," c. 1880s, oak base with turned feet, built from nickel-plated brass, fifty (plus five) bakelite beads per rod, $750+.

Oak base, fifty (plus five) composition beads per rod, nickel-plated brass hardware, c. 1890s, excellent original condition, $750.

Oak based, this is Brunswick-Balke-Collender's finest offering in mantle top scorekeepers. Fifty (plus five) composition beads, rare oxidized copper finish, sea horse motif marquis, turned oak feet, VERY RARE piece, excellent original condition, $1,750 to $2,000.

Unbelievable "Akam" company 1870s cast iron peacock motif mantle top style scorekeeper. Diminutive wooden beads with acorn style tabs. Painted with beautiful iridescent colors, beads suspended by brass wires, stretched between two stunning "long horn" horns. Each brass cable has an ingenious "tightener" at one end. This is the only one we've ever seen in twenty-six years. Restored, $7,500.

Late 1800s Thurston brand scorekeeping device, mahogany with ivory buttons to move the slides. Typically used for keeping score in a game called "Life Pool." Quite rare, excellent original condition, $1,000+.

Rare "Stevens & Sons" "life pool" scoreboard, c. late 1800s, mahogany with lots of ivory accents and beautiful mother of pearl buttons in the interior. An exceptional example, $1,000+.

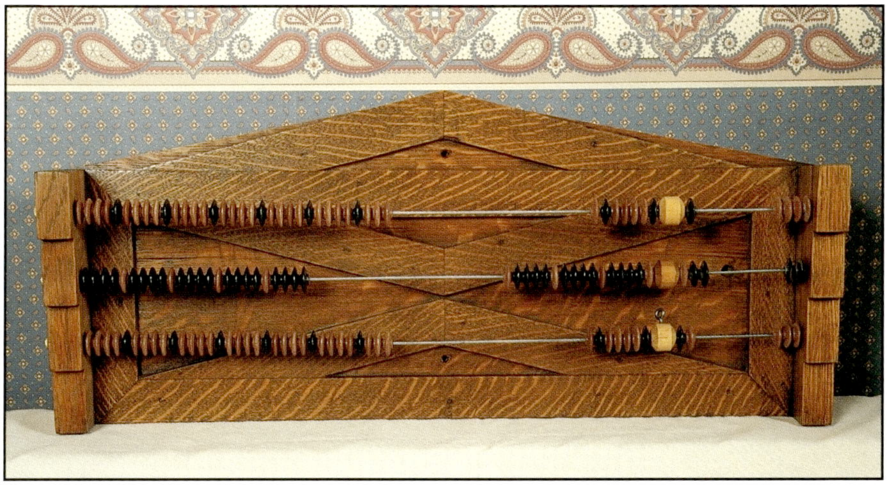

Early 1900s, oak three tier scorekeeper in mint condition, composition beads, forty (plus five) beads per rod. This is a great looking mission style piece and very hard to find, hangs on the wall, $1,300.

Oak and ebonized oak "Pin Pool" scorekeeper from the Brunswick-Balke-Collender Co., c. 1890s, small compartments on left were for placing your "pea" in when playing the game of "pea pool." This concept developed because of the strong tendency for some players to cheat. This board could be used to keep score for a variety of billiard games. Outstanding original condition, $795+.

Early 1880s version of the "Pin Pool" scoreboard. Several manufacturers sold this identical device, but most, by far, were sold by the Brunswick-Balke-Collender Co. Restored, numbers replaced, ornately framed, $950.

We believe this is an A. Gunklach Co. brand "Pin Pool" board from the 1870s. It is the only example we've ever seen. Nifty brass buttons for drawer sliding, beautifully made from select poplar, a fabulous example, $2,500+.

Oak Pin Pool scorekeeper with gold stenciling on ebonized background. Round brass "pea" holders on top, small shelf on bottom for miscellaneous items and chalk. Rare, $1,500 to $2,000.

Oak, Brunswick & Balke pin pool scorekeeper, "New York" style, patented June 20, 1871. Tiny red celluloid markers, brass cups for peas, mint condition, ultra rare, $3,500.

Cream of the crop Brunswick & Balke Co. "Hotel Style" pin pool scorekeeper. Walnut with gold gilt stencil on ebonized background, two locking drawers for miscellaneous accessories, restored, new stencil, c. 1870s, $7,500..

Very rare and unusual FLOOR MODEL bead style scorekeeper. Oak, c. 1880s, beautifully turned throughout, $3,500.

Chapter X
Chairs and Lights

Early billiard chairs and benches are delightfully comfortable, but, unfortunately, are surprisingly difficult to find. Given all the pool rooms that existed for so very many years, they should be quite common. I wish they were, but they're not.

But, without a doubt, the MOST difficult billiard piece to acquire is a *legitimate,* and *authentic,* antique billiard light. Most folks settled for a simple, generic ceiling unit in their home billiard rooms. Relatively ordinary looking gas fixtures, simple kerosene models, or very basic, early electric examples lighted most billiard parlors. Only under exceptional circumstances, where only the *best* would do, would the truly imposing examples be found. If you've searched, you already know, when you find one, BUY IT!

Mahogany billiard bench, c. 1920s, by Brunswick-Balke-Collender, restored, $2,150.

Birch billiard spectator chair, c. 1920s, restored, $975+.

Oak billiard spectator chair, c. 1900s, leather seat, restored, $1,250+.

Oak billiard spectator chair, plank seat, c. 1900s, restored, $1,250+.

RARE example of a very unusual design in billiard spectator chairs. It has a "rush" seat and is "mortise and tenoned" as well. Outstanding original condition, early 1900s, $3,500+.

Hard rock maple billiard spectator chair with a leather seat, c. 1880s, restored, $1,500+.

Oak billiard spectator chair with inset cane seat, restored, c. 1900s, $1,500+.

Birch billiard spectator chair with leather seat, restored, c. 1890s, $1,500+.

Maple billiard spectator chair with a plank seat and footrest, c. 1900s, restored, $1,500.

Oak billiard spectator chair with rare herringbone caned seat, c. 1880s, the catalog calls this style the "Collender" model, restored, $1,500+.

Maple billiard spectator chair with unusual herringbone caned seat, hard to find this seat style, c. 1880s, restored, $1,500+.

Oak billiard spectator chair, c. 1880s, "Collender" style, restored, $1,500+.

Beautiful golden maple "Collender" style billiard spectator chair with rare herringbone caned seat , with footrest, c. 1880s, restored, $1,750+.

Similar oak Collender style billiard spectator chair with herringbone seat, no footrest, nicely turned rungs, c. 1880s, restored, $1,500+.

Oak Collender style billiard spectator chair, factory "no footrest" model, c. 1880s, herringbone caned seat, restored, $1,500+.

Rare example of billiard spectator chair in oak, c. 1880s, unusual bentwood arms, pressed cane seat, with footrest, a very sought after Brunswick-Balke-Collender design, restored, $2,000+.

Maple 1880s Collender style billiard spectator chair with pressed cane seat, with footrest, restored, $1,500+.

L: RARE factory made "child's billiard spectator chair," c. 1890s, leather seat, oak finish, footrest, $2,250+. R: Earliest style of billiard spectator chair you'll see. 1870s vintage, rare ash example, large, stunning, restored, $2,500+.

Rare wrought iron and brass billiard light with hammered tin shades. Circa 1890s, excellent original condition, $6,500+.

Black wrought iron framed billiard light with metal shades (textured to simulate green leather), c. 1900s, excellent original condition, $7,500+.

Gorgeous, all polished brass, early oil billiard light. Circa 1880s, electrified, milk glass shades and smoke bells with spun brass tanks, $8,500+.

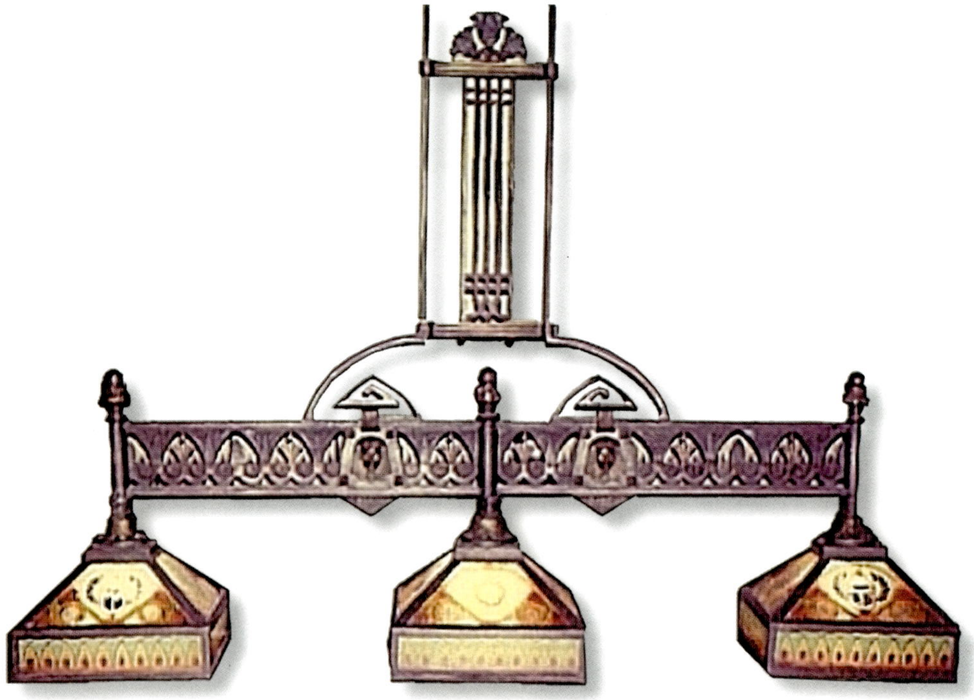

Massive, ornate cast iron billiard light with Egyptian motif. Reverse painted shades, electric, c. 1890s, $15,000+.

Exceptionally ornate cast brass gas billiard fixture, electrified, with different cameo glass plaques on either side, mahogany frame, and dozens of cut glass prisms. Circa 1880s, $15,000+.

An 1870s example of a Brunswick & Balke Co. kerosene billiard light. Tin shade, (restored), two font model, cast iron font frame, exceptionally rare item, $7,500.

An 1880s example of a four burner original gas billiard fixture from Brunswick-Balke-Collender, restored and electrified, ultra rare piece, $8,500+.

Extremely ornate, solid cast bronze, original gas and candle billiard fixture, c. 1860s, electrified, later period shades, very spectacular piece, $18,500+.

Above:
Incredible cast iron and brass billiard fixture. Original electric, c. 1890s, reverse painted shades with multiple coat of arms. Note the two cast bears on the upper corners. This light at one time hung in the billiard room of a magnificent home built by one of the founders of the city of Bettendorf, Iowa. One of only two known to exist, $50,000+.

MASSIVE gas billiard chandelier, c. 1870s, 5' 2" tall, 5' wide, shown here with contemporary double-cased shades. This is one of the most spectacular billiard lights we've ever seen, solid cast bronze, $35,000+.

Chapter XI
Billiard Cues

Complicated category, cues! Tables and cues comprise the two most diverse and prolifically changing entities in the world of billiards. Many, many decades of relentless competition to lead the field in sales and business success resulted in a literally amazing array of both spectacular tables and, the singularly most important component the typical billiard fanatic has always demanded, excellent cues. The seemingly infinite combinations of exotic woods and natural substances used to create the sometimes truly stunning tools of the trade have endowed us today with this most fascinating, though little understood, billiard collectible of all. The variations to be found are intimidating, to say the least, but rare and unique examples are incredibly scarce and seldom sold. Cues created especially for European aristocracy, America's wealthiest patrons of the sport, and those designed as *trophies* for men's clubs, and state, national, and international competitions are very seldom found and very highly prized.

The prices listed for the following cues are based on the assumption that the stick in question has neither an ivory ferrule, which increases the value of each cue by $100, nor a mother of pearl or ivory nameplate, which increases the value of each cue by $250, unless otherwise specifically noted in the cue's individual description.

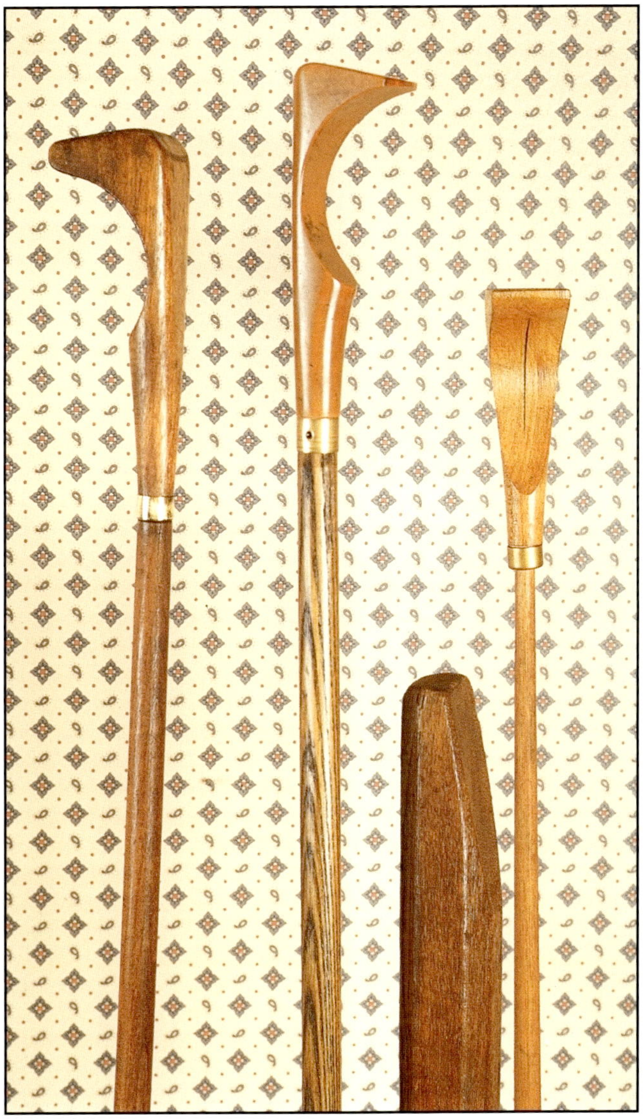

Three examples of what was called a "mace." The player shot with both ends of this cue. These were first used in the late 1700s and continued well into the 1800s. The "cupped head" was for addressing the ball you were shooting with when it was trapped tightly against the rail. It was also sometimes used for "slinging" the ball, like with a hockey stick. These are great museum pieces and get quite expensive. The shorter, more stout cue is without a doubt the earliest cue we've been able to find in our twenty-six years of collecting. It has a gradually sloping butt end for addressing balls when frozen to the rail and a well worn striking tip and is made from one piece of solid white ash. This cue is the style from the 1500s and 1600s and is ordinarily only seen in very early prints showing members of the aristocracy busily playing billiards. One of the maces clearly shows its "sightline" in the inside head area. The heads are found made from white ash, maple, and the extremely hard and durable boxwood to name just a few. Maces, $1,500+ each. Any seventeenth, eighteenth, or nineteenth century cue (also called a mace in their era), $2,000+.

All of the following cues are priced on the assumption that they are in good to very good condition. Slightly less than straight is not a major factor in late nineteenth century cues as they are typically for display only. These first four are all late 1800s examples of Brunswick-Balke-Collender cues. L to R: Model #4, one piece cue with NO splice, in other words, from one piece of wood, $100. Model #5, another NO splice cue that has been grain painted to simulate a splice, $150. Model #10, an actual splice in this cue in the rounded "Vignaux" style, $200. Model #15, a four point spliced cue, $175.

This is an eight cue set of model #10s, with the harder to find "Vignaux" style splice, showing several of the genuinely exotic woods they were available in. Here are some of the different choices there were: ebony, rosewood, cocobolo, amaranth, mahogany, sabacue, coraline, zebra, walnut, dagaine, sapote, purple heart, cherry, hard rock maple, and white ash. These particular eight early examples have more or less "square butts" and are all in pristine original condition. They are from the 1880s from the Brunswick-Balke-Collender Co. They are original non-ferruled, yet leather tipped, cues as well! Ebony, rosewood, and cocobolo examples, $1,000+; other "fancy wood examples," as they referred to them, $800+.

The next four are all from the same 1899 Brunswick-Balke-Collender catalog that the previous examples were from. Incidentally, we have found many very mint condition Brunswick-style cues that never did have a company decal. We are convinced that these were examples sold by other firms who purchased their cues from the same sources that Brunswick did before they began making their own line. L to R: Model #20, with a beveled or "Berger" style butt, $150. Model #18, with a "Vignaux" style three veneer splice, $250. Another model #20, without the beveled butt, with red decal, $175. Model #12, the cork wrapped offering, with standard four point splice, $400+.

More 1890s Brunswick-Balke-Collender models, showing a few of their "ornamented butts" (carved). L to R: Model #20, carved butt, rosewood, $550+; Model #20, carved butt, $550+; Model #10, carved butt, left spiral, $450+; Model #10, with extra veneers in splice, carved butt, right spiral, $500+.

Left to right: Model #10, "turned butt" carving, $400+; Model #20, rare carving style, $450+; Model #10, rare carving style, $500+; Model #10, rare carving style, ebony wood, $800+.

Left to right: Four Model #20s and a Model #10, all in hard to find carving styles, all in the Brunswick-Balke-Collender catalog. First cue, $450+; all others, $550+.

Four early-to-mid-1900s cues. L to R: First cue has a clear plastic sleeve over the leather butt wrap for displaying the owner's name, brass joint, $600+. Next cue has an ivory joint, leather wrap, and an unusual rectangular ivory nameplate, $750. Next is an early one-piece "Willie Hoppe," with engraved signature, in a rare rosewood example, excellent condition, $450. Last is another "famous player" cue, brass joint, corrugated rubber wrap, and is engraved with the name "Harold Worst," $350.

Late 1800s to early 1900s examples. L to R: Rare double "butterfly" spliced model #30, one piece cue, $800+; model #21 (because of the leather wrap), $400+; model #12, with cork wrap, (later, renamed the model #22), $400+; three consecutive model #26 1/2 examples, the first is silk wrapped, has a plastic name sleeve, and sports the appropriate four point splice with FOUR additional beautifully colored veneers. The second has a cork wrapped butt. The last is made from solid macasser ebony. Each of these cues has a value of $1,250+.

Left to right: Vignaux style, two veneer splice, three veneer border to mother of pearl nameplate, ebony butt plate, $800. Vignaux style, two veneer splice, celluloid nameplate, $675. Vignaux style, three veneer, double side-by-side butterfly splice, ivory joint, mother of pearl rectangular nameplate, three veneer butt plate, $900+. Vignaux style, three veneer, double butterfly splice, $700.

Left to right: Model #30, double butterfly spliced, early square butt, ebony wood, $950. Odd purple heart, maple, and walnut four point AND butterfly spliced, $675. Unique "elliptically spliced veneers" in butt with two-veneer butterfly splice above, rare, $1,000+. Classic multiple veneer, double-reversing pointed and butterfly style splice, with three veneer surrounded mother of pearl nameplate, in a rosewood butt, and a rare buckhorn ferrule, $2,000+.

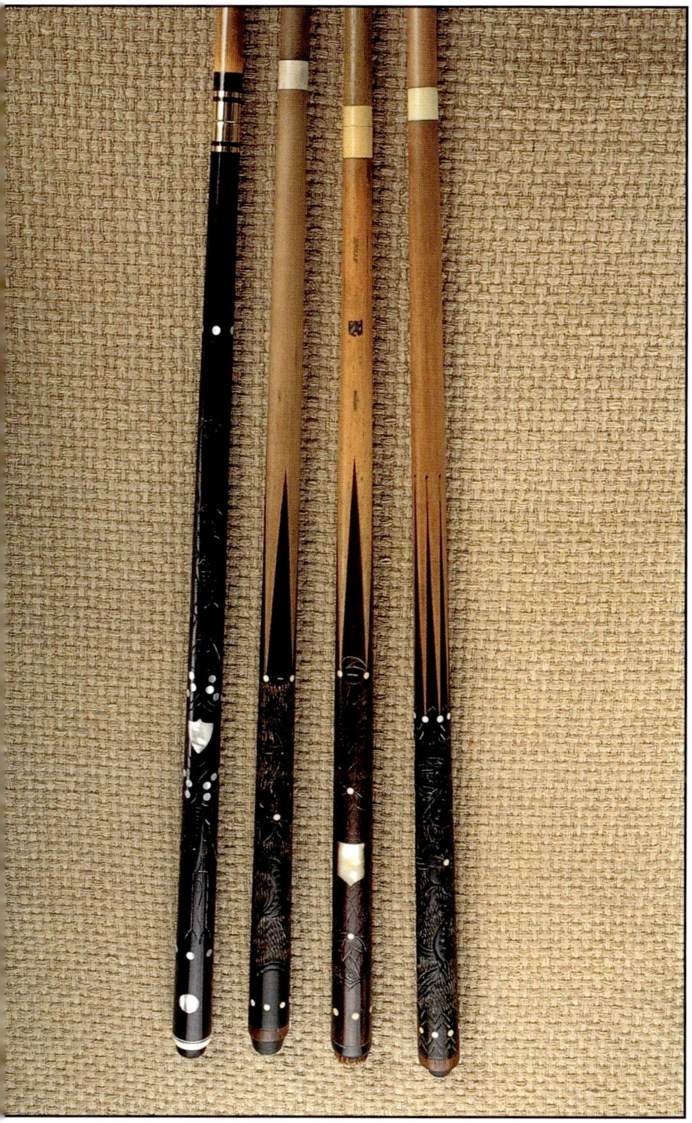

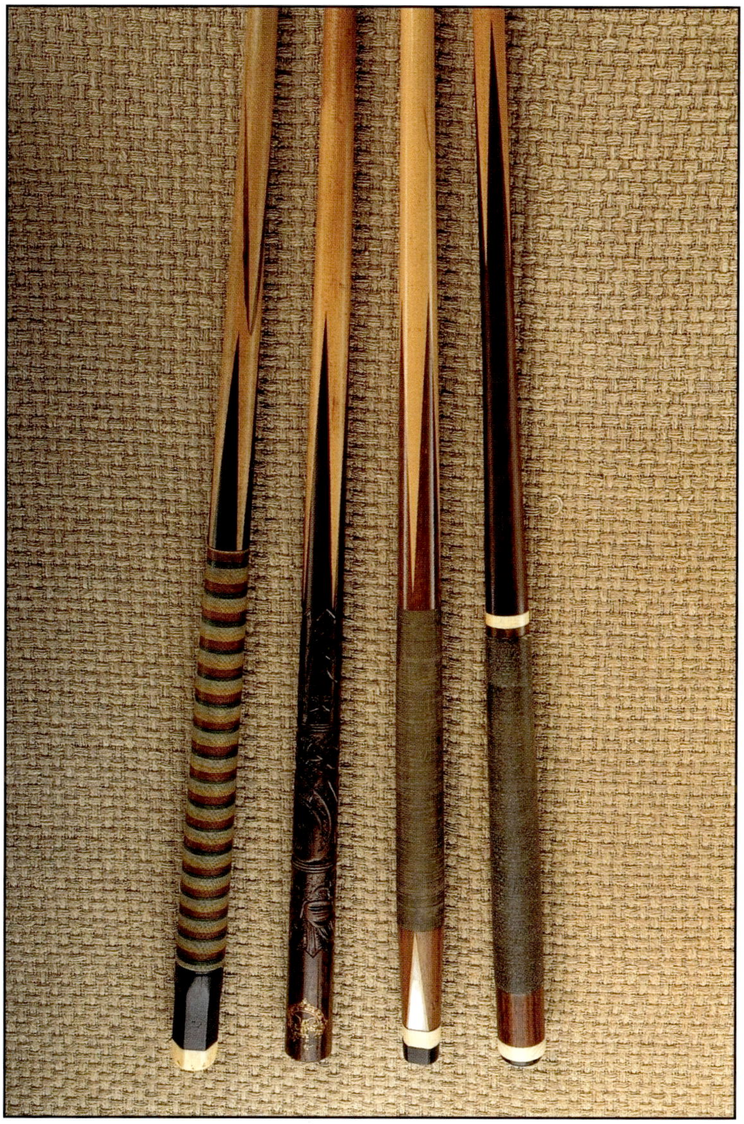

Left to right: Early Sampaio brand, hand carved with heavy mother of pearl inlay work, full rosewood butt sleeve(no splice), $1,500+. Three consecutive differently carved examples of circa 1880s, French made, two piece, "Hiolle" brand cues: left to right: ebony, four point splice, $1,500; rosewood, four point splice, $1,500; ebony, RARE eight point splice, top of the line, $2,750+.

Left to right: Ultra rare model #210, "Hexagonal" butt cue, with a rare rainbow pattern silk wrap, ebony butt, ivory butt plate, unique double set of four point splicing, with one extra walnut veneer in the upper splice, $4, 500. Extremely scarce model #27, "Chinese Carved Butt" cue, walnut, nice original decal, near mint condition, $3,100. Model #220, "Fishpole Style," walnut wood, linen wrap, mother of pearl nameplate, ivory and ebony combination butt plate, very rare, $1,800. The previous three cues were all available in the late 1800s. This next cue is from the early 1920s and is called the "Hub" cue. It has an ivory butt plate, an ivory collar half way up the butt, at its first joint, and another ivory collar at the mid-way joint (not shown in photo), as well as an ivory ferrule. This example is made from walnut and has a linen wrap. It is in super condition and this particular example was sold by the J. E. Came Co., $2,500+.

Left to right: "Faux Bamboo" cue, late 1800s, $550. Ebony four point splice, RARE twine wrap, rare brass butt plate, beveled butt, $500. Rosewood four point splice, linen wrap, rare scrimshawed ivory weight indicator, $550. Model #16, four point splice, spliced ebony shaft, $650. Model #16X, linen wrap, spliced ebony shaft, $750.

Left to right: RARE "Eisenmeister" woven silk wrap, two piece, ivory joint collar, rosewood spliced shaft, excellent B.B.C. decal, $1,500+. Rare *mottled* version of the scarce Brunswick-Balke-Collender "Vulcanite" model cue, ivory collar, ebony spliced shaft, $3,500. "Merry Widow," model #28, ivory collar, linen wrap, cherry butt and matching spliced cherry shaft, excellent decal, $2,500. Model #20x, linen wrap, spliced ebony shaft, excellent factory decal, $500+. Model #220, "Fishpole" cue by Brunswick-Balke-Collender, ivory and ebony butt plate, ebony butt, fiber and ivory collar, mother of pearl nameplate, rare, $2,400. Model #20X, four point splice, spliced ebony shaft, mother of pearl nameplate, $800.

Left to right: These are all rare examples of c. 1920s cues from the Albert Pick Co. The "Vincent" model, linen wrap, ivory joint, with spliced rosewood shaft, $2,500+. The "Vincent," with large ivory and black fiber butt plate, linen wrap, ivory joint, $2,250. The "Alcazar" model, brass joint, rare design, $3,000 to $3,500.

Left to right: Late 1800s four point splice, rosewood, rectangular mother of pearl nameplate in center of butt, ivory weight indicator, $900. Ebony butt with spliced ebony shaft, linen wrap, rectangular mother of pearl nameplate, $800. Double butterfly spliced with three veneers and an ivory nameplate, $1,500. Four point splice, linen wrap, rectangular mother of pearl nameplate, spliced ebony shaft, $800.

Left to right: RARE double carved design in butt, four veneer four point splice, mother of pearl nameplate, $2,300+. Beautifully carved butt, four point AND three veneer butterfly splice, ivory collar, spliced ebony shaft, SIGNED mother of pearl nameplate, ivory ferrule, $3,500+. RARE carved butt design, four veneer four point splice, mother of pearl nameplate, $2,500+. RARE double carved design in butt, four point splice, SIGNED mother of pearl nameplate, $2,500+.

All but the second cue from the left are Model #26 1/2 examples. The #26 1/2 model sports a display of three, four, or five very thin, colored veneers in the butt-sleeve-to-forearm splice. They do appear without a mother of pearl nameplate, but all in this group do have this additional feature, which, in addition, is also bordered by a grouping of thin inlaid veneer strips. Values, left to right: Plain butt, pearl nameplate, $1,500. Ebony wood butt, spliced ebony shaft, SIGNED pearl nameplate, ivory collar, linen wrap, (not a #26 1/2) four point splice, $2,500. Plain butt, spliced ebony shaft, pearl nameplate, $2,000. Linen wrap, spliced ebony shaft, pearl nameplate, $1,800+. Plain ebony butt, pearl nameplate, $1,750. Linen wrap, ivory collar, SIGNED pearl nameplate, $2,500+. Ebony butt, leather wrap, ivory collar, spliced ebony shaft, SIGNED pearl nameplate, $3,500. Ebony butt, very rare cork wrap example, ivory collar, spliced ebony shaft, pearl nameplate, $3,600.

Left to right: Unique ebony 1800s vintage cue with extensive mother of pearl inlay, four point splice, a pearl nameplate on one side and an ivory nameplate (triangle) on the other, ivory butt plate, ivory and fiber collars, ivory ferrule, most probably a "trophy cue" and one of a kind, $10,000+. Fabulous concentrically graduated inlay design, rare woods in a macassar ebony butt, ivory butt plate, brass and fiber collars, ivory ferrule, unmistakably from the hand of the renowned ivory turner and cue maker, George Britner, $5,000+. Heavily carved with flower designs, four veneer four point splice, ivory ferrule, wood triangle inlaid in butt bordered by veneer strips, late 1800s, $2,250. Carved with flowers, four point splice, ivory collar, ivory ferrule, spliced ebony shaft, SIGNED pearl nameplate, $3,600+.

Left to right: Here are three different c. 1800s examples of cues from the German cue maker, B. Finck & Co. Ebony butt with extensive, fine crisscross inlay and an ivory weight spot, ivory collar and ivory ferrule, spliced ebony shaft, $5,500. This interesting and rare "zebra" style of composition sets these next two cues apart; the cue on the left has seventeen splices between ebony and maple with a walnut insert at the base of the butt, $5,500+, while the one on the right has thirteen ebony to maple splices with a rosewood insert at the butt base, $4,500+. The last example has an unusual repeating series of concentrically carved circles around the butt and sells for $600 to $700.

Four very scarce, middle 1800s, "butterfly" spliced style European designed cues. Rather expensive examples in their day, they are easily distinguishable by the unusual patterns of inlay work at the base of their butts. These attractive and popular component patterns, first developed by early European cue manufacturers, were later closely replicated by a few of the American billiard firms. In the late 1800s, Brunswick, and a few other major manufacturers, began producing their own lines of nearly identical models. Their American counterparts incorporated only very subtly differing features to avoid patented design conflicts. L to R: A double butterfly spliced cue with a base wood of ebony and a wood triangular butt insert, $2,250+. A double butterfly with one set of reversing points splice, triangular wood insert, $3,250+. Double butterfly and one set of reversing points with ebony and ivory inlays in butt insert, $5,000+. TRIPLE butterfly splicing with multiple wood butt insert, very rare, $6,500+. All four of these cues have a triangular wood, ivory, or mother of pearl insert on the opposing side of the butt, typical of the finer European specimens.

Here are five very scarce, late 1800s, American made beauties. L to R: A model #34, FOUR veneer, triple butterfly splice, with an additional set of four reverse round-ended veneers in the lower splice, ivory butt plate and ferrule, SIGNED mother of pearl nameplate, $8,000+. Model #36, SIX veneer triple butterfly splice, ivory butt plate, SIGNED pearl nameplate, very good original Brunswick-Balke-Collender decal (not shown), ivory ferrule, $10,000+. Model #33, THREE veneer triple butterfly splice, ivory collar, ivory ferrule, rare original brass butt plate, ivory nameplate, ebony butt with rarely found diamond pattern carving, $6,500+. Model #25, FIVE veneer double butterfly splice, fiber collar, ivory ferrule, pearl nameplate, ebony butt (extremely scarce example), $5,500+. Model #23, THREE veneer double butterfly splice, spliced ebony shaft, pearl nameplate, $2,800+.

Here are four variations of the ultimate factory made billiard cue. Sold by several different manufacturers, this model is typically referred to as the #360. Sold by the Brunswick-Balke-Collender Co. as the model #360 to designate this particular basic design, it was also sold by other firms, in which case it would not have a Brunswick decal. Found with six colored veneers in its construction, and occasionally with a spliced ebony shaft, this model is considered by most collectors to be "the one to collect." ALL models should have the characteristic mother of pearl nameplate, bordered by three or four veneers as well, and one or two ivory collars at the joint. The pin in the joint should be in the shaft on all original factory made examples and the shaft should be noticeably shorter than the butt, as opposed to them being the same length, as in a standard cue. L to R: #360 (these were typically used as "First Prize" trophies for major billiard tournaments in the late 1800s and early 1900s), multiple veneer TRIPLE butterfly splice, plain butt, ivory collar, ivory ferrule, spliced ebony shaft, mother of pearl nameplate (not shown), excellent original Brunswick-Balke-Collender decal, $8,000+. #360, same cue with rare ebony butt and leather wrap, decal in only fair condition, $8,500+. Ultra scarce #360 in that it boasts a CARVED butt, this lacks the spliced ebony shaft, but has a SIGNED mother of pearl nameplate, mint decal, $15,000+. And finally, a linen wrapped #360, standard shaft, double ivory collars, SIGNED pearl nameplate, $8,500+.

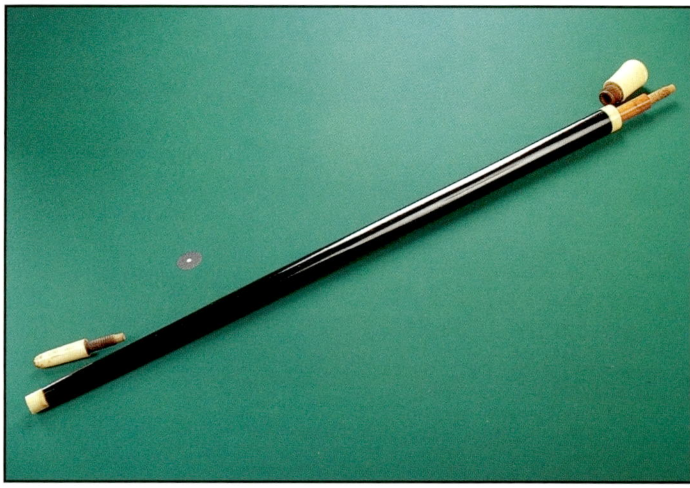

Left cue (of two shown in the rack in the first photo) and close up: A very rare, French made, Jules "Adorjan" FOUR piece cue. With a walnut butt, a burgundy leather wrap, a maple forearm and first-half of shaft, and a beautiful ebony fore-shaft, this early billiard cue, created by a world-class professional player, was definitely "avant-garde" for its day. An 1800s example, this RARE classic possesses an unusual feature which, because it breaks down into sections, enables the player to alter the overall weight and balance of the cue *while* competing. The joints at either end of the forearm are cleverly designed to accept interchangeable "weights" of various degrees. The shaft, as well as being interchangeable between maple and ebony for maintaining the cue's balance, also afforded the shooter a choice of "tapers" to keep in stride with the type of game being played, $4,500+. Right cue (of two displayed in the first image) and close up: This is what is known as a combination "Cue / Cane"! There are plenty of 1940s and newer examples of this type of billiard collectible, but THIS is the real thing. This late 1800s cue / cane is made of ebony and trimmed entirely in ivory. All the joints have *wood threads* and the stamp on this German made specimen is "J. B. Dorfelder." The ferrule is a rare "state of the art" ivory example that is threaded at the center to allow for a quick fix when in the middle of an important match, a very rare item indeed, $2,000+.

I doubt if you're going to find another one of Alfredo De Oro's personal pool cues, but just in case you do, here's the scoop on this one. This is basically a model #26 1/2, later known as the "Titlist" style butt. It has the multiple colored-veneer strips bordering the four point splice. It has a leather wrap (replaced for restoration purposes), an ivory ferrule, ivory joint collar, and even an ivory butt plate. De Oro's nameplate is done in celluloid, another medium used for this purpose in the late 1800s. The fact that De Oro was one of the premier billiard players of all time, winning several national and world tournaments, makes this a cue for the truly serious collector. We value it at $10,000+.

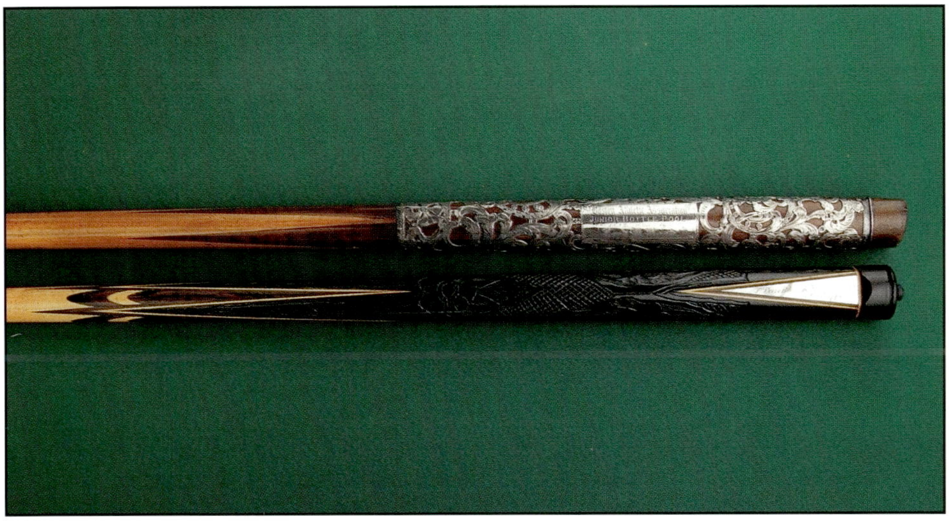

Top cue: An otherwise fairly ordinary, four point splice cue. It has a walnut butt, featuring the trademark "Berger" bevel, and an ivory collar and ferrule. But this one-of-a-kind example is actually a "Trophy" cue. Made from solid sterling silver, the beautiful and highly detailed engraved wrap, featuring flowers, vines, and a gorgeous horse head, displays the name of the proud winner of the "Junior Bottle Pool" tournament held by the "Boston Athletic Association" in 1892. Excellent condition, $10,000+. Bottom cue: Deeply carved flowers into a beautiful ebony butt, with four-veneer BOTH rounded and pointed splice, ivory ferrule, ivory collar, and a unique ebony turned butt cap, with a SIGNED mother of pearl nameplate listing both the date and "1st Prize" winner's name for an 1898-99 season of billiards, excellent original condition, again, one of a kind, $10,000+.

Here are three very different examples of late 1700s to early 1800s "marquetry" cues. All three have ivory or mother of pearl triangles on both sides of their butts. The middle cue is an ultra rare two piece example. All three cues have ivory butt caps with the one on the left having a thin layer of leather as well so that a player could shoot with either end if necessary. Only the jointed example has an ivory and ebony ferrule arrangement, with the left and right cues being more typical of the period and were intended to be used with only leather or, early on, nothing at all. The inlay is identical on both sides of these remarkable and intricate masterpieces. Ordinarily, these were specially made for royalty only. Many exotic veneers were used in their highly detailed designs. At 180 to 225 years old, these cues bring truly premium prices, $10,000+.

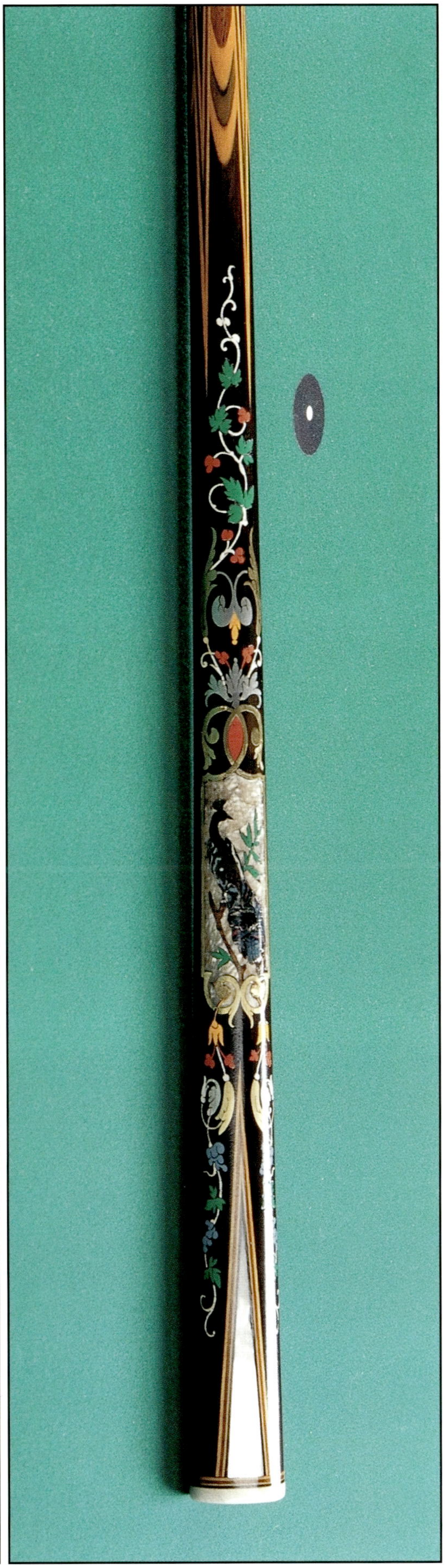

THIS is as fine a cue as was ever made. With four lustrous colors of *ENAMEL*, crimson, emerald, violet, and gold, used for the foliage and tiny, delicate vines, a spectacular abalone-feathered peacock, with a rosewood breast, perched proudly on a walnut branch, imbedded in a crushed mother of pearl window, actually framed in brass, with still more intricate brass and pewter inlays throughout the flowery design, this magnificent specimen takes a back seat to *nothing* ever made. It has an ultra fine linear "stitching" affect in inlaid wood bordering the incredible panorama, which appears on both sides of this masterpiece. With a brilliant triangular mother of pearl insert, bordered by more fine colored veneers on both sides as well, and a stunning white ivory butt plate, climbing to the forearm of the cue, we find a spectacular five wood "reversing" butterfly AND four-point style splice, not once, but TWICE, as we travel up the abruptly tapered shaft toward the 1770s ferrule-less tip. This is a full fifty-seven inches of literal "billiard jewelry"! The case is another story! The tiger striped mahogany custom built carrying case is exquisitely finished and lined with, what else, billiard felt. It bears an engraved spelter plaque that reads "Mr. Claude Falkiner / Presented by ALCOCK & CO. PTY. LTD. / MELBOURNE / 1924," sports a leather handle, and it has a lock and key. Claude Falkiner was at one time a world champion billiard player and we believe that this cue was one of the trophies passed from winner to winner from the late 1700s to possibly as late as the early 1900s. Definitely a one of a kind item, and perhaps the finest example of late eighteenth century cue craftsmanship in existence, $50,000+.

Chapter XII
Ball Racks

Consider this: *carom tables*, those without pockets, simply did not require a wall fixture for holding loose balls. Consequently, wall ball racks, especially Victorian examples, are extremely hard to come by. Here are both some ordinary and some relatively unique examples.

The least expensive ball rack offered by Brunswick in the late 1800s. Oak frame with ash backboard, refinished, $450.

Oak with ash backboard ball rack with factory locking cupboard doors. Numbers were for individual players as these were used to keep score, player by player, c. 1895, restored, $795.

Nine shelf scorekeeping ball rack, in oak, with attractive cornice complete with dentil molding. First found in the 1890s catalogs. Restored, $550 +.

Mahogany Brunswick-Balke-Collender nine shelf ball rack, early 1900s, restored, $795.

Birch early 1900s nine shelf ball rack with celluloid inlay at top. Restored, $795.

Brunswick Balke Collender oak nine shelf ball rack with celluloid inlays, restored, new decal, early 1900s, $795+.

Oak eight shelf ball rack, side loading, with wall protector plate, hard to find style, restored, early 1900s, $795.

Great, definitely mission style, oak ball rack, c. 1890s, restored, $950.

Oak with ebonized side rails, this is a very early ball rack example in the larger nine shelf variety, outstanding original condition, c. 1890s, $695.

Oak side loading ball rack with ornate carved base trim and crown, eight shelf, c. 1890s, restored, $795.

Oak eight shelf Brunswick-Balke-Collender ball rack with impressive fluted vertical rails and shapely crown, heavily quarter sawn wood, c. 1890s, restored, $895.

Oak Brunswick-Balke-Collender seven shelf ball rack with nice crown and extension shelf for storing brush, chalk, etc., c. 1890s, $750.

Oak eight shelf ball rack with ash backboard, fluted rails with nice cornice with dentil molding, restored, c. 1890s, $795.

Early Victorian style oak ball rack with wonderful crown and nine shelves. Restored, c. 1880s, $950.

Nine shelf (eight player) oak ball rack from the Wallie Dorr Billiard Co., fancy carved cornice, excellent decal on rack skirt, restored, c. 1890s, $695.

Four shelf oak ball rack, side loading, with great carved crown, c. 1890s, restored, $695.

Oak ball rack from the Kansas City Billiard Table Co., loads on the right side, UNLOADS on the left side. When the door is opened, sloping shelves roll balls to the left side of the rack, where they fall down to a waiting wicker ball basket. Restored, early 1900s, $900+.

Eight shelf oak ball rack, side loading, with carved crown, c. 1890s, restored, $895.

Great quarter sawn oak 1890s "National" brand ball rack with fluted blocks, top and bottom, fluted rails, super dentil molded cornice, and shaped skirt, c. 1890s, restored, as nice as you'll find in this style, $1,500.

Rare Julius Balke brand ball rack, cherry with some ebonizing, carved skirt, c. 1860s, holds fifty-six balls!! Restored, $2,100.

Walnut, with some ebonizing and gold gilting, J. E. Came Co. ball rack. Nine shelf, c.1870s, very rare example, great crown, outstanding original condition, $1,295.

Another rare example of the Julius Balke Co. ball racks, c. 1860s to 1870s. Balls sit in holes, very unusual design, ten shelves, holds four complete sets of fifteen balls!! Walnut, restored, $2,000+.

Walnut Brunswick-Balke-Collender 1880s vintage ball rack. An unusual example that accepts balls from EITHER side! Nine shelf, restored, $1,500+.

"Eastlake" model, by J. M. Brunswick & Balke Co., side loading, nine shelf (eight player), rare bird's-eye maple and inlaid example. Restored, new stencil, c. 1870s, $3,500+.

Early J. M. Brunswick & Balke Co. butternut wood ball rack, "Non-Pariel" model. Nine shelf, c. 1870s, restored with original decal, $1,500.

Rare "Brilliant Novelty" model Brunswick-Balke-Collender ball rack. Nine shelf, cherry, heavily inlaid, great crown and skirt, restored, new stencil, c. 1880s, $3,500+.

Brunswick Balke Collender manufactured model of the rack designed by the National Billiard Table Co. (which they bought out), c. late 1800s, restored, rosewood and grain-painted poplar with gold gilt highlights, eight shelf, restored, new stencil, side loading, slightly different version of the "Monarch" model, $3,500+.

Exceptional early Victorian oak ball rack. Heavy carving, great crown and skirt, carved rails (pillars), rare pea pool bottle compartment, nine shelf, c. 1880s, restored, $3,500+.

Genuine "Monarch" model by the J. M. Brunswick & Balke Co., c. 1870s, rosewood, eight shelf, side loading, outstanding original condition, heavy gold gilt work, $3,500+.

The Duesenburg of factory built ball racks. A twelve shelf, Victorian-style, walnut masterpiece. From The J. M. Brunswick & Balke Co., c. 1870s, restored, $6,500+.

Brunswick Balke Collender mahogany vertical stacking mechanical ball rack. When the brass button was pushed at the rack bottom, balls would funnel down, move to the center chute, and drop into a leather or wicker ball basket. Hard to find model, early 1900s, restored, new stencil, $1,500 to $2,000.

An 1880s Brunswick-Balke-Collender mechanical releasing ball rack. Oak, nickel-plated release lever, some ebonizing, with extended shelf for ball receiver. When the release bar is lowered slightly, shelves tip slightly to let the balls roll side to side until they reach the bottom, where they are gathered into an oak triangle and tray device with which they are then brought to the table. VERY RARE piece, complete with oak ball box and oak triangle with cheese-cloth lined base, restored, shown "shelves flat" and "shelves tilted." $2,500+.

Eight shelf (seven player) oak Brunswick-Balke-Collender mechanical releasing ball rack from the 1880s to 1890s. This version has a small brass lever in the lower left corner that activates the releasing feature. A wicker basket hung from a hook under the bottom right hand corner to accept the falling balls. Great crown, restored, new stenciling, shown "shelves flat" and "shelves tilted." $2,500+.

Ultra rare "Whitney's Patent Ball Rack" by Brunswick & Balke, c. 1870s, ebonized oak, eight shelf, gold gilt work, nickel-plated hardware, great crown, original oak ball collector and serving tray, restored, shown "shelves flat" and "shelves tilted." $5,500.

Chapter XIII
Cue Racks

Virtually everyone that purchased a table also selected a cue rack of some type to hold the cues. The following are both some standard and some premier examples that could be found in either the pool hall or the ballroom. Some tables actually had cue racks designed specifically as mates to create a more balanced setting. Floor model cue racks, which are quite scarce, will sometimes fetch higher prices than the simpler styles of tables they may be found with!

Elegant serpentine designed mahogany cue rack, c. 1860s, maker unknown, restored, $1,500.

Brass cue locks closeup

Factory storage unit for 6 decks of cards closeup

Mahogany parlor style rack, private brass cue locks, beveled mirror, RARE factory card-deck compartment, restored, c. 1890s, $3,500+.

An 1890s oak cue rack, from the "National Billiard Table Co.," mint condition, $2,500+.

Rare cast iron cue rack from the Akam Billiard Table Co., c. 1870s, missing artwork on the top section, $2,250.

Victorian era oak Brunswick-Balke-Collender cue rack, c. 1890s, mint condition, $3,500.

Cherry Brunswick & Balke cue rack, c. 1870s, restored, new stencil, $2,500.

Walnut, c. 1870s, H. W. Collender cue rack, very rare example, restored, original decal, $4,000.

Walnut, c. 1870s, Brunswick & Balke "Queen Anne" model cue rack, restored, new stencil, $3,500.

"Manhattan" model cue rack by Brunswick-Balke-Collender, oak, c. 1880s, mint condition, $4,500.

"Union League" model oak Brunswick-Balke-Collender cue rack, c. 1880s, mint condition, $4,000.

Rare bird's-eye maple inlaid "Eastlake" model cue rack by Brunswick & Balke. c. 1880s, restored, new stencil, $4,500.

Rare "Brilliant Novelty" model Brunswick-Balke-Collender cue rack, c. 1880s, restored, new stencil, unusual cherry example, heavily inlaid, $5,500.

Exceptional example of an H. W. Collender cue rack, c. 1870s, walnut, very fine condition, some restoration, $6,500.

Rare, early Oliver Briggs walnut cue rack. Restored, c. 1870s, $3,250.

Cherry "Brilliant Novelty" cue rack, ultra-rare early version by Brunswick & Balke, c. 1870s, original stenciling, restored, $6,500.

Very early oak Brunswick-Balke-Collender cue rack with factory attached mechanical ball rack. Opening center door releases held balls in a basket. Restored, c. 1880s, $5,500.

"Queen Anne Private Cue Rack" (New York style), manufactured by Brunswick and Balke Co. FOR Isaac Taylor, oak, c. 1880s, very rare inlaid example with locking drop down privacy door, outstanding original condition, $5,750 +.

Walnut "private" model cue rack, c. 1870s, double door example, restored, new stencil, by Brunswick-Balke-Collender, $5,000.

Extremely rare cherry Brunswick-Balke-Collender individual locking doors cue rack, beautifully inlaid to match the Brilliant Novelty model pool table, c. 1880s, $7,500+.

The epitome of all Victorian cue racks, "The Excelsior Private Cue Rack," by Brunswick & Balke, c. 1870s, fully restored, walnut, holds twenty-four cues, staggering them from front to rear, $15,000+.

Oak Brunswick-Balke-Collender floor model rack, c. 1890s, one of their nicest examples, $2,250+.

Oak, c.1880s, floor model cue rack from Brunswick-Balke-Collender. Restored, holds twelve cues, beautifully turned pillar, $1,500 to $2,000.

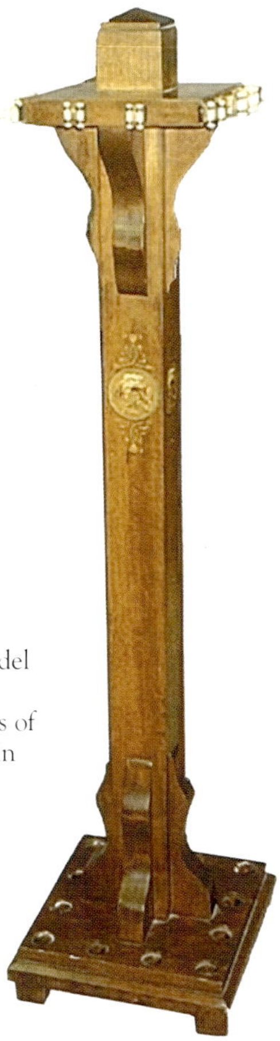

A "Wendt" manufactured floor model cue rack with bone retaining clips. Has a flowery decal on all four sides of the tower. A hard to find example in mint condition, c. 1900, $2,100.

Oak, round floor model cue rack. Burled elm top plate, excellent example, c. 1880s, $1,750 to $2,250.

Exceptional early oak floor model cue rack. Revolving example, c. 1870s, restored, a very rare piece, $4,500.

Gorgeous walnut revolving floor model cue rack, c.1840s. Note the perch for the occasionally not needed fourth ivory billiard ball on the top of the rack. Rare and exceptionally select wood, restored, $4,250.

Ebonized cherry revolving cue rack, c. 1870s, outstanding model and probably one-of-a-kind. Manufactured by Brunswick & Balke, $12,500+.

Oak Brunswick-Balke-Collender billiard sideboard, c. 1890s, made well into the early 1900s, holds twelve cues. Note the pea pool scorekeeper incorporated into the piece. Hard to find, restored, $5,000+.

Circa 1890s oak Brunswick-Balke-Collender billiard sideboard (or "buffet"), holds sixteen cues, pea pool scorekeeper above the ball storage compartments, with game "bead" scorekeeper in the upper opening, and cups for chalk on the buffet deck. Restored, $5,500+.

Earlier 1880s version of the Brunswick-Balke-Collender billiard cue "buffet" in oak. Note the cups for chalk on either side of the sideboard deck. Rare model, $6,500+.

Incredible W. H. Griffith c. 1860s walnut billiard sideboard. Holds eighteen cues. Has two slides for scorekeeping beads, a drawer for chalk, brush, balls, collapsing triangle, etc., a white marble deck, beautifully burled, carved lady's head on a pierce carved crest. Restored, ultra rare item, $25,000+.

Custom made for an (apparently) important customer, this unique billiard cue closet has two shallow drawers for chalk and other accessories, four shallow compartments for miscellaneous items, and an interior that will accommodate six personal cues. Note the scorekeeper device on the top. A very unusual piece, $3,500+.

Early 1900s birch (stained mahogany) cue "closet," holds six cues on either side, holds around ten hats and coats inside, from Brunswick-Balke-Collender, $2,250+.

These were primarily found in billiard parlors. The twelve drawers hold ten cues each for a total of 120 customer cues. This is an oak example by Brunswick-Balke-Collender, c. 1910, and has a large storage area in the bottom. Original condition, $3,000+.

An early 1870s renaissance style mahogany billiard cue closet that hung on the wall. Locking storage compartment for balls, etc., at bottom. Designed to accommodate up to 60" snooker cues, it has a specially created area that will accept maces (very early cues with mallet-type heads). It was probably built for an aristocrat and is one-of-a-kind. $12,500+.

Rare oak corner billiard cue closet, closed and open. This stunning piece of billiard furniture has curtain rods to afford privacy, if wanted. Mint original condition, $6,500.

Early Brunswick-Balke-Collender two piece cue rack. Made from ash, their least expensive offering from the period, c. 1880s, $800.

Very difficult to find "Step Banner" model cue rack by Brunswick & Balke, c. 1870s, rosewood and grain-painted poplar to simulate rosewood, $5,000+.

Rare Jacob Strahle brand version of the Monarch style two piece cue rack. Ornately designed, it will accommodate twelve cues. Poplar wood, c. 1870s, restored, $4,500.

The king of the two piece wall racks, this is the "Monarch" model in rosewood. Outstanding original condition and extremely rare, this model is from J. M. Brunswick & Balke and easily brings $5,500 or more when in pristine condition or properly restored.

Believed to be an early H. W. Collender cue rack, in walnut, this example has a cue butt deck designed to accept the rectangular heads of maces as well as for the larger square butts of the earliest cues. Circa 1860s, it holds thirteen cues, $3,500.

Another example of the wonderful racks designed by W. H. Griffith, a predominant manufacturer from the Victorian period, this rack is made from rosewood and dates from roughly the 1850s to the 1860s. It holds fourteen cues and will fetch around $3,500 if mint or appropriately restored.

Believed to be a W. H. Griffith brand rack, this is another example from the 1860s and is also in walnut. It, too, is designed to accommodate maces or cues with square butts. Holds thirteen cues, $3,500.

A beautiful specimen from the "O. D. Benjamin Billiard Table Co." Made of walnut, c. 1860s, restored, this rack actually "threads" together at the four corners and it holds fourteen cues, $3,500.

Very unique design. An early 1870s Brunswick & Balke cue rack in rosewood and very figural bird's-eye maple, it holds fourteen cues. $5,000+.

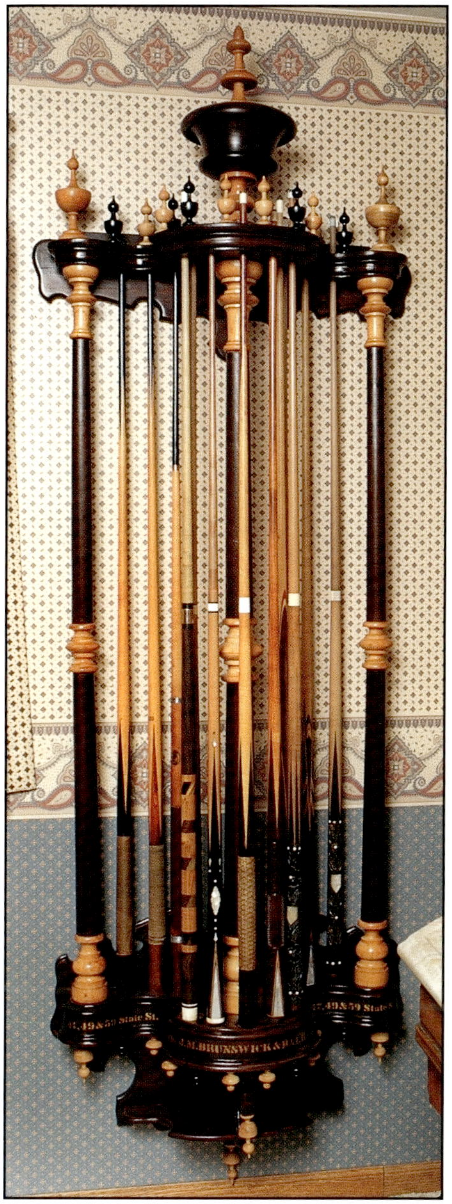

Spectacular "Non-Pariel" model cue rack by "The J. M. Brunswick & Balke Co.," c. 1870s, rosewood and hard rock maple. Serpentine configuration with heavy use of finials, this is a two piece rack with three large, turned pillars spanning the distance between the top and bottom decks. There is a storage shelf on the lower section for chalk, etc. Outstanding original condition, $9,500+.

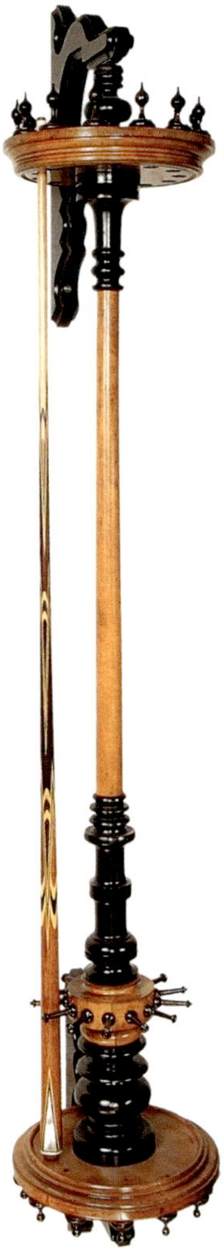

Rare "rotary" cue rack from the "E. Brunswick Billiard Table Co." Rosewood and maple with some ebonizing, this is a stunning example of an extremely hard to find model. Minor restoration, $8,500+.

Rare, factory made "single" cue, "locking," or "private" cue holder. Mahogany, c. 1905, neat design, $500.

Another rare rack from the Akam Billiard Table Co. from the late 1870s. Akam's merchandise was made almost entirely of cast iron and brass. This cue rack is brass with a brass tube over a cast iron separator post. There is an Akam brand billiard table in the billiard table chapter with elephant heads for legs, and a score-keeper with a peacock theme in the scorekeeper section. Beware of reproductions. Holds twelve cues, $3,000 to $3,500.

Chapter XIV
Billiard Tables

Surprisingly few people are aware of the enormous number of distinctions that were created to attract the attention of billiard table buyers over the past few hundred years. The diversity and quality are both amazing and exciting. These tables range from subtly attractive to incredibly ornate and the values are decided by this one most important factor, together with *where* the tables are marketed, and, more often than not, *who the sellers and buyers are*! The range of the cost of antique tables is extraordinarily broad, with the most competitive prices being found in the Midwestern U. S. As with almost any antique, wholesale prices are normally only a fraction of what the professionally restored piece will fetch on the retail market. The rule of thumb is to work to purchase the finest table you can comfortably afford AFTER having done enough research to determine that it will increase in value. Nearly every true antique table (those manufactured before, let's say, 1925) is a sound investment. As the retail values differ tremendously as you shop around the country, patience will often find you a "best deal" eventually, but be sure you are comparing apples to apples. There *IS* a difference between *refinished* and *restored*. Our twenty-six years in the antique billiard table business has been literally replete with coincidence and surprise. We're now thinking of retiring when our current inventory of antique tables has been sold, but plan to continue dealing in the more unusual collectibles.

We offer a professional written appraisal service for antique pool tables, typically pre-1930, for $45. Because of the profuse technical differences between so many similar-looking old pool tables, we have elected not to speculate as to what they may sell for just *here* or *there*. The scope of the antique pool table retail market is SO broad that we feel every consideration merits individual attention.

Conclusion

Now, close your eyes and try to imagine the addictive ambiance of a classic game of billiards. Whether in a ballroom atmosphere of exquisite beauty and Victorian etiquette or in a dark and smoky back street tavern, the game is the same! Folks from all walks of life, of both genders, and from all over the globe have adored this game for hundreds of years. They still do. This book is meant to show you why.

Here is a little poem I wrote back in 1984 that seems to articulate the tension and excitement that can sometimes evolve during an important game of billiards.

"The Hustle"

Well grab yourself a seat along the bar and have a beer, you won't believe the story that you're about to hear.

It all began at the bar that night, I don't recall the year, but this is how it happened, and, yes, it happened here.

Behind the bar the barmaid scanned the booths for needed drinks, when, all at once, into the room this stealthy figure slinks.

He slowly saunters through the joint, he gives the maid a glance, for sixty seconds, nothing moves, the place is in a trance.

He pauses by the jukebox, where the tiny colored lights, for just a moment danced upon his blinding pearly whites.

He squinted through the darkness, slipped off his tattered cloak, swept back his tousled silver hair with one hypnotic stroke,

Then strolled across the room to where the old pool table stood, and tapped his fingers gently on the scarred but pretty wood.

Don't know what made me do it, the place was packed that night, but as he plucked that cue ball from beneath the smoky light,

From somewhere deep within my soul the haunting challenge came. They say I said, "Hey, rack 'em up, if you wanna shoot a game!"

He said, "O. K., but just for fun," as he racked, then grabbed a stool. Then added, "Take it easy, I've played very little pool!"

I pulled a damn good house cue off the wall and grabbed some chalk. I dusted down the tip real hard and watched him like a hawk.

I'm not sure why the crowd had gathered near to watch us play, but someone yelled, "So bust 'em, if you got no more to say!"

When, as I leaned to break 'em, in the corner of my eye, I saw the ivory fingers, and I felt my throat go dry.

I stared for just a moment at the worn and lifeless fist. I'd heard the tale, but always thought the man did not exist.

I slowly raised my head until I saw his chiseled face. His eyes were old, but crystal clear, though smoke now filled the place.

But as I pondered who he was, another guy yelled, "Break"! And so the game began and you could feel that table shake.

But, when the last small spheroid came to rest upon the slate, not ONE damn ball was down and now MY turn had come to wait.

He slithers to the cue rack and he grabs an old house stick. Then turns to me and asks, "I guess this means I get to pick?"

"Yeah, that's the way it's played", I said, "now show us what ya' got, but don't forget that, when you miss, I only need one shot!"

Then, with his wooden weapon poised upon that ivory fist, "You've HAD your shot," he softly said, "'cause I have never missed!"

With whittled ivory fingers nestled 'neath the powdered tip, his stroke was soft and silky with a firm but gentle grip.

"The five ball in the corner," was the first I heard him call. The crowd had gone dead quiet, as I watched the first one fall.

The cue ball found the seven, frozen tight, and knocked it loose. I'd broken well, the rest were out, as I heard him mumble, "Deuce."

The two fell hard, I saw the old man's eyes, well, kinda squint. The tip had fallen off his cue, and God, that thing was bent!

Then a tiny grin began to crawl across his face, he pointed at a corner pocket, "Guess I'll play the ace."

But then it happened, "whitie" gave the nine this little kiss, and there he stood, not one good shot, if he was gonna miss,

The time had come, so I said smartly, "What's it gonna be?" He slowly raised his head, he found my face, and said to me,

"Would you like to lay a little money on the line?" I glanced back at the table; he was snookered on the nine!

"You're on," I quipped, and then, and WHY, I'll never understand, I glared into his gentle eyes and said, "How 'bout a GRAND?"

The crowd drew down around us tight, the barkeep killed the box. The old man scanned the room and found this flashy little fox.

"Would you please hold the money?" were the only words he said. Then something deep inside me told me, I was good as dead.

He counted out a thousand bucks, then gave it to the chick. I glanced back at the table, at his bent and tip-less stick.

"Your money, friend," he taunted, so I matched the emerald wad. "Now, let's see you get out of this," I sneered, and gave the lay a nod...

"Seven, in the side, five rails," was all the old man said. The damn thing went so easy you'd have sworn the shot was dead!!

His leave was great for anything, but the best shot was the six, and I remember noticing, no matter what he picks,

The leave is automatic, and before the six had dropped, he was on the three and stroking, and as the cue ball stopped,

He drilled it in the side, then drew it back to nail the four, in less than fifteen seconds he had run to just one more...

The eight was sitting lonely on the corner pocket lip. With nothing lying in the way, he let the old cue slip.

The crowd of people roared, though they were s'posed to be MY friends. He shook my hand and whispered, "This is how it ALWAYS ends"!

I never saw that guy again, and I never caught his name. And, no, I won't forget that night, that face, that fist, that game!

US $69.95

9 780764 317002 56995

ISBN: 0-7643-1700-8